MEDIA IN POSTAPARTHEID SOUTH AFRICA

MEDIA IN POSTAPARTHEID SOUTH AFRICA

Postcolonial Politics in the Age of Globalization

Sean Jacobs

INDIANA UNIVERSITY PRESS

This book is a publication of

Indiana University Press
Office of Scholarly Publishing
Herman B Wells Library 350
1320 East 10th Street
Bloomington, Indiana 47405 USA

iupress.indiana.edu

© 2019 by Sean Jacobs

All rights reserved

No part of this book may be reproduced or utilized in any form or by any means, electronic or mechanical, including photocopying and recording, or by any information storage and retrieval system, without permission in writing from the publisher. The paper used in this publication meets the minimum requirements of the American National Standard for Information Sciences—Permanence of Paper for Printed Library Materials, ANSI Z39.48-1992.

Manufactured in the United States of America

Library of Congress Cataloging-in-Publication Data

Names: Jacobs, Sean, author.
Title: Media in postapartheid South Africa : postcolonial politics in the age of globalization / Sean Jacobs.
Description: Bloomington : Indiana University Press, 2019. | Includes bibliographical references and index.
Identifiers: LCCN 2018048041 (print) | LCCN 2018052372 (ebook) | ISBN 9780253040572 (web PDF) | ISBN 9780253025319 (hardback : alk. paper) | ISBN 9780253025425 (pbk. : alk. paper) | ISBN 9780253040596 (ebook epub)
Subjects: LCSH: Mass media—South Africa—History—20th century. | Mass media—Political aspects—South Africa. | South Africa—Politics and government—1994-
Classification: LCC P95.82.S6 (ebook) | LCC P95.82.S6 J33 2019 (print) | DDC 302.230968—dc23
LC record available at https://lccn.loc.gov/2018048041

1 2 3 4 5   24 23 22 21 20 19

For Jessica, Rosa, and Leo

Contents

ix
Acknowledgments

1
Introduction

15
1. The Mandela Channel

35
2. Branding the Nation in Prime Time

63
3. The Aspirational Viewer

87
4. *Big Brother* MultiChoice

109
5. HIV-Positive Media

137
6. The Second Afrikaner State in Cyberspace

171
Conclusion

181
Index

Acknowledgments

MEDIA IN POSTAPARTHEID *South Africa* is the culmination of years of engagement with South African media politics. It bears the imprint of my studies as well as of a range of interlocutors in South Africa, the United Kingdom, and the United States who have provided valuable comments, references, the gift of their time, and encouragement over many years, sometimes without knowing it. However, I take full responsibility for the conclusions I have reached.

This book has a long genesis, originating in my time as a graduate student in political science at Northwestern University in the mid-1990s (on a Fulbright scholarship). There, I wrote a thesis on the introduction of commercial satellite television into South Africa. I subsequently returned to South Africa to work as a political researcher for a democracy think tank, the Institute for Democracy in South Africa. That job involved ample media punditry and piqued my interest in media's role in shaping political struggles. I spent the second half of 1998 researching state-media relations at Harvard's Shorenstein Center. Between 2000 and 2004, I researched and later wrote my doctoral dissertation on public mediation after apartheid by analyzing a series of elite media debates with specific reference to economic policy and social movement protest.

After completing my PhD in politics at the University of London in 2004, I returned to the subject of popular media, as I had realized that most South Africans do not experience the momentous changes to their country as elite debates (in op-ed columns or even news magazine programs on television) but through mass popular media like soap operas, reality television and advertising, and the internet.

In 2005 I took up a joint appointment in the departments of communication studies and African-American and African Studies at the University of Michigan, where I first started thinking about the topics in this book and published separately about reality television and rhetorical struggles over the AIDS pandemic.

I have presented some of the ideas in this book at academic conferences and in invited talks as well as written about my thoughts on the blog I founded in 2009, *Africa Is a Country*. It is these insights that I bring together in this book.

Two of my most important interlocutors are Herman Wasserman and Wendy Willems. Herman is my closest friend and our collaboration probably my longest, dating back to Cape Town in the early 1990s. Wendy and I met in Harare, Zimbabwe, in the late 1990s, and we have maintained a friendship and enjoyed debates about media that have spanned continents.

Various others were generous with ideas, support and time over the years. They include David Styan, my former PhD advisor at Birkbeck College, University of London; Sunil Agnani; Akin Akedosan; Farzanah Badsha; Omar Badsha; Patrick Bond; Mamadou Diouf; Susan Douglas; Peter Dwyer; Ntone Edjabe; Ebrahim Fakir; Jonathan Faull; Benjamin Fogel; Krista Johnson; Ron Krabill; Dan Magaziner; Elzbieta Matynia; Marissa Moorman; Martin Murray; Lene Øverland; Suren Pillay; Anne Pitcher; Aswin Punathembekar; Lucia Sacks; the late Elaine Salo; Paddy Scannell; Brent Simons; Dylan Valley; and the late Marilyn Young.

Andrea Meeson, Camilla Houeland, Kenichi Serino, Jessica Blatt, and Caitlin Chandler made edits on various drafts of chapters or to the full manuscript.

Gavin Silber, Mandisa Mbali, Doron Isaacs, Nathan Geffen, Brad Brockman, Anso Thom, Ashwin Desai, Achal Prabhala, Mia Malan, Kerry Cullinan, Zachary Levenson, Brett Davidson, Steven Friedman, Lily Saint, and Andrea Meeson gave comments on the chapter on HIV/AIDS social movements. Matthew Crouse, Neil McCarthy, Akin Omotoso, Vanessa Jansen, Rosa Keet, Mfundi Vundla, and Kethiwe Ngcobo agreed to be interviewed about South African soap operas. Peter Bruce, Peet Kruger, Mondli Makhanya, and Mathatha Tsedu agreed to be interviewed for a journal article about the media and xenophobia in 2003. Those interviews proved very useful in forming a picture of South African media after the transition. Interactions with Christi van der Westhuizen, Thomas Michael Blaser, Tom Devriendt, and Jacob Boersema and their collective researches especially influenced my thinking about Afrikaner identity politics. Over the years, many other South African media workers and journalists—too many to recount here—gave informally of their time to chat about the sector; a lot of those discussions made it into my formulations and conclusions.

Aubrey Bloomfield, Yael Even Or, Adam Esrig, and Pablo Medina Uribe assisted with research. Thanks also to my colleagues and students in the Graduate Program in International Affairs at The New School and previously at the Center for Afro-American and African Studies as well as Communication Studies at the University of Michigan, where I floated some of these ideas in classes and seminars. For four summers in a row between 2012 and 2015, I accompanied groups of New School graduate students as part of the International Field Program to Cape Town. These two-month visits proved valuable in updating my conclusions about what was happening to media in South Africa.

Earlier versions of some of the content in chapter 4, *Big Brother* MultiChoice, were explored in "*Big Brother*, Africa Is Watching," *Media, Culture and Society* 29, no. 6 (2007): 851–868.

Though the material is new and the focus different, I have written before about the themes in chapter 5, HIV-Positive Media, in "Media, Social Movements and the State: Competing Images of HIV/AIDS in South Africa," coauthored with Krista Johnson and published in *African Studies Quarterly* 9, no. 4 (Fall 2007): 127–152.

I could not have asked for a more patient editor, Dee Mortensen, who stuck with me throughout this process. Special thanks also to Paige Rasmussen at Indiana University Press for working with me.

My children, Leo and Rosa, have to listen to me endlessly drone on about South Africa and Africa. It is so they do not forget who they are. It was fun watching South African television commercials, clips from soap operas, and parliamentary debates with them on YouTube. I can still hear them on the latter: "Can we watch 'Point of Order' again, Dad?"

Finally, to Jessica Blatt, my partner in life and one of the smartest and most perceptive people I know. She read most of the manuscript, shot down my worst ideas, and helped me formulate some of the best. She loves me more than I deserve, and, more than anyone, has made me a better writer.

MEDIA IN POSTAPARTHEID SOUTH AFRICA

Introduction

SOUTH AFRICAN BREWERIES (SAB) has long dominated the national beer market and is associated with the country's most popular sports teams. In 2002 SAB acquired the US company Miller Brewing. While one of SAB's brands, Castle Lager, became South Africa's most recognizable brand of beer, SABMiller became a multinational corporation, the world's second largest beer brewer, and a global brand.[1] Notwithstanding this expanding profile, much of SABMiller's branding continued to emphasize its South African roots.

One of SABMiller's most popular television commercials first aired in 2004 on the tenth anniversary of South Africa's first democratic elections. The commercial opens with scenes of crowds across South Africa gathering on streets, on beaches, and in fields. The camera zooms in on a crowd that is noticeably diverse in terms of class, race, age, and gender. Gradually, each person picks up a stretch of rope from the ground and starts pulling. In the next few fast-cut scenes, viewers note the dramatic effects of the crowds' collective effort, literally felt around the world. A guard at Buckingham Palace in London feels the earth move under him; a window cleaner on scaffolding in Manhattan shakes. The South Africans are drawing the world toward them. Globally recognizable landmarks like the Statue of Liberty in New York City, Pão de Açúcar (Sugarloaf Mountain) in Rio de Janeiro, and the Sydney Opera House in Australia are dragged into sighting distance of Cape Town's Table Mountain.[2] A rousing South African pop song with lyrics in English and Zulu, sung by white pop singer Johnny Clegg, plays in the background.[3] As the crowds admire their handiwork, a voice-over drives the point home: "At the South African Breweries, we have always believed that our country's most precious asset is its people. And that by harnessing the power of our nation, we can all achieve the extraordinary. The South African Breweries, inspired by a nation."[4]

Only a decade earlier, on April 27, 1994, South Africans had voted in their country's first democratic elections. The elections represented a break with nearly three hundred and fifty years of colonialism and apartheid. For the bulk of the twentieth century, only white people had the right to fully participate in South Africa's political institutions and governance structures as citizens. The "nation" effectively meant the white nation. Black subjects operated in a separate, unequal world of Bantustans (homelands) and faux citizenship; they had their own "nations," though, unlike white people, they had no say in how South Africa was governed. White people also controlled television, advertising, and newspapers, among other things.

The liberation movements that fought apartheid imagined a socialist, nonracial vision for South Africa. But that vision was subject to censorship, exile, and the shutdown of media outlets that openly identified with antiapartheid movements. South African brands operated within the bounds of the white-controlled public arena, isolated even further after the early 1980s by cultural sanctions and economic boycotts imposed by Great Britain's Equity Actors' Union and some Hollywood producers and actors.

Since 1994, political discourse has been driven by the imperatives of national unity and public consensus around a singular South African political identity. The SABMiller television commercial distilled that message into an idealized vision of South Africa's present and its future possibilities. This new political consciousness was not sui generis but rather the outcome of a multipronged set of conscious political projects symbolized and pushed forward by political leaders such as Nelson Mandela, Desmond Tutu, and Thabo Mbeki.

Mandela especially built a public persona grounded in conciliatory and consensus politics. His legendary appearance at the 1995 Rugby World Cup final in Johannesburg brought together a host of these themes. At the time, rugby was still considered a white man's sport, even though black men's participation in rugby dates back to the sport's introduction in the region in the late nineteenth century. The national team, the Springboks, was associated with white masculinity and was exploited by Afrikaner nationalist ideologues as a reflection of regime strength and white people's dominance during apartheid.[5] Since the early 1980s, South Africa had been subjected to a sports boycott. Test rugby matches between the Springboks and old rivals like New Zealand's All Blacks and Great Britain's Lions were particularly affected, with few nations willing to play in South Africa. In the wake of Mandela's release and the unbanning of liberation movements in 1990, South Africa was slowly allowed back into test rugby. By the time of the 1995 Rugby World Cup final, many aspects of the game were still overwhelmingly white, including the administration of the game, the audience (primarily only white people could afford tickets), and the makeup of the Springbok team, which had only one black squad member. Nevertheless, the fact that South Africa was chosen to host the Rugby World Cup was seen as the culmination of the normalization of relations between South Africa and the rest of the world and an endorsement of the political transition. At the start of the 1995 final match between the Springboks and the All Blacks, Mandela dressed in a replica of the SABMiller-sponsored Springbok team shirt and appeared on the field to rally the South African team and (mostly white) fans in the stadium as well as those watching on television. Mandela's carefully calculated actions were later credited with symbolically doing more than any other political leader to reconcile local white citizens with his presidency and the new South Africa. This series of events later got a Hollywood ending, becoming the basis for a feature film directed by Clint Eastwood that celebrated the Springbok victory and Mandela's actions as a symbol of reconciliation and forgiveness between white and black South Africans.[6]

Archbishop Desmond Tutu, the head of the Anglican Church in South Africa in the 1980s and 1990s and a Nobel Peace Prize winner, will be remembered for popularizing the slogan "rainbow nation" as a catch-all for South African identity. The idea was that South Africa consisted of many colors, living together and building a new country. While criticized for playing down race and class inequalities in favor of South African unity, rainbowism proved particularly effective in shaping journalistic, advertising, and branding discourses about the country and its people. Thabo Mbeki, Mandela's successor as president of South Africa, similarly popularized an inclusive African identity for all South Africans under his "African Renaissance" label, which emphasized black renewal and South Africa reconnecting to the African continent.

Government ministries built the attainment of a singular national consciousness into their policy goals, whether reforming education or housing. So did public commissions like the Truth and Reconciliation Commission (TRC), which dominated media headlines between 1996 and 1998. In such formulations, especially at the TRC, South Africa's greatest asset was its ability to transcend its seemingly intractable social problems.

SABMiller's marketing campaigns drew heavily on this symbolism and claimed for the company a link to the glorious, patriotic camaraderie associated with the end of apartheid, the country's transition to liberal democracy, the construction of a rainbow nation, and South Africa's aspirations as a global player. SABMiller's actual history was deeply intertwined with colonialism and apartheid, including the promotion of segregated drinking cultures and exploitation of cheap labor. However, in its new South African advertising, the company embodied the triumphant and expectant messages of the political transition. Whereas apartheid emphasized divisions, the "new" nation was pulling as one, according to SABMiller. Whereas apartheid symbolized sanctions and isolation, now South Africa—and SABMiller—was part of the world and ready to do business with it. The story of South African unity was so compelling that it was bringing the world together.

The 2004 SABMiller commercial was good marketing: its brands now dominate over 90 percent of beer sales in South Africa. But it also highlights the growing importance in South Africa of popular media—such as television commercials, television soap operas, reality television, and the internet—in the construction and reconstruction of a new national identity and politics.

Though South Africa had a well-developed media sphere under apartheid, and commercials were commonplace since at least 1978 (television was only introduced in 1976), the apartheid state worked hard to control what kinds of messages were conveyed by commercials, television dramas, or variety shows and what was being reported or discussed on news programs. This oversight was made easier by the fact that until the late 1980s, the state broadcaster was the only one licensed to provide broadcasting services. Postapartheid, in a free media environment, the state's control over media processes would weaken and South African broadcasting would witness the addition of private broadcasters, including satellite television. As a result, advertising copywriters, creative directors, and the people behind television soap operas and reality shows took on increasingly decisive roles in envisaging the terms of the new South Africa.

With the opening of formerly white-controlled, heavily propagandistic media spaces, television commercials, soap operas, reality television, and social media became public spaces. There South Africans could reflect on and work through—with varying degrees of resolution—debates, contests, and projections about the country. Popular media also become the place where South Africans could publicly define the country's relation to the rest of the continent and the broader world. In general, in popular media, corporate interests and national political agendas aligned together to construct a mostly neoliberal, uncritically capitalist and consumerist vision of South African social life. But this also created or opened spaces for social movements to shape discourse. In some cases, this could mean that forces that did not celebrate the new dispensation could use the internet to deepen the terms of the new democracy. Others could use it to reject the new South Africa and imagine a segregated future.

This book explores these various dimensions through a series of case studies. Some examples include moments that illustrate how an alliance between rainbowism and consumer capital drove the new South African narrative in advertisements and soap operas and then exported that vision to the rest of the continent via reality television. Other examples explore the politics of groups who dissent from the postapartheid consensus and as a result seek out alternative media spaces such as the internet.

In the cases explored in this book, media provide a window to the competing narratives of the vital social transition from a society organized around apartheid and opposition to it to the consumerist, aspirational, capitalist, individualist reality of contemporary South Africa. They offer a way to narrate and analyze the reconstruction of a kind of South African citizenship in the wake of state-sponsored white supremacy and its nationalist, socialist, and leftist opposition. We see South African media consolidate and enact the victory of a particular image of what South Africa ought to be. That projected image and the subsequent messaging is then broadcast across Africa as a neo-Pan Africanist or commoditized idea of what the continent ought to be and South Africa's place in it. We also see the emergence of new sites of contestation and resistance to these processes.

Organization of the Book

Chapter 1 reviews the broad outlines of South Africa's media history, homing in on a series of media events associated with the transition and the new democracy: Mandela's release from prison in 1990, his April 1993 television address in the wake of the murder of popular communist leader Chris Hani, the first democratic election in 1994, the 1995 Rugby World Cup, and the proceedings of the TRC (1996–1998). While these events may be familiar to many readers, the argument here is that these media events not only inaugurated a democratic age but also a media age. The claim of this book is that media events like these ushered in an intensified, mediated politics that has defined political life in South Africa since the beginning of the second decade of democratic rule. In this context, journalists, screenwriters, television producers, advertising creatives, and activists on social media become crucial political actors, helping to set the terms of debate about the meaning of citizenship.

Chapter 2 explores the textual and technical worlds of television commercials. As the SABMiller case described earlier suggests, South African television commercials are notable for their politicized rhetoric and for invoking a certain rendering of history and the political present, whether they are marketing cars or beer or promoting company brands. The chapter explores how South Africa's political and business elites understand the mystique of liberation, the political transition and democracy ("the past," "overcoming," and "the nation") as commercial resources and as something ordinary people want to be associated with. The elites recognized that public acceptance of rainbowism was decisive for the success of the government's political programs and was good for business. Here we see the mutual imbrication of corporate brands and the state. The branding favored by South African companies celebrates the neoliberal settlement in the country and dovetails nicely with state projects that imagine postracial futures and a globalized South Africa.

Chapter 3 builds on the analysis of advertising by examining soap operas aired on the country's public broadcaster, the South African Broadcasting

Corporation (SABC). Soap operas became one of the key sites for the production of South African national identities and for reflecting on political and social changes. Soap operas also provided models for changing racial attitudes and aspirational politics among black South Africans. Crucially, private producers and SABC commissioning editors of these soap operas were guided by a socially driven understanding of media—one shared with the public broadcaster's board. As a result, soap operas commissioned by the SABC were encouraged to explicitly engage with the political transition as well as imagine or create original values for a new South Africa. This chapter discusses two of the longest-running and top-rated soap operas on South African television, which dominated television schedules on the SABC for the first two generations or so of South African freedom: *Generations*, broadcast between 1994 and 2014, and *Isidingo* (the need), which made its debut in 1998 and is still on the air. *Generations* was set in an all-black media company and was explicitly geared at upwardly mobile black viewers. *Isidingo* revolved first around the happenings in a mining town and later moved to a television studio. *Generations*' plotlines and characters reflected the aspirational politics associated with South Africa's black middle and working classes. It also highlighted discourses of black economic empowerment favored by Mandela's successor, Mbeki. *Isidingo* reflected the compromises and reconciliatory politics of the political and economic transition and marketed itself as "one-nation viewing"—a show equally for black and white viewers.[7] Overall, the idea with both programs—and with soap operas on the SABC in general—was to cultivate a particular kind of viewer, the aspirational viewer, one who was open to the promises of capitalism and the market economy and thus would thrive under the new conditions of political and, presumably, economic freedom.

Chapter 4 explores the business strategies of MultiChoice, the South African–owned satellite television company that dominates television production and broadcasting on the continent. As a result of its success, MultiChoice became an important vehicle through which South African corporations coordinated their expansion into the rest of Africa. In the process, MultiChoice reimagined ordinary South Africans' relationship with other Africans (at least on-screen) and reshaped popular culture elsewhere on the continent. The chapter explores these developments on two fronts: first, reality television and, second, MultiChoice's attempts to gain a share of the huge profits generated by the southern Nigerian film industry known as Nollywood.

The first half of the chapter focuses on the reality show *Big Brother Africa*. A South African production company owns the African franchise rights to the Dutch show *Big Brother*; it broadcasted *Big Brother Africa* live from a house in South Africa's commercial and media capital, Johannesburg. Twelve contestants were drawn from twelve countries across the continent, including Kenya, Angola, Nigeria, and the hosts South Africa.[8] The composition of the cast set *Big*

Brother Africa apart from most other editions of the show elsewhere in the world as well as previous series in South Africa, which were mostly nationally based. As a result, the show projected pan-Africanist sensibilities. The main effect of the format, however, was to expose millions of Africans to South Africa's political and social discourses. Some African governments and political and cultural elites objected to *Big Brother Africa*. Ordinary Africans, however, sought out the program. In some cases, *Big Brother Africa* became the space where Africans could openly and matter-of-factly debate identity, class, and gender politics in their own countries—debates from which they were otherwise shielded, whether by censorship or "tradition."

The chapter also explores MultiChoice's relationship to Nollywood, the world's second largest producer of movies by volume. Much of Nollywood's wealth was built informally in terms of distribution and exhibition networks; this film industry had been relatively independent of global corporations. MultiChoice understood that Nollywood was the most financially profitable entertainment outlet available in West Africa and wanted in on it. The question was whether MultiChoice could succeed where global media networks had thus far failed—that is, could it become involved with a local media culture and local production and distribution systems without necessarily destroying them and remain profitable. As this chapter shows, MultiChoice's strategy was to commodify and standardize Nollywood rather than eliminate it. By 2012, MultiChoice was screening Nollywood films around the clock on its bouquet of "Africa Magic" channels, including Hausa- and Yoruba-specific channels. In the process, MultiChoice became the largest screener of televised Nollywood movies.

Big Brother Africa was unique in its early use of interactive technology such as text messaging and later social media to engage audiences around the continent. While viewers voted contestants out via text message, the show also used audience texts to create a live stream of comments and discussion. Text messages by viewers, and later Twitter and Facebook comments, scrolling across the bottom of the screen became integral to the show's success. That ticker also became a space where viewers could express open dissent with their respective governments' or local religious authorities' opposition to *Big Brother Africa*. As we see in the remaining two chapters, groups like AIDS campaigners and Afrikaner nationalists, who were not included in nation-building discourses, similarly found space in interactive online technologies to develop alternative politics.

In Chapter 5, I explore the politics of the Treatment Action Campaign (TAC), an AIDS campaigner group that dissented from the postapartheid consensus very early on in its critique of the ruling African National Congress's (ANC's) handling of the AIDS crisis. From 1998 through the first decade of the 2000s, South Africa faced an HIV epidemic of enormous proportions. It was made worse by President Mbeki, who denied the causal link between HIV and AIDS, claimed that antiretrovirals were toxic, and refused to support a government-funded scale-up of HIV treatment. Mbeki's claims were unfounded and dismissed as bunk by the medical establishment, but he sought out and enjoyed the support of AIDS denialists (who referred to themselves as "dissidents") online. However, TAC was much more effective at using the internet to advance its own narratives and build transnational alliances for its work. One consequence of TAC's work was that Mbeki was forced to resign one year before the end of his presidential term while TAC won its demands for a government-funded AIDS treatment plan. This chapter focuses on TAC's use of media communication tools, both off- and especially online, which it used to mount a successful critique of the limits of rainbowism and the failures of neoliberal governance.

Chapter 6 moves on to a different kind of counternarrative, exploring the relationship between media and the formation of white, especially Afrikaner, political identities after apartheid. For much of its history in the twentieth century and coinciding with apartheid, Afrikaner political identities remained monolithic and stable. The boundaries of Afrikanerdom were effectively policed by a small, contained elite in the state, security forces, schools, Afrikaans universities, clergy, and Afrikaans media. The end of apartheid disrupted this status quo, and Afrikaner identities were suddenly up for grabs: Who would define Afrikaner identity after apartheid and how would they go about it? And what implications, if any, would the changing political environment and a revolution in media technology have for white South African, especially Afrikaner, identities? In this chapter, I argue that media technologies were key to the emergence of new identity entrepreneurs among white South Africans who would tap into and exploit global discourses of identity, including those around "minority rights" and "victimhood." I argue that two sets of factors combine to explain the formation of postapartheid Afrikaner political identities: the first is the impact of globalized discourses circulating online about identity—about "victims" of cultural domination. The second refers to the symbiotic relationship that develops between media-savvy figures or movements (identity entrepreneurs) and established Afrikaans media companies.

The conclusion speculates about what the declining influence of mass party politics, print journalism, and other traditional media means for identity formation, cultural politics, and political representation. It also draws preliminary insights about the impacts of new forms of mediated communication (various web news affiliations, YouTube videos, increasing narrow casting of satellite television channels, and mobile technology) on political life.

Why This Book

Media in Postapartheid South Africa explores the workings of popular and social media in creating new visions of the South African nation for consumption at home and on the rest of the continent. As the nation is reimagined by corporations and the state, so is citizenship—around the ability to consume but also around ways to influence political processes. We can identify glimpses of the emerging terms of political contestation in South Africa and social and commercial configurations elsewhere on the continent. In this text, I join the scholarly move in political science away from studying familiar categories for gauging political change—that is, the agencies of the state, political party politics, and elite media (journalism, opinion editorials, television news, etc.) already covered so well by mainstream political scientists, historians, and other traditional social scientists—toward studying media symbolism, ritual, culture, and ideology. Here Fredric Jameson's "sweeping hypothesis" that third-world artistic texts be read as "national allegories" may be useful for how we understand the role of soap operas or advertising in a place like South Africa and how we "read" them. Jameson argues that "third-world texts, even those which are seemingly private and invested with a properly libidinal dynamic—necessarily project a political dimension in the form of national allegory: *the story of the private individual destiny is always an allegory of the embattled situation of the public third-world culture and society*" (emphasis in original).[9] The move to the popular—and to culture—reflects a transition in political life globally that is also observed in South Africa. As Ron Krabill and I, drawing on public deliberation theory, have argued elsewhere about postapartheid South African politics, the larger context for the growing role of media in political processes is the decline of mass political parties and social movements. There are several key characteristics of this new politics. For one, political debate becomes tied to election cycles. As for the language of politics, it is conducted mostly on television in a code discernible to political elites (especially political journalists and political party operatives) that excludes ordinary people in the process.[10] We also witness that more indirect forms of politics—like civil society and social movements—replace old-style political parties. Media substitute for and resemble the public sphere to a large degree. The day-to-day restructuring of social and political life is given some sense of collective shape and meaning through mass media.[11] Politics increasingly reflects the style of entertainment. More specifically, media characterized as "news" or as "news analysis" decline in impact relative to popular entertainment media in shaping popular opinion.[12]

Another focus is social media's role in politics. Though television has made powerful forays into political and cultural life in South Africa and Africa, it is in the social media frontier where, as writer and social commentator Binyavanga Wainaina suggests, a new African intellectual history is being written.[13] In South Africa, as elsewhere on the continent and in the developing world, struggles over political meaning between key political actors now play out online. Political identity, long the preserve of the state or political elites, is increasingly the domain of popular cultural figures and popular media.[14] Social media applications such as Twitter and Facebook (and Facebook Live) have become integral to the communication strategies of social movements and political parties. South Africa is no different. This book explores aspects of these emerging politics in two of its chapters. For example, how TAC maneuvered interactive media had profound implications for government policy and social movement activism not just in South Africa but further afield. At the same time, the case of online Afrikaner nationalism reminds us that the internet (and social media)—usually held up as democratizing agents and associated with media development—can also serve to entrench media inequalities or foster antidemocratic politics.

For much of its history, South Africa has been treated as an exceptional country by scholars, analysts, and activists (whether those rationalizing apartheid or those struggling to imagine an alternative vision of the nation). On the surface, exceptionalism made sense: the country was the last holdout among the twentieth century's racial and colonial states; further, its liberation movement took place after an international consensus on human rights and nonracism had already emerged—at least at a rhetorical level. Add to all this the myth of the rainbow nation, the singular and outsized celebrity and legend of Nelson Mandela, and the much-touted reconciliatory nature of South Africa's transition to democracy. Together, these factors contribute to the view of South Africa as an exceptional nation. A closer look suggests South Africa exemplified phenomena that were and are globally commonplace: apartheid as a form of colonialism, an elite political transition (with its government of national unity and truth commission) similar to transitions elsewhere in Latin America and Southeast Asia, and the adoption of neoliberal economic policies. In addition, the growing clout of multinational corporations and the privatization of key public services are, similarly, part of a broad, general global story. The same story could be told about South Africa's media, especially the emergence of a liberal media environment and the turn to the popular.

South Africa has long been viewed as separate from the rest of the African continent. Despite appearances, however, South Africa's economic history and its political struggle have always been closely intertwined with the rest of the continent—a process intensified after apartheid. Anthropologists Jean and John Comaroff refer to postapartheid South Africa as the "America of Africa."[15] Although the country was until recently isolated from the rest of the continent and operated as a racist dictatorship, in the past twenty years it has emerged as a major territorial, economic, political, and media powerhouse on the African continent. South Africa now inhabits an intermediary position as simultaneously a regional superpower and a link between its neighbors, the region, and the world. South African businesses dominate economic relations with immediate neighbors and in the southern African region.[16] Although there is a long tradition of scholarship about South African capitalist and military expansion and engagement with the rest of the continent—dating back to the mining industry of the nineteenth century and continuing during apartheid and the Cold War—fewer works have paid attention to the cultural and specifically media elements of South Africa's expansion into the continent. South Africa's postapartheid media elites and corporations shape consumption patterns, continental political identities, and understandings of political citizenship in key ways. This book builds on and joins budding scholarship on these connections.[17]

Finally, media scholarship on African media operates with a focus on what is broadly termed "media development"—that is, what is lacking in African media or African public spheres, or how much catching up there is to do terms of technology, access, or resources—and debates about freedom of expression, democracy, and press freedom. But as a number of scholars have pointed out, while useful for the funding agendas of Western agencies, these approaches and data mean little for or do not tell us much about African media and audiences. Achille Mbembe, for example, notes that while "we now feel we know nearly everything that African states, societies and economies *are not*, we still know absolutely nothing about *what they actually are*" (emphasis in original).[18] Filling this gap requires a break with normative, instrumental frameworks to more descriptive and analytical approaches. It also requires breaking with glib celebrations of creativity and inventiveness of "the local" to confront questions of power, especially of neoliberalism.[19] So, the focus in this book is on what *is* there: what content gets produced, how it is produced, and the politics that flow from those processes. It takes popular media seriously.

For a long time, most third-world societies and media systems were deemed to be receptacles and carbon copies of northern cultural products and ideas. That idea has been thoroughly debunked for the most part, except when it comes to African cultural production. However, more recently a number of theorists have challenged the general outlines of the former approach. In some cases, theorists and researchers have suggested Africa as a useful place from where to study rampant globalization, neoliberal reform, or the limits and potential of liberal democracy.[20] In the early 2000s, cultural theorist Paul Gilroy, for example, viewed South Africa "and its lessons as the best hope for a politically realigned world," according to Audrey T. McCluskey. Gilroy made the following plea: "It is my hope that, not Europe and the North Atlantic, but the post-colonial world in general, and South Africa in particular, will in due course, generate an opposed and yet equivalent sense of what our networked world might be and become."[21] Rather than acting mostly as amplifiers of social conflict and politics—as they do in traditional first-world markets—media in postcolonial, including African, societies have emerged as the "authoritative cultural archive."[22] Television, radio, digital culture, print journalism, sound culture, and social media dominate our political and social lives. Media are how most people learn about globalization, scandal, consumption, and politics. Media are the vehicles through which the past and present are mobilized and, crucially, through which a range of new regional or "middle" powers attempt to increase their influences. Prominent among these middle powers are Qatar's various Al Jazeera channels, the pan-South American Telesur news service, the export of Brazilian or Turkish soap operas to the Arab world and Lusophone African states, and Mexico's various private television firms that broadcast in and control Latino markets in the United States. South Africa's media corporations like MultiChoice or, until recently, the continental version of the public broadcaster, SABC Africa, can also be counted among these. Thus, Jamaicans watch South African soap operas like *Generations*; Americans can access the cable channel Africa TV, which is mostly a bouquet of South African productions (including morning shows); and Nigerians can watch Nollywood "on-demand" on satellite television services run by South African–owned MultiChoice.

This book is about South African identity in the context of globalization and postcoloniality and where media is increasingly available everywhere: on phones, on television and radio sets, and, even now, still in print. The choices made by media powers (whether editors, writers, advertisers, or the state itself) help to configure, define, and limit who "the people" know themselves to be. But, of course "the people" now also make their own media. And increasingly it is social media driven by public debates and desires that is most influential in shaping not just South African society but political identities elsewhere on the continent.

Notes

1. In October 2016, SABMiller became a business division of Brazilian beer company Anheuser-Busch InBev, making it part of the largest brewery in the world. Dealbook, "SABMiller, From Local Brewer to Global Leader, *New York Times*, August 17, 2011, https://dealbook.nytimes.com/2011/08/17/sabmiller-from-local-brewer-to-global-leader/; Robb M. Stewart, "Foster's Shareholders Approve SABMiller Bid," *Wall Street Journal*, December 1, 2011, https://www.wsj.com/articles/SB10001424052970204012004577071092363029270; Jonathan Jannarone, "SABMiller Gets a Lot Out of Africa," *Wall Street Journal*, May 23, 2013, https://www.wsj.com/articles/SB10001424127887323336104578501223302283786.

2. See Ngiyadela, "South African Breweries Advert," YouTube, June 3, 2007, https://www.youtube.com/watch?v=SxILx2qGOHE.

3. Stuart William and Mark Brzezicki, "Osiyeza," EMI Music Publishing, 1993.

4. Ngiyadela, "South African Breweries Advert."

5. I discuss this event and its political import in more detail in chapter 1.

6. *Invictus*, dir. Clint Eastwood (Liberty Pictures/Warner Bros., 2009).

7. Kulani Nkuna, "Isidingo Tackles Abuse," *The Citizen*, October 12, 2013, https://citizen.co.za/lifestyle/your-life-entertainment-your-life/97388/exploring-abuse/.

8. Even *Big Brother Naija*, the Nigerian iteration of the show, was based in South Africa.

9. Fredric Jameson, "Third-World Literature in the Era of Multinational Capitalism," *Social Text* 15 (1986): 69.

10. Sean Jacobs and Ron Krabill, "Mediating Manenberg in the post-Apartheid Public Sphere: Media, Democracy and Citizenship," in *Limits to Liberation after Apartheid: Citizenship, Governance and Culture*, edited by Steven L. Robins, 157–172 (Cape Town: James Currey, 2005).

11. Ibid., 158.

12. Sonja Narunsky-Laden's work explores some of these aspects in relation to popular print magazines aimed at black consumers. See, for example, Sonja Laden, "Who's Afraid of a Black Bourgeoisie? Consumer Magazines for Black South Africans as an Apparatus of Change," *Journal of Consumer Culture* 3, no. 2 (2003): 191–216; and Sonja Narunsky-Laden, "Identity in Post-Apartheid South Africa: 'Learning to Belong' through the (Commercial) Media," in *Power, Politics and Identity in South African Media*, edited by Adrian Hadland, Eric Louw, Simphiwe Sesanti, and Herman Wasserman, 124–148 (Pretoria: HSRC Press, 2008).

13. Binyavanga Wainaina, public remarks, Yale University, New Haven, CT, October 8, 2014.

14. See, for example, Ron Krabill, *Starring Mandela and Cosby: Media and the End(s) of Apartheid* (Chicago: University of Chicago Press, 2010); and Herman Wasserman, *Tabloid Journalism in South Africa: True Story!* (Bloomington: Indiana University Press, 2010). For work outside South Africa but with similar approaches and focuses, also see Aswin Punathambekar, *From Bombay to Bollywood: The Making of a Global Media Industry* (New York: New York University Press, 2013); and Arvind Rajagopal, *Politics after Television: Hindu Nationalism and the Reshaping of the Public in India* (Cambridge: Cambridge University Press, 2001). See also the articles and essays by Moradewun Adejunmobi, Wendy Willems, Jonathan Gray, Katrien Pype, and Paddy Scannell in a special issue on "Media in Africa" that I edited for *Popular Communication: The International Journal of Media and Culture* 9, no. 1 (2011).

15. Jean Comaroff and John Comaroff, *Theory from the South: Or, How Euro-America Is Evolving toward Africa* (Boulder, CO: Paradigm, 2012), 14.

16. See Roger Southall, "Is Lesotho South Africa's Tenth Province?" *Indicator SA* 15, no. 4 (1998): 83–89; P. Mathoma, "South Africa and Lesotho—Sovereign Independence or a Tenth Province," in *South African Yearbook of International Affairs, 1999/2000* (Johannesburg: South African Institute of International Affairs, 1999); and Alex Duval Smith, "Lesotho's People Plead with South Africa to Annex Their Troubled Country," *The Guardian*, June 5, 2010, https://www.theguardian.com/world/2010/jun/06/lesotho-independence-south-africa.

17. This book builds on and complements the media research of, among others, Iginio Gagliardone on media technologies in Ethiopia (how new technologies entrench authoritarian politics); Victoria Bernal's ethnography of Oromo identity politics; Tendai Chari's work on Zimbabwe's diaspora and online media; and Mehita Iqani's work on consumption in *Consumption and Media in the Global South: Aspiration Contested*. Media scholar Wendy Willems's broad theoretical reflections on popular culture and the African public sphere are also useful markers; so is the volume, with its broader remit, on "transcultural political economy" edited by Paula Chakravartty and Yuezhi Zhao. Iginio Gagliardone, "The Techno Politics of the Ethiopian Nation," in *Knowledge Development and Social Change through Technology: Emerging Studies*, edited by Elayne Coakes, 206–222 (Hershey, PA: IGI Global, 2011); Victoria Bernal, "Diaspora, Cyberspace and Political Imagination: The Eritrean Diaspora Online," *Global Networks* 6, no. 2 (2006): 161–179; Tendai Chari, "Longing and Belonging: An Exploration of the Online News-Consumption Practices of the Zimbabwean Diaspora," in *Journalism, Audiences and Diaspora*, edited by Ola Ogunyemi, 235–249 (New York: Palgrave Macmillan, 2015); Mehita Iqani, *Consumption and Media in the Global South: Aspiration Contested* (New York: Palgrave-MacMillan, 2015); Wendy Willems, "Interrogating Public Sphere and Popular

Culture as Theoretical Concepts on Their Value in African Studies," *Africa Development* 37, no. 1 (2012): 11–26; Wendy Willems, "Beyond Normative Dewesternization: Examining Media Culture from the Vantage Point of the Global South," *The Global South* 8, no. 1 (2014): 7–23; and Paula Chakravartty and Yuezhi Zhao, eds., *Global Communications: Toward a Transcultural Political Economy* (Lanham, MD: Rowman and Littlefield, 2007).

18. Achille Mbembe, *On the Postcolony* (Durham: Duke, 2001), 9, quoted in Willems, "Beyond Normative Dewesternization," 18.

19. Willems, "Beyond Normative Dewesternization," 19.

20. Comaroff and Comaroff, *Theory from the South*, 1. See also Francis Nyamnjoh, "De-Westernizing Media Theory to Make Room for African Experience," in *Popular Media, Democracy and Development in Africa*, edited by Herman Wasserman (New York: Routledge, 2010): 19–31.

21. Paul Gilroy, "Cosmopolitanism Contested: What South Africa's Recent History Offers to a World in Which Solidarity Has Become Suspect" (keynote lecture, Celebrating Ten Years of Democracy, Wiser Conference, University of Witwatersrand, Johannesburg, South Africa, May 10, 2004), 1–2, quoted in McCluskey, *The Devil You Dance With* (Chicago: University of Illinois Press, 2009), 1.

22. Ravi Sundaram, "Postcolonial Media after the Informal" (public lecture, State Library of Victoria, Melbourne, Australia, March 24, 2011).

CHAPTER 1

The Mandela Channel

IN THIS CHAPTER, I review the broad outlines of South Africa's media history, honing in on a series of media events associated with the nation's transition from institutional apartheid to the new democracy. In short order, they are Nelson Mandela's release from prison in 1990; Mandela's April 1993 television address in the wake of the murder of Chris Hani, a popular communist leader; the first democratic election in 1994; the 1995 Rugby World Cup (which I have already discussed to some extent in the introduction); and the proceedings of the TRC between 1996 and 1998. These events, familiar to many students of South African politics, are recounted here because they helped to inaugurate not only a democratic age but a media age—specifically a television age—in South Africa. Equally, they ushered in an intensified, mediated politics that has defined political life in South Africa since the beginning of the second decade of democratic rule. This is a political epoch in which journalists, screenwriters, television producers, advertising copyeditors or creatives, and activists on social media became central actors in South Africa's political drama and in the process helped define the terms of debate over the meaning of citizenship in postapartheid South Africa.

The life trajectory of the most visible South African public figure of the twentieth century, Nelson Mandela, captures this transformation well. It begins with Mandela walking out of a prison outside Cape Town on Sunday, February 11, 1990, after spending twenty-seven years behind bars, most of them on Robben Island off the coast of Cape Town. Mandela's first steps as a free man were also South Africa's first "media event" in which all South Africans were participants.[1]

I remember the lead-up to Mandela's release. At the time, I was a student at the University of Cape Town and also a journalist at the campus newspaper. I watched the live broadcast of Mandela walking out of prison with my family in a township about nine miles from the city. For viewers in my family and community—who had mostly known political censorship—it was a new experience. Many of us had never seen images of Mandela because his likeness had been banned by the state from the time he was sentenced to life imprisonment in 1964. His likeness and voice mostly existed in yellowed images passed along by hand or on pirated copies of documentaries made by foreign television and film crews. Now he was live on state television, walking triumphantly out of the gates of Victor Verster prison outside Paarl with his then wife, Winnie Madikizela-Mandela, at his side. Television viewers watched on the SABC as Mandela's motorcade sped to the city. Then, before a crowd of tens of thousands in front of the Cape Town City Hall, in a city still governed by a white mayor, Mandela declared himself "not a prophet, but a humble servant of you the people" and drew from his now famous 1964 statement at the Rivonia Trial where he was sentenced to serve a life sentence on Robben Island: "I have fought against white domination and I have fought against black domination. I have cherished the ideal of a democratic and free society in which all persons live together in harmony and with equal opportunities. It is an ideal, which I hope to live for and to achieve. But if needs be, it is an ideal for which I am prepared to die."[2] Mainstream media—both local and major Western sources—fretted about Mandela thanking the South African Communist Party for its principled support or for not denouncing armed struggle, but this did not take away from the historical significance of the event as well as its media implications.

A few days earlier, on February 2, 1990, F. W. de Klerk, the last white president of South Africa, had delivered an explosive speech to Parliament that was carried live on the SABC. De Klerk announced the release of Mandela and remaining political prisoners and the unbanning of the ANC and other liberation movements. Most of the resistance movements had been banned from public life (and the media) for nearly three decades. In the days before the opening of Parliament, local and international presses had widely speculated that De Klerk would make a major announcement (it was an open secret that the government and the ANC had been negotiating behind closed doors). Nevertheless, there was still skepticism about whether De Klerk would follow through—he had a reputation as a hard-liner in the National Party—so many television viewers did not tune into his speech.

It is clear from the sequence of events surrounding Mandela's release, including De Klerk's speech days earlier, that the South African government understood its media power and was keen to control how the news would be received. For example, in the lead-up to Mandela's release date, De Klerk and his advisors worked hard to create a media image of the president as a reformer, someone who had taken bold steps in his decision to release Mandela and lift the ban on what was arguably the most popular and powerful liberation movement on the continent during the twentieth century.[3] De Klerk and his advisors knew they would negotiate themselves out of power. What they wanted to secure was their legacy—how they would be perceived for posterity (in this they were aware of the fate of former Soviet leader Mikhail Gorbachev, who in the wake of *perestroika* and *glasnost* was generally viewed as a pragmatic, bold reformer in Western media). They also wanted to control public opinion of the ensuing negotiations between the government and the ANC.

A week before Mandela's release and to ensure that the government dominated the front pages of Sunday newspapers (the most popular newspapers in South Africa at the time), De Klerk's office released an official photograph of the president posing next to Mandela. In the photograph, the two men stand stiffly beside each other in a study. The focus is on De Klerk, who smiles confidently at the camera, while Mandela looks away, awkward in an ill-fitting gray suit. The government arranged for every press conference or announcement by De Klerk's office about Mandela's release to be broadcast live. Its intent was clearly to spotlight De Klerk as an able statesman driving the political transition to democracy.[4] This was a definite departure from the norm of how successive South African governments had treated the press and radio and television journalists—that is, with contempt. The apartheid government had little time for media, with the exception of the pro-apartheid Afrikaans press, the SABC, and local and international media that acknowledged the supposed unique predicament of white people in South Africa and who could be counted on to rationalize apartheid to readers and listeners back in their home countries.

That said, the National Party government had a deep sense of the agenda-setting function of broadcast media. Frederik van Zyl Slabbert, a white parliamentary opposition leader, recalled in his 1985 memoir how National Party government ministers put state media, especially the SABC, in the service of the local version of the Southern strategy used by the Republican Party in the United States. The strategy involved the National Party presenting itself as the only bulwark against "black radicals" and majority rule on the one hand and as the only "moderate" alternative to more extreme white supremacist elements in white politics on the other. In this case, a cabinet minister told Slabbert: "Come election time, all we do is show Eugene Terre'Blanche [a local buffoonish neo-Nazi] giving his Nazi salute on TV and your voters will flock to our tables in the northern suburbs of Johannesburg."[5]

The Introduction of Television

Television as a broadcast medium came relatively late to South Africa. The apartheid government passed laws regulating television as early as 1949 but only introduced a national television service in 1976. Albert Hertzog, the cabinet minister responsible for broadcasting services in the 1960s and early 1970s, once famously described television as "that evil black box; sickly, mawkish, sentimentalist, and leading to dangerous liberalistic tendencies." Hertzog claimed that these "dangerous liberalistic tendencies" induced by television were foreign ideas. They originated outside South Africa, especially in the United States. In 1964 Hertzog, in graphic terms, warned the all-white Parliament about the negative effects of television: "It is afternoon and the Bantu [black] houseboy is in the living room cleaning the carpet. Someone has left the television set on. The houseboy looks up at the screen, sees a chorus-line of white girls in scanty costumes. Suddenly seized by lust, he runs upstairs and rapes the madam."[6] For National Party politicians, television normalized integration propaganda and, worse, promoted sameness. J. C. Otto, a National Party member of Parliament (MP), imagined a global conspiracy, invoking veiled anti-Semitic stereotypes: "What happened in regard to the Freedom Riders in the U.S.A.? There the television cameraman came along to photograph everything. There too the black man was represented as being the oppressed and ultimately emerged as heroes. The overseas money magnates have used television as a deadly weapon to undermine the moral and spiritual resilience of the white man."[7] In the end, the frustrations of most white South Africans—who felt cut off from the West and therefore were missing out on global events—led to the government changing its mind. It did not help matters that South Africa was also lagging behind more than 130 nations—including a number of African nations, much to white people's and the government's embarrassment—that already operated public and commercial television services. South Africa thus became "TV's final frontier in the industrial world."[8]

After the launch of SABC TV, the apartheid regime and the National Party predictably dropped their opposition to television and proceeded to trumpet the virtues and supposed benefits of the medium with the same fervor as they had previously rejected it. But this enthusiasm for television did not mean the apartheid rulers would abandon state control or overt political interference. For the bulk of the remaining period of apartheid rule, South African television was effectively an arm of the state and became the key means with which to build consensus for government policies and to cater exclusively to the anxieties and desires of the white minority.[9]

Documentary filmmaker Kevin Harris recalls the television of his childhood:

> In those days, television was white. There was no black television. It was a service for the white viewer. Their whole thrust was to make one-dimensional films about life in South Africa. Soap operas, that kind of thing, . . . reflected a white society as whites saw it. You had black townships like Soweto, which was [hidden] over the hill. Basically, black people came into your homes to work for you during the day and at night they went back to their homes. Television very much endorsed and propagated that [ideology]. It was broken down into [separate programming by race]. . . . White South Africans were not confronted with what was happening in their name.[10]

The SABC's programming was replete with regular broadcasts of military parades, state funerals, and heavily censored news bulletins that consistently disparaged any form of resistance, demonizing protesters as "Russian-trained," "terrorists," or as "agitators." A heavy dose of Calvinist Christianity shaped broadcast schedules: "Daily transmissions were bookended by stern scripture readings, the first lesson usually broadcast at more or less the same time that rival television channels [in South Africa] nowadays air their early evening dramas."[11]

It is necessary to emphasize the point that when television was first introduced to South Africa, apartheid as a system of rule still appeared invincible: white people were politically united behind the National Party (voting for it with large majorities in parliamentary elections), the economy was booming, and all the major liberation movements were banned, exiled, or experiencing a lull in activity. The resistance leaders of the main organizations that dominated the 1950s and early 1960s were either in prison, in exile, or had been murdered or co-opted. In 1973 the apartheid regime successfully suppressed a major worker's strike and in June 1976 achieved the same against a national school boycott that became known as the Soweto uprising. One year later, in September 1977, South African police murdered Steve Biko, a key leader of internal resistance and Black Consciousness thinking.[12] Despite the official pronouncements by the apartheid regime and its Western allies, the white government could count on quiet but unwavering support—including access to weapons technology and sanctions-busting—by major Western governments such as the United States, Great Britain, and West Germany as well as countries like Israel, some South American dictatorships, and US-aligned African states. Official US policy, for example, was cold toward liberation movements and found convoluted justifications for white rule inside Cold War logics.[13] On the cultural front, boycotts by the British Equity Actors' Union and parts of Hollywood put limits on the kinds of shows South Africans could see on their television screens.

In 1982 the SABC launched a second set of channels. While TV1 (as the original channel became known) remained exclusively targeted at the white population, the new channels (TV2 and TV3) were split between various segments of the black population defined by language and region. Yet apart from the language and regional divisions, which appeared logical on the face of it, the new "black" stations vigorously policed and promoted "tribal identities." Programmers emphasized differences between "ethnicities," insisting that black people appearing on-screen wear "traditional" outfits while performing "traditional culture" and use "uncontaminated" African languages (meaning free of any English influence) in dramas or music videos, with little mention of white control into their worlds.[14] This policy was, of course, at odds with the extent to which black South Africans were urbanized and languages were mixed as well as the reality of black people's integration into capitalist processes of production and exchange. (This would also extend to television advertising, as I show in chapter 2.)

On the surface, apartheid appeared intact, but troubles loomed for the South African regime, white politics, and mainstream culture more broadly in the mid- to late 1980s. The economy was undergoing the beginnings of a recession, and white people—though still voting for the apartheid government in large numbers—were experiencing a decline in living standards and feeling isolated from the rest of the world, especially Western Europe, with which most of them identified or aspired to culturally. Most significantly, the effects of sports and cultural boycotts as well as the impacts of broadening economic sanctions made leisure travel and access to luxury commodities difficult. Also during this period, key factions within the white business establishment—weary of the cost of strikes and political unrest on their bottom lines—began to doubt the apartheid government's ability to implement reforms and solve the political and economic crises. Many business representatives, members of the Afrikaner intelligentsia, and white liberals initiated talks with "credible black leaders" (by which they meant the ANC) to end apartheid.[15]

Outside South Africa, the most prominent liberation movements proved very successful in their diplomatic campaigns to isolate the regime. Culture and media became a major part of this strategy, with the ANC co-opting artists to its campaigns. Some of these included underwriting larger efforts by prominent US musicians in 1985 to boycott performing in South Africa (the "Sun City" campaign); input into film and television depictions of the struggle (such as *Cry Freedom* in 1987, *A World Apart* in 1988, and *A Dry White Season* in 1989);[16] producing dramas with a clear antiapartheid message; and, most crucially, consciously equating the struggle against apartheid with charismatic leadership, especially that of Nelson Mandela.

The 1980s also witnessed a resurgence of black protest, labor strikes (following the legalization of black-led trade unions in 1979), and significant white resistance to constitutional reforms to provide minimal rights that would open political activity to black people. In the latter case, it culminated in the formation, in 1983, of the United Democratic Front (UDF), the first major mass movement to challenge the apartheid regime since the murder of Biko in 1977.[17] Then, in 1985 a new national and politically radical trade union federation, the Congress of South African Trade Unions (COSATU), was formed. COSATU quickly allied with the UDF, in the process birthing an even more formidable mass movement. The politics of the UDF and COSATU harked back to the popular resistance movements of the 1950s and emphasized what they termed nonracialism in contrast to racial divisions enforced and fostered by apartheid or the Black Consciousness politics of Biko. Crucially, COSATU, the UDF, and their allies proved adept at media production, launching newspapers, producing and making films, and training a new generation of media workers and critical media consumers. The UDF and COSATU would also lead the first campaigns to democratize and deracialize South African media, lobbying to turn the SABC into a public broadcaster, build "community" radio, and break apart the exclusively white control of print media.[18]

The Reform of Media

By the end of the 1980s, TV2 and TV3 began to reflect the changing class structure and political economy of black South Africans. While some of the shows on these channels repeated and reflected old, outdated tropes, other programs began to depict black people employed in manufacturing inside "white South Africa." Those shows were complemented by American sitcoms and dramas (especially police dramas, often dubbed into Afrikaans or Zulu) that featured intermingling of races and desegregated workplaces. Game shows, soap operas about urban black life, and variety and talent shows that mixed modern music genres quickly became standard fare on these channels. Around this time, the SABC also began broadcasting *The Cosby Show*. This series about a black middle-class family in New York City became popular with viewers of all races but especially white South Africans. As a result, some white South Africans (including De Klerk) have argued ex post facto that *The Cosby Show* had a significant impact on white South Africans' attitudes toward their black countrymen and in the process contributed to white South Africans' willingness to endorse negotiations to end apartheid. Research, however, suggests that *The Cosby Show*'s impact was derived more from its shared popularity and as a shared cultural experience across races. The effect, argues media sociologist Ron Krabill, who did research into *The Cosby Show*'s run on South African television, was that South Africans of all races could imagine some sort of future beyond apartheid.[19]

That all South Africans watched television shows like *The Cosby Show* together has led some to suggest that the apartheid media system exhibited mass media characteristics or approximated some kind of public sphere. The evidence cited for this includes, first, the fact that the apartheid state staged its own televised media events—whether live broadcasts of military parades, the opening of Parliament, or the funerals of its presidents and prime ministers—and that these events were consumed collectively. Second, that although state and commercial media presented apartheid visions of the nation and the people to audiences, the latter often read or experienced those media—especially radio dramas—differently, undermining its original intent. On the second, historian Jacob Dlamini, for example, recalls listening to a Radio Zulu presenter prefacing every propaganda item on the evening news with "Bathi ngithi (they say I must say this)."[20] Similarly, black audiences adopted the sounds and images of white American popular culture, transmitted via Hollywood films, as their own. As McCluskey points out, "Hollywood American movies provided an escape for black South Africans that prompted their realization that the world is bigger than South Africa. As young adults, blacks copied the styles of their heroes, the American movie stars of the 1940s and 1950s—both black and white—including the music, clothes, and dance styles."[21]

However, the language politics of the SABC, which strictly prohibited language mixing and privileged Afrikaans and English over indigenous languages, militated against the formation of a public sphere. For example, when commercials were introduced on the SABC in 1978, they exclusively targeted white audiences only. While over time some commercials featured race mixing, generally these commercials featured black people either as rendered background actors, extras, or bystanders, or they were left out of the picture altogether.[22]

This then was the media environment into which Nelson Mandela reentered public life on February 2, 1990. Most striking was the role and place of the SABC. It was the only news broadcaster in South Africa, and, crucially, it controlled live news broadcast feeds from South Africa. In the case of Mandela's release, for example, television viewers from around the world, not just in South Africa, experienced Mandela's release via an SABC video feed and, if they watched in English, an SABC audio feed. Thus, viewers around the world, not just in South Africa, witnessed the spectacle of a veteran SABC journalist, Clarence Keyter, a white South African who was not known for his independence, struggling to describe the events from outside prison gates.

If the SABC's control stood out, just as noticeable was how visibly ill at ease Mandela appeared with the technology and conventions of media-driven politics. American television interviewers in South Africa in particular remarked on his 1960s-era tone and presence: "His bearing, his diction warped time. He would pluck carefully at the creases of his trousers before taking his seat. 'Quite so,' was his standard form of agreement. Asked what films he watched, he spoke movingly of Carmen Miranda and Cesar Romero as if their hits had premiered last Saturday around the corner at the Odeon."[23] Media observers noted that Mandela was ignorant of the "Reaganite dicta that facts impede communication and that one should meet a media question with a media answer."[24]

This view of Mandela as naïve about public relations and media strategies is an oversimplification. There is enough evidence that Mandela and other ANC leaders of his generation had a clear sense of media's public opinion function from early on in their activism. For one, the ANC as an organization encouraged a media politics; it published its own newspapers from its launch in 1912, had good relationships with the most prominent black journalists of the time, and its leaders were encouraged to cooperate for media profiles. *Drum Magazine*—a white-owned but largely black-staffed South African popular print magazine that built a reputation for chronicling black life (unusual then) from the 1950s on—was particularly favored by ANC leaders. Mandela, for example, agreed to feature in interviews and pictorials of himself and his equally photogenic second wife,

Winnie, going about their daily routine at home and in social settings. These profiles humanized ANC leaders and made media stars out of the Mandelas.

When Mandela was on the run from the police in the early 1960s—before his life sentence—he gave a series of interviews to journalists in his various hideouts. In one particular case in 1960, a television journalist from the British ITN network interviewed Mandela at a secret hideout near Johannesburg. The journalist introduced Mandela as "the most dynamic leader in South Africa today," and because of a now-famous Mandela declaration on armed struggle, the interview took on a mythical status.[25] Mandela reveled in the media's description of him as the "Black Pimpernel"—a local adaptation of the Scarlet Pimpernel; the original was a fictional character who avoided capture during the French Revolution. Mandela wrote approvingly about how the "Black Pimpernel" became part of his and the ANC's media strategy: "I would feed the mythology of the 'Black Pimpernel' by . . . phoning individual newspaper reporters from telephone boxes and relaying to them stories of what we were planning or the ineptitude of the police."[26]

Similarly, Mandela exploited media tropes of black politics to his own and the ANC's advantage. For example, though the young Mandela built a public profile as a lawyer with a practice in downtown Johannesburg, he also played up the media's fascination with his family relationship to traditional chiefs and the Xhosa royalty. On the day of his sentencing in 1964, Mandela arrived dressed in the ceremonial outfit of a Xhosa chief. Images of "Chief" Mandela were plastered on front pages, and video of that entrance—often slowed down for effect—became a staple for years to come. The whole performance was a deliberate strategy to make a very public and symbolic connection with a long history of black resistance for Mandela supporters and particularly for the media. The gambit worked: the *New York Times*, for example, referred to Mandela and his co-accused as "the new George Washingtons and Ben Franklins" of their time.[27]

While Mandela was in jail, the state banned all images of him, along with speeches or quotes or attributions thereof, yet he retained a prominent media presence through his likeness on posters, in countless songs composed in his honor, as a recipient of honorary doctorates, and from the 1980s on, through music concerts that became impressive live television events.[28]

Nevertheless, the media landscape that Mandela encountered on his release in 1990 was profoundly different from the one that he left behind in 1964. More intense and fast-paced, these profound changes may explain his clumsy media reactions. However, the force of Mandela's personality and the appeal of the ANC among the majority of South Africans meant that despite the apartheid government's best efforts, it could not control how black South Africans would experience the media event of his release or how Mandela or the ANC would shape or frame it to their political advantage. Throughout this, Mandela made a point of downplaying his personal charisma and insisting that he was merely an ordinary servant of the people and loyal ANC member, but he could not prevent the new media politics from turning him into a twenty-first-century media star.

Much of the writing about South Africa's political transition marks the final of the 1995 Rugby World Cup as the high convergence point of media and politics. Yet that pinnacle was actually reached two years earlier, in April 1993. The tragic murder of Chris Hani, the ANC's second most popular figure after Mandela, triggered this media transition. Hani, a member of the ANC's national executive committee, was also a former head of the ANC's military wing and leader of the South African Communist Party (a key ANC ally). There was a general sense among ANC rank and file that Hani should follow Mandela as president of the country and not Thabo Mbeki (who eventually succeeded Mandela in 1999).[29] At the time, the ANC had resumed negotiations with the South African government after accusing the De Klerk administration of fomenting intra-black violence. Most white people (including elements in the mainstream press) viewed Hani as a radical even though he had publicly committed himself to negotiations. Days before Hani was murdered, he had implored ANC members to become "combatants for peace."[30]

Hani was gunned down on April 10, 1993, by a white right-wing activist associated with groups opposed to even mild changes to the apartheid status quo. Janusz Waluś, a Polish immigrant and member of Eugène Terre'Blanche's Afrikaner Weerstandsbeweging (AWB; Afrikaner Resistance Movement), shot Hani in the driveway of his new house in Boksburg—"a mostly white working class suburb that Chris was seeking to integrate"—just east of Johannesburg.[31] The police later arrested a Conservative Party MP, Clive Derby-Lewis, who had conspired with Waluś to murder Hani.[32]

Following Hani's murder, the country seemed balanced on a knife's edge, with daily news reports of mass marches, protests that turned violent, and attacks on police and state property. Scores of people were killed, and the ANC threatened to suspend constitutional negotiations.[33] De Klerk and his political advisors had lost the confidence of white citizens and were unable to respond to the anger of the black majority over Hani's murder. At this point, De Klerk turned to Mandela, requesting the latter to deliver a live television address to the nation that would also be broadcast on radio. Three days later, on April 13, South Africans tuned into the SABC and saw Mandela sitting at a desk in the style associated with US presidents. He gave a short speech that emphasized national unity ("*we* are a nation in mourning") and appealed to "all South Africans to stand together against those who, from any quarter, wish to destroy what Chris Hani gave his life for—the freedom of all of us." Mandela began his remarks: "Tonight I am reaching out to every single South African, black and white, from the very depths of my being. A white man, full of prejudice and hate, came to our country and committed a deed so foul that our whole nation now teeters on the brink of disaster. A white woman, of Afrikaner origin, risked her life so that we may know, and bring to justice, this assassin."[34]

This live television broadcast was remarkable for a number of reasons: it was a mass-media event hosted on the SABC, which up to that point had been a virtual propaganda arm of the apartheid regime and was still ridiculing the ANC as terrorists and communists. Crucially, South Africans got a glimpse of Mandela as President more than a year before he was elected to that position. In effect, this media event symbolized a de facto handover of political power from the apartheid rulers to the ANC.[35] It also suggested that only television provided the kind of communicative space—immediately accessible, widely shared, and visually emotive—required for the political moment.[36] Mandela's flawless, pitch-perfect, and authoritative performance was subsequently credited—by ordinary South Africans and media and political commentators alike—with calming the mood and speeding up constitutional negotiations, thus paving the way for the first democratic elections a year later. As Mandela himself reflected, "In this instance, it was the ANC, not the government, that sought to calm the nation."[37] Desmond Tutu later told a journalist, "I loved Chris [Hani] very, very deeply, and it was one of the most devastating moments and the anger was palpable. Had [Mandela] not gone on television and radio . . . our country would have gone up in flames."[38]

Mandela's imprint on South Africa's media politics became even more acute in the wake of the 1994 democratic elections. A number of media events would cement his media legacy. Two of these, from the later 1990s, were particularly important and retained their symbolic power long after he was gone from the political scene: the 1995 Rugby World Cup final and the public hearings of the TRC held between 1996 and 1998. Both events stand out not merely for how Mandela used them but also for how they came to be appropriated for various causes and explanatory schemas—popular and scholarly—about South Africa and about media's role in political life.

Though South Africans of different class and ethnic backgrounds have played organized rugby since the late nineteenth century, white Afrikaner sports officials, along with the ruling party and its media, consistently worked to make explicit links between rugby, white identity, Afrikaner nationalism, the state, and sporting prowess. Rugby was organized along racial lines from its inception. Predictably, it reflected racial inequalities in terms of access to opportunities.[39] Early on, white sports officials succeeded in convincing the International Rugby Board (IRB) that the white rugby association was the legitimate representative of the local game. During the 1970s and 1980s, however, antiapartheid sports groups disrupted Springbok tours and succeeded in getting South Africa banned by the IRB in response to apartheid policies and the South African Rugby Union's silence on these policies.

In the late 1980s, rugby was turned into a professional game. The inaugural Rugby World Cup was scheduled for 1987, hosted by New Zealand. South Africa, predictably, was not invited. By the time of the next tournament—in 1991—Mandela had already been freed from prison, but South Africa had not been readmitted to international rugby. For the next tournament, in 1995, South Africa was not only deemed fit to compete, it was awarded the right to host it. White South African rugby administrators read this as an endorsement of how they managed the game, despite black critics pointing out that the sport remained unequally divided along racial lines and showed little sign of transforming. The white board also had the support of mainstream, mostly white, newspaper headline writers and sports journalists, who agreed with the South African Rugby Board. Mainstream sports opinion interpreted the country's return to international rugby and hosting of the World Cup as affirmation of the country's "successful" political transition. Yet any observer could see that the Springboks was an overwhelmingly white team—with only one black player, winger Chester Williams, in a squad of thirty. Williams was featured heavily in advertising and the promotional material for the Springboks as well as in media to market the tournament, yet he enjoyed little playtime on the field.[40] As for the crowds at matches, they replicated racial divisions in South Africa (mostly white people could afford the steep ticket prices), and many of the white fans openly waved the discarded orange, white, and blue flag of the colonial and apartheid regimes and sang offensive songs.[41] The Rugby World Cup and the events around it would have faded into memory for most people outside of rugby circles except for what happened next: Mandela and the ANC decided to exploit the final to publicly promote its new nation-building agenda and to assuage white people's fears about the new South Africa.

In what became a political and media legend, Mandela appeared before the crowds at the tournament final wearing a Springbok team shirt with the number six—the number of the Springbok's white captain, Francois Pienaar. The overwhelmingly white crowd began to chant Mandela's name. It immediately became clear to those in Ellis Park Stadium and those watching at home as well as the media that Mandela had confronted and used what was seen as unacceptable about the tournament to his advantage. His public act also served to motivate the team—the Springboks won the game and the championship—and lifted the crowd and millions of people watching via television inside and outside South Africa. Viewers saw white fans—many who openly opposed the ANC and the political transition—chanting Mandela's name.[42] The effect was palpable: "The camera zooms in on Nelson Mandela standing on the field in a packed stadium. He is wearing a number six jersey instead of the customary Madiba shirts. His fist is clenched, not in the black power salute, but in triumph as alongside him Francois Pienaar lifts the Webb Ellis trophy [the World Cup] into the sky. For a few short moments South Africans in their lounges, pubs and shebeens are euphoric."[43]

Writer J. M. Coetzee, an open critic of the Springboks, the rugby establishment in South Africa, and of seductive rhetoric of the political transition, had to concede: "The country—it is even possible to say the country as a whole—experienced a flush of pride in the achievement of a team that had become, or was on the brink of becoming, their team."[44] In the days and years after the final, television and newspaper images of Mandela's action and the reactions to it would have the effect of solidifying a certain mainstream view of South Africa's transition: of the rainbow nation undergoing a peaceful transition and of Mandela and the ANC reconciling with white South Africa. For a long time after, commentators and mainstream editorial writers both inside and outside South Africa asserted the positive impact of the televised spectacle of the 1995 Rugby World Cup final on race relations. Many suggested that it was this event above all else that cemented the favorable view Mandela enjoyed among white South Africans until his death in December 2013. The over-the-top sentiments of British journalist John Carlin are a representative stand-in. (Carlin authored the 2008 bestselling book, *Playing the Enemy: Nelson Mandela and the Game That Made a Nation*, which formed the basis of the 2009 Hollywood film *Invictus*, a recounting of the events of the 1995 Rugby World Cup final.) Carlin said, "Behind the spontaneous clamor from the white Ellis Park crowd—that 'Nelson! Nelson!'—lay eloquent and convincing evidence that [Mandela's] hard toil had paid off. . . . They were crying out for forgiveness and they were accepting his, and through him, black South Africa's generous embrace."[45] By contrast, historian Albert Grundlingh rightly concludes that Mandela's appearance at the final was in many senses a cliché, "an orchestrated media affair."[46] About *Invictus*, film critic Ella Taylor had this to say: "As history, it is borderline daft and selective to the point of distortion."[47] As for Mandela, three years after the World Cup final, he announced that a government commission of inquiry into rugby in South Africa was being formed, primarily to tackle the failure of rugby administrators to deal with the continued dominance of white people both in administration and on the field in top-level rugby. For challenging racism in rugby, Mandela was taken to court by the same rugby administrators who three years earlier had embraced him.[48] Nevertheless, these kinds of criticisms as well as black South Africans' frustrations with the terms on which the new South Africa was negotiated—that is, mostly favorable to the country's white minority—did not dull enthusiasm for supposed meaning and impact for Mandela's actions at the 1995 Rugby World Cup final.

The TRC has enjoyed the same symbolic power as the 1995 Rugby World Cup for South Africans. It may be no small coincidence that Mandela signed the TRC into law less than one month after the last match of that final. Like the World Cup, the TRC was a media spectacle par excellence: the TRC's public hearings were held in church halls, municipal buildings, and community centers that would hold only a couple of hundred people, but it was broadcast live on public radio and television and was complemented by weekly magazine programs with highlights from the testimony, transforming the commission into a media event in which millions participated.[49] This led to conclusions such as Krabill's: "South African mass media have served as both essential actors in the TRC drama, as well as the stage on which much of the drama has been performed."[50]

The effects of the blanket media coverage and the TRC's media-friendly format only contributed to its media legend: so much so that Max du Preez, executive producer and anchor of the weekly *The TRC Special Report* on the SABC, concludes that the TRC hearings were "perfect for television journalism." "It was not a story about politicians," he explains, "it was about the way ordinary men, women and children felt about the horrors of Apartheid. The TV cameras could take the close-ups of these feelings into every living room in the country . . . For the first time, the nation acknowledged the victims. They told us that when they gave their evidence, they knew they were not talking just to the commissioners, but they were talking to the whole nation. That was the impact of the TV coverage."[51]

Alex Boraine, deputy chairperson of the TRC, later suggested that wall-to-wall media coverage of the commission's proceedings had turned the TRC into "truly a national experience rather than restricted [it] to a small handful of selected commissioners."[52] This openness was in marked contrast to truth commissions in Latin America that predated the TRC, the proceedings of which were usually held behind closed doors.

Despite the heavy media presence and the theatrical and emotional nature of the public hearings, the idea that the TRC provided unmediated access to authentic truth did exist. But as Catherine Cole, who has studied the relationship between human rights and performance, observes, "In actuality these public hearings were highly mediated." The TRC served as "casting director," determining which victims would have the privilege of experiencing public hearings. "In addition, the media selected which portions of each daylong hearing would be broadcast on television and radio, or splashed across the newspaper headlines."[53] Du Preez confirmed this activist role of the media covering the TRC by going "beyond just telling the story." Journalists actively encouraged the process of reconciliation started by the commission by arranging meetings between victims and perpetrators.[54] The TRC, however, was a negotiated truth and largely left in place gross economic inequalities.[55]

In conclusion then, a new kind of politics emerged from these media events—mostly overdetermined and always underanalyzed. The claim of this book is that media events like Mandela's release; his prefigurative "presidential" address in 1993; a series of regular, televised general elections since 1994; the 1995 Rugby

World Cup final; and the mediation of the TRC all act together as precedents for a more intensified and less formal mediated politics that has become commonplace in South Africa since the second decade of democratic rule. In fact, I suggest that most postapartheid political developments and controversies play out in public as live, highly mediated events—as we see in the following chapters—deliberately framed by journalists, television soap opera scriptwriters and producers, advertising copyeditors, or participants on social media.[56] To understand the interaction of mass media in society, we need to extend our analyses in nontraditional ways—that is, away from politics (with a capital P) or megamedia events and the sorts of spectacles covered in this chapter—to more everyday use and interactions with media. This involves looking at how people engage with their social worlds and how those social worlds are mediated or constructed by media companies and public officials through, for example, television commercials, soap operas, or on social media. That is the work of the remainder of this book.

Notes

1. Daniel Dayan and Elihu Katz (*Media Events: The Live Broadcasting of History* [Boston: Harvard University Press, 1992]) first introduced the idea of the "media event." That concept has since been critiqued and expanded by, among others, Nick Couldry, *Media Rituals: A Critical Approach* (New York: Routledge, 2003); Douglas Kellner, *Media Spectacle* (New York: Routledge, 2003); and Frank Bösch, "European Media Events," EGO (European History Online), December 3, 2010, http://ieg-ego.eu/en/threads/european-media/european-media-events. See also Arvind Rajagopal, *Politics after Television: Hindu Nationalism and the Reshaping of the Public in India* (Cambridge: Cambridge University Press, 2001).

2. Nelson Mandela, "South Africa's New Era; Transcript of Mandela's Speech at Cape Town City Hall: 'Africa It Is Ours!,'" *New York Times*, February 12, 1990, https://www.nytimes.com/1990/02/12/world/south-africa-s-new-era-transcript-mandela-s-speech-cape-town-city-hall-africa-it-is.html.

3. See Martha Evans, "Mandela and the Televised Birth of the Rainbow Nation," *National Identities* 12, no. 3 (2010), 314.

4. Ibid., 313.

5. Frederik van Zyl Slabbert, quoted in Mbulelo Mzamane, "Celebrating Thirty Years of Television in South Africa" (speech delivered at the inaugural Golden Plumes Awards, Johannesburg, December 14, 2006). See also Lee Edwards, *Mediapolitiek: How the Mass Media Have Transformed World Politics* (Washington, DC: Catholic University of America Press, 2004); and Evans, "Mandela," 309.

6. Albert Hertzog, quoted in "South Africa: The Other Vast Wasteland," November 20, 1964, 40, cited in Rob Nixon, *Homelands, Harlem and Hollywood: South African Culture and the World Beyond* (New York: Routledge, 1995), 52.

7. J. C. Otto, Hansard, September 19, 1966, Col. 2407, quoted in Nixon, *Homelands*, 53.

8. Nixon, *Homelands*, 45.

9. For this history, see Ruth Tomaselli, Keyan Tomaselli, and Johan Muller, eds., *Broadcasting in South Africa* (Chicago: Lake View Press, 1989); and Robert B. Horwitz, *Communication*

and Democratic Reform in South Africa (Cambridge: Cambridge University Press, 2001). See also chapter 4 of this book.

10. Kevin Harris, quoted in Audrey T. McCluskey, ed., *The Devil You Dance With* (Chicago: University of Illinois Press, 2009), 61.

11. Sean O'Toole, "An Unmistakably White Question Mark," in *Extra!*, edited by Candice Breitz (Johannesburg: Standard Bank, Goethe Institute, Iziko Museums, and Goodman Gallery, 2012), 9.

12. Dan Magaziner, *The Law and the Prophets: Black Consciousness in South Africa, 1968–1977* (Athens: Ohio University Press, 2010).

13. Sasha Polakow-Suransky, *The Unspoken Alliance: Israel's Secret Relations with Apartheid South Africa* (New York: Pantheon, 2010). See also Chris McGreal, "Worlds Apart," *The Guardian*, February 5, 2006, https://www.theguardian.com/world/2006/feb/06/southafrica.israel; and Chris McGreal, "Brothers in Arms—Israel Secret Pact with Pretoria," *The Guardian*, February 6, 2006, https://www.theguardian.com/world/2006/feb/07/southafrica.israel.

14. This language purity and separation continued well into the new South Africa. See, for example, filmmaker Beathur Baker's comment in an interview about her experiences working on film sets: "[White filmmakers] would insist that [black] actors speak textbook versions of Zulu or Xhosa, which is so different from the colloquial way that people speak on the street" (Beathur Baker, quoted in McCluskey, *The Devil You Dance With*, 21). However, conditions around language did improve after 1994. The director Angus Gibson describes some of the pushback to the mixing of languages in the groundbreaking television drama *Yizo Yizo* (This Is It) about a troubled high school in a Johannesburg township: "In terms of local television, there has been a kind of apartheid thing about purity of language. So everybody spoke 'pure' Zulu or Xhosa or Sotho. It was this weird thing on television of this antiquated language being spoken. Obviously, it was part of the divide-and-rule notion [inherited from apartheid].... [On *Yizo Yizo*] for the first time, people mixed languages in a way that people mix in this country. We were careful to cast families in ways that were realistic. Language is spoken like you hear it on the streets here" (Angus Gibson, quoted in McCluskey, *The Devil You Dance With*, 55).

15. Alan Cowell, "South Africa without Apartheid," *New York Times*, June 22, 1986, https://www.nytimes.com/1986/06/22/business/south-africa-without-apartheid.html. Also see Patti Waldmeir, *Anatomy of the Miracle: The End of Apartheid and the Birth of the New South Africa* (New York: W. W. Norton, 1997).

16. See *Cry Freedom*, dir. Richard Attenborough (Marble Arch Productions/Universal, 1987); *A World Apart*, dir. Chris Menges (Film Four International/Atlantic Releasing Corporation, 1988); and *A Dry White Season*, dir. Euzhan Palcy (Davros Films/MGM, 1989); Artists against Apartheid, *Sun City* (Manhattan Records, 1995).

17. See Inneke van Kessel, *Beyond Our Wildest Dreams: The United Democratic Front and the Transformation of South Africa* (Charlottesville: University of Virginia Press, 2000); Gail Gerhart and Clive Glaser, *From Protest to Challenge: A Documentary History of African Politics in South Africa, 1882–1990*, vol. 6, *Challenge and Victory, 1980–1990* (Bloomington: University of Indiana Press, 2010); Gregory Houston, *The National Liberation Struggle in South Africa: A Case Study of the United Democratic Front, 1893–1987* (Farnham, UK: Ashgate, 2015); and Jeremy Seekings, *The UDF: A History of the United Democratic Front in South Africa, 1983–1991* (Suffolk, UK: James Currey, 2000).

18. For an overview of these processes, see Horwitz, *Communication and Democratic Reform*; and Guy Berger, "Towards an Analysis of the South African Media in the Transformation, 1994–99," *Transformation* (1999): 82–116.

19. Ron Krabill, *Starring Mandela and Cosby: Media and the End(s) of Apartheid* (Chicago: University of Chicago Press, 2010). Ron Krabill is also quoted in "'The Cosby Show's' Legacy

in South Africa," *The World*, Public Radio International, May 28, 2016, http://www.pri.org/stories/2016-05-28/cosby-shows-legacy-south-africa.

20. Jacob Dlamini, *Native Nostalgia* (Johannesburg: Jacana Media, 2009), 36; Liz Gunner, "Resistant Medium: The Voices of Zulu Radio Dramas in the 1970s," *Theater Research International* 27, no. 3 (2002): 259–274.

21. Audrey T. McCluskey, ed., "Introduction," in *The Devil You Dance With* (Chicago: University of Illinois Press, 2009), 4.

22. See Horwitz, *Communication and Democratic Reform*; Dan Magaziner, "Two Stories about Art, Education and Beauty in Twentieth Century South Africa," *American Historical Review* 118, no. 5 (2013): 1403–1429.

23. Nixon, *Homelands*, 179.

24. See Nelson Mandela, *Long Walk to Freedom: The Autobiography of Nelson Mandela* (Boston: Little, Brown, 2000); Sonja Laden, "Who's Afraid of a Black Bourgeosie? Consumer Magazines for Black South Africans as an Apparatus of Change," *Journal of Consumer Culture* 3, no. 2 (2003); Rob Nixon, "Mandela, Messianism and the Media," *Transition* 51 (1991): 42–55; Nixon, *Homelands*, 179; and John Carlin, *Playing the Enemy: Nelson Mandela and the Game That Made a Nation* (London: Penguin, 2009), 83.

25. Alexis C. Madrigal, "Nelson Mandela's First TV Interview, May 1961," *The Atlantic*, December 6, 2013, http://www.theatlantic.com/international/archive/2013/12/nelson-mandelas-first-tv-interview-may-1961/282120/.

26. Mandela, *Long Walk to Freedom*, 114.

27. Nixon, *Homelands*, 178.

28. Nixon, "Mandela," 42–55.

29. Kenneth S. Zagarki, "Rhetoric, Dialogue and Performance in Nelson Mandela's 'Televised Address on the Assassination of Chris Hani,'" *Rhetorica and Public Affairs* 6, no. 4 (2003): 709.

30. Ibid., 710.

31. Mandela, *Long Walk to Freedom*, 607.

32. Adrian Guelke, "Political Violence and the South African Transition," *Irish Studies in International Affairs* 4 (1993): 59–68.

33. For some analysis and perspective on these events, including the impact of Hani's death on mid-1990s transitional politics, see Terry Bell and Dumisa Ntsebeza, *Unfinished Business: South Africa, Apartheid, Truth* (New York: Verso, 2003); Patrick Bond, *Elite Transition: From Apartheid to Neoliberalism in South Africa* (London: Pluto Press, 2000); and Hein Marais, *South Africa: Limits to Change: The Political Economy of Transition* (London: Zed, 2001).

34. Nelson Mandela, "Television Address to the Nation by ANC President Nelson Mandela on the Assassination of Chris Hani," ANC.org, April 13, 1993, http://anc.org.za/content/television-address-nation-anc-president-nelson-mandela-assassination-chris-hani.

35. Guelke, "Political Violence," 60; BBC Newsnight, "How Mandela Responded to the Assassination of Chris Hani," YouTube, December 9, 2013, https://www.youtube.com/watch?v=lOn24d9xwYQ.

36. Krabill, *Starring Mandela and Cosby*, 138.

37. Mandela, *Long Walk to Freedom*, 609.

38. John Carlin, "Interview: Archbishop Desmond Tutu," *Frontline*, PBS, accessed April 2, 2014, http://www.pbs.org/wgbh/pages/frontline/shows/mandela/interviews/tutu.html.

39. See Albert Grundlingh, Albert Mauritz, Andre Odendaal, and Stephanus Burridge Spies, *Beyond the Tryline: Rugby and South African Society* (Athens: Ohio University Press, 1995); and Albert Grundlingh, "Playing for Power? Rugby, Afrikaner Nationalism and Masculinity in South Africa, c. 1900–70," *International Journal of the History of Sport* 11, no. 3 (1994): 408–430.

40. Ashley Hammond, "Chester Williams: The Success of the Rainbow Nation Was Only Temporary," *Gulf News*, July 31, 2015, http://gulfnews.com/sport/rugby/chester-williams-the-success-of-the-rainbow-nation-was-only-temporary-1.1559367; Jim White, "Interview: Chester Williams," *The Observer*, November 17, 2002, *The Guardian*, https://www.theguardian.com/sport/2002/nov/18/rugbyunion.jimwhite; Albert Grundlingh, "From Redemption to Recidivism? Rugby and Change in South Africa during the 1995 World Cup and Its Aftermath," *Sporting Traditions* 14, no. 2 (1998): 67–86; Jacqueline Maingard, "Imag(in)ing the South African Nation: Representations of Identity in the Rugby World Cup 1995," *Theatre Journal* 49, no. 1 (1997): 15–28.

41. See Lynette Steenveld and Larry Strelitz, "The 1995 Rugby World Cup and the Politics of Nation-Building in South Africa," *Media, Culture and Society* 20, no. 4 (1998): 609–629; and Ashwin Desai and Zayn Nabbi, "Truck and Trailer: Rugby and Transformation in South Africa," in *State of the Nation: South Africa 2007*, edited by Sakhela Buhlungu, John Daniel, Roger Southall, and Jessica Lutchman, 402–426 (Cape Town: HSRC Press, 2007). See also the contributions from Albert Grundlingh in "Roundtable on *Invictus*," *Safundi: The Journal of South African and American Studies* 13, no. 1–2 (2012): 115–150; as well as Carlin, *Playing the Enemy*; Grundlingh, "From Redemption to Recidivism?"; and Maingard, "Imag(in)ing the South African Nation."

42. Barney Roman, "What Does a Scrum Mean in Zulu," *Mail and Guardian*, May 19, 1995, https://mg.co.za/article/1995-05-19-what-does-a-scrum-mean-in-zulu; John Carlin, "Nelson Mandela Unites a Nation with His Choice of Jersey," *The Guardian*, January 7, 2007, https://www.theguardian.com/sport/2007/jan/07/rugbyunion.features1.

43. Mzamane, "Celebrating Thirty Years."

44. J. M. Coetzee, "Retrospect: The World Cup of Rugby," *Southern African Review of Books*, no. 38 (July/August 1995), http://web.archive.org/web/20001001002444/www.uni-ulm.de/~rturrell/antho4html/CoetzeeJ.html.

45. John Carlin, *Playing the Enemy: Nelson Mandela and the Game That Made a Nation* (Penguin, 2008), 250 quoted in Evans, "Mandela," 322.

46. Grundlingh, "From Redemption to Recidivism?," 83.

47. Ella Taylor, "Reconciliation, If Not Truth, in Clint Eastwood's 'Invictus,'" *Village Voice*, December 8, 2009, https://www.villagevoice.com/2009/12/08/reconciliation-if-not-truth-in-clint-eastwoods-invictus/.

48. Chris Thurman, "Louis Luyt—Rugby Boss, Propagandist, Fertiliser Man and 'Scumbag,'" *Business Day*, February 6, 2013, http://www.bdlive.co.za/opinion/2013/02/06/louis-luyt--rugby-boss-propagandist-fertiliser-man-and-scumbag.

49. Joe Thloloe, "Showing Faces, Hearing Voices, Tugging at Emotions: Televising the Truth and Reconciliation Commission," *Niemann Reports* 52, no. 4 (1998): 53–54, http://niemanreports.org/articles/showing-faces-hearing-voices-tugging-at-emotions/.

50. Ron Krabill, "Symbiosis: Mass Media and the Truth and Reconciliation Commission of South Africa," *Media, Culture and Society* 23 (2001): 568.

51. Max du Preez, quoted by Thloloe, "Showing Faces," 53–54, http://niemanreports.org/articles/showing-faces-hearing-voices-tugging-at-emotions/.

52. Alex Boraine, quoted in Catherine Cole, *Performing South Africa's Truth Commission: Stages of Transition* (Indianapolis: Indiana University Press, 2010), 5.

53. Catherine Cole, "Performance, Transitional Justice, and the Law: South Africa's Truth and Reconciliation Commission," *Theatre Journal* 59, no. 2 (2007), 180.

54. Thloloe, "Showing Faces," 53–54.

55. McCluskey, "Introduction," 3.

56. Sam Mkokeli, "ANC Turns Tables on Media with News Analysis," *Business Day*, December 5, 2011, http://www.bdlive.co.za/articles/2011/12/05/news-analysis-anc-turns-tables-on-media-with-news-analysis; Mandy de Waal, "Marikana—The Matter of Embedded Journalism," *Daily Maverick*, August 24, 2012, https://www.dailymaverick.co.za/article/2012-08-24-marikana-the-matter-of-embedded-journalism/#.WzPou9JKiUk; Jane Duncan, "SABC: Marikana and the Problem of Pack Journalism," SABC Online, October 7, 2012, http://abahlali.org/node/9253/; Kwanele Sosibo, "Marikana and the Brand Journalist," *Mail and Guardian*, December 23, 2014, https://mg.co.za/article/2014-12-22-marikana-and-the-brand-journalist; Dan Magaziner and Sean Jacobs, "Notes from Marikana, South Africa: The Platinum Miners' Strike, the Massacre and the Struggle for Equivalence," *International Labor and Working Class History* 83 (Spring 2013): 137–142; Nick Davies, "Marikana Massacre: The Untold Story of the Strike Leader Who Died for Worker Rights," *The Guardian*, May 19, 2015, https://www.theguardian.com/world/2015/may/19/marikana-massacre-untold-story-strike-leader-died-workers-rights.

CHAPTER 2

Branding the Nation in Prime Time

Television commercials in South Africa are striking in how they openly draw on and reflect political debates with a degree of explicitness and candor rarely observed elsewhere. More significantly, these commercials consistently refer to, imagine, and construct a very specific set of tropes about national identity and political and economic development. Often these tropes incite debates about the end of apartheid, the role and impacts of race in society, poverty, affirmative action (variously known in South Africa as employment equity, transformation, and black economic empowerment, or BEE), and economic development as well as South Africa's place in a globalizing world.

Advertising in South Africa is a window through which South Africans see not only representations of themselves but also their roles in relation to the nation and what passes for the global community. Advertising is also a generative space where identities evolve on multiple levels.[1] Postapartheid South Africa has not been simply inscribed with homogeneous identities from the top down. In fact, culture and history is mined and reimagined by and through the advertising industry to create images that mutually construct the nation.[2]

With few exceptions, neoliberal economics is the dominant frame of these television commercials. The political rhetoric embedded in them along with the invocation of a certain rendering of history mainly support a neoliberal ideology. Elsewhere, marketing scholars Adesegun Oyedele and Michael Minor have described this process as "a romanticized view of middle-ground politics promoted by political establishments both at the national and international level." It has proven to be most decisive in countries "undergoing major ideological change."[3] South Africa would appear to be a perfect case study.

People working in marketing and advertising in South Africa are not ignorant of their power. As the chief executive officer (CEO) of a leading marketing research company put it in 2013, "There is a vacuum in terms of moral leadership in the world and brands and companies have to take the initiative in filling that moral vacuum. . . . I've always believed that companies have replaced the church [in providing moral leadership]. Currently it's in the corporate environment where issues such as appropriate behavior, morality, ethics and contributions to communities are being discussed. . . . Brands and companies are slowly but surely beginning to fill the moral vacuum. . . . We need iconic brands and it is these brands that take control of community development and that contribute to Ubuntu."[4] [Ubuntu refers to people's shared humanity and is a philosophy derived from the Nguni-speaking communities of Southern Africa.]

By the early 1990s, the depiction of social reality in South African advertising amounted to a representation that gravitated "towards the most idealized of its forms conducive to the consumption appeal being propagated." Alexander Holt argues that the "most pervasive forms of ideology" in these commercials depicts "bourgeois identity," and as a result, "this ideology is propagated through the positive stereotypes in the mass media with which we so readily (and often unconsciously) identify. These positive stereotypes play a role in class formation, or in the forms of socialization that give the appearance of classless social structures in postindustrial societies."[5]

The South African advertising industry is not terribly self-reflective. Despite the power of advertising and commercials in South African public life, most studies of advertising in South African trade journals as well as online, on blogs, or in news media limit their scope to questions of market penetration or brand loyalty. Globalization is a homogenizing process in these accounts.[6] The annual Loerie Awards (for the brand communications industry) and media columns on advertising very rarely go beyond counting accolades, backslapping, and remarking on how the industry competes well against first-world firms. There appears to be little appreciation for the idea that images of the nation created through advertising are important sites of study.[7]

Conventional Wisdom

The conventional wisdom about advertising in more intensely mediated societies is that it mainly wants to carve up populations and identify and manufacture niche consumer identities—whether selling beer, cars, or bank services or promoting corporate identities. South African television commercials, like commercials everywhere, are primarily about representing and selling brands. However, television commercials in South Africa are striking in how they openly draw on and reflect political debates with a forthrightness rarely observed elsewhere. They also aim to enforce a certain kind of politics or political ideology.

Globally, while many brands have profited from associations with identity-based political movements (such as feminism, gay rights, and black nationalism)—and vice versa—advertising agencies and their clients usually shy away from connecting brands with contentious political issues. Politics may show up, but usually in a humorous or noncontroversial manner. The advertising campaigns for Molson Canadian, a product of the Molson beer company (now the Molson Coors Brewing Company [MCBC]), illustrate this point.[8] Explicit reference to Canadian nationalism is a recurring trope in Molson's ad campaigns. One memorable campaign was Molson's "I Am . . ." television ad campaign in 2000. The ad focused on "Joe," a white actor representing the "average Canadian."

In the commercial, Joe stands on a stage and proceeds to articulate what defines him as Canadian. Joe's "rant" consists of debunking a series of Canadian stereotypes said to originate with Americans. The commercial won a number of advertising prizes and spawned similar commercials in a number of European countries. It was also parodied at the American Academy Awards, debated on talk radio, and lampooned by French-speaking comedians (the Québécois feel marginalized in mostly English-speaking Canada). However, throughout this "public debate," the media, marketers, and television audiences (as well as those who viewed the ad online) were clearly in on the joke.[9]

Similarly, American television commercials often make explicit ties to the country's flag and American patriotism. However, overuses of these national symbols (whether to sell cars or to recruit volunteers to serve in the country's armed forces) render them somewhat banal. Such commercials are stripped of any meaningful content beyond a direct relationship with the product being promoted that declares its "American-ness." At best, ironic sentiments drive much of the American advertising that engages with political campaigns or social issues. Occasionally, American television commercials tackle politics in a serious way, but when brands are attached explicitly to party politics, negative reactions often follow. Thus, politicized brands are discouraged, at worst excised for overstepping the boundaries between commerce and political commentary. US advertisers shy away from including or referencing overt politics in product branding.[10]

"It's Halftime in America" is one of the best examples of a politicized ad. The January 2011 commercial for US car manufacturer Chrysler starred famed American actor Clint Eastwood and was a commentary on the US government's bailout of the auto industry. Its cultural significance stemmed from its being first broadcast during the halftime show of that year's Super Bowl football game in Indianapolis, Indiana. The Super Bowl is the biggest sports-related media event in the United States. Commercials that air during the Super Bowl's halftime show are imbued with some cultural power. They are written about by journalists and are featured on news shows and in business pages as well as social media for days and weeks afterward. In the Chrysler commercial, Eastwood is shown walking on a darkened Detroit street while delivering a soliloquy about unemployment, economic recession, and the Obama administration's bailout of the auto industry, which is presented as a patriotic act.[11]

Reaction was swift. The Super Bowl was hardly over before Republican Party operatives accused Eastwood of shilling for Barack Obama's reelection campaign. Obama had bailed out car manufacturers and, as the *New York Times* reported at the time, this did not sit well with conservative critics, including George W. Bush's former chief campaign strategist, Karl Rove. The Republicans would usually have no problem with bailing out American industry. Nevertheless, Rove judged the commercial as "political payback and accused the automaker of handing the president a prime-time megaphone in front of one of the largest television audiences of the year."[12] Republicans also resented the fact that Obama's advisors publicly praised the commercial. Eastwood denied that the commercial had any politics: "The ad doesn't have a political message. . . . It is about American spirit, pride and job growth."[13] The implication of the media storm was clear: for some in America's political and media classes, political themes had to be avoided in television commercials.

In South Africa, commercials with a political undertone are quite common and noncontroversial, but occasionally they do clash against actual politics. The advertising campaigns for Nandos, a South African fast-food company with global ambitions, is a case in point. Nandos regularly incorporates contemporary political references (race, class, electoral politics, and identity, etc.) into its campaigns. The brand's television and print commercials usually manage to combine a quick-off-the-mark, topical sense of the news with a particularly South African brand of wit and irony. However, any political critique embedded in Nandos commercials is made undone by the fact that even the objects of Nandos's "commentary" (usually politicians) play along and laugh at the jokes or puns made at their expense. For example, a popular local politician, Julius Malema, could see the humor in a 2009 Nandos commercial featuring his puppet likeness that mocked his delivery style and his rhetoric.[14] The "politics" of these commercials as well as any political agenda Nandos may have had are rendered moot. What matters instead is that Nandos's bottom line benefits from all the media attention, which is good for business either way.

Television, Advertising, and Apartheid

As I argue in chapter 1, the ideological function of SABC television under apartheid was to reinforce white dominance and provide cover for the myth of separate racial identities. Television commercials, first shown on the SABC in 1978, were no different. Races were not allowed to mix (the SABC required advertisers to shoot two separate, identical commercials, one with black actors and one with white actors) and neither were languages. Advertisers were required to use "the Xhosa or Zulu equivalent of Victorian English"—for example, "the soap that cleans your teeth" for toothpaste.[15] Commercials were also replete with patronizing racist and colonial stereotypes.[16] Take one of the most recognizable commercials of the early 1980s for Rolux lawn mowers.[17] An actor playing the role of "explorer" David Livingstone is shown clearing a path through "Africa" with a lawn mower as his black bearers follow behind him. This was, of course, deliberate: "From the point of view of ethnographic reconstruction, the representation in [this commercial] bears some realism to the White lifestyle during the [1970s in] apartheid [South Africa]."[18]

These commercials contained no reference to the local political context, whether they were selling consumer products—including television sets, furniture, personal grooming products, and food and beverages—or financial services, especially banking.[19] An early 1980s car commercial for Ford Sierra XR6 opens with a long shot of a car traveling on a deserted road in the countryside at night.[20] Soft music plays, and the scene cuts to a young, well-groomed white man driving the car. He pulls up as a fashionably dressed white woman waits for him by a small helicopter. He exits the car and walks toward her. In the final scene, the two of them embrace, accompanied by the overlaid tagline, "Man and Machine in Perfect Harmony." The commercial could have been shot anywhere in 1980s Western Europe or North America. Other times, cultural genres popular among black South Africans were appropriated and included in ads but without breaking through the apartheid imagination. A 1984 commercial for Toyota Corolla tracked innovations in the vehicle's design by linking them with trends in global popular music between 1975 and 1984. Two young dancers in bright colors that contrast with the colors of the cars perform dances like the moonwalk and the robot. Both the dancers in the commercial are white.[21]

Some television commercials would occasionally break with the tight consensus on racial domination by mildly referencing local realities in featuring black characters. This was especially the case during the "era of reform"—that is, the mid- to late 1980s, when the government began negotiating with banned opposition movements (like the ANC) and relaxing restrictive race laws around housing or job opportunities for blacks. In these ads, black characters—still marginalized—might be depicted in nontraditional roles such as financial service or office work. At most, these black characters were filmed as indistinct faces in large crowds, whether outdoors (for example, in parks or in separate cars on the same roads) or in more indoor public settings such as banks, offices, and bars, though the scenes were still dominated by white characters. Even when these images were edited together, in close-up shots, black actors were most often filmed to appear separately from white actors—for example, in office spaces with all-black colleagues.

These black figures rarely had speaking parts. A 1984 commercial for Standard Bank, for example, opens with light, cheerful music ("It's yours because we're always striving together / It's yours because we're always working it out together") with scenes of large crowds—though still mostly white people—entering and leaving office buildings, riding escalators, or walking down busy streets.[22] In some frames, the crowds are multiracial. These scenes are then intercut with profile shots of black and white professionals smiling and looking straight into the camera. Only the white actors, however, have speaking parts. The commercial ends with a middle-aged white actor—presumably depicting someone of authority within the bank, perhaps the bank manager—sitting in an office chair and saying in an upbeat voice, "The key is initiative. My bank's got it."

Few apartheid-era television commercials strayed very far from the core commitments of that system, with the everyday realities of black citizens absent and lacking even gussied-up, aspirational visions of black life that the Standard Bank commercial presented.[23] The effect of this commercial landscape was clear: "the media agenda . . . was set up in such a manner that advertisers were to some extent contributing to the construction of separate social realities for blacks."[24] The major exception were the commercials for SAB's Castle Lager beer from the 1980s through to the 1990s in which white and black men socialized together in multiracial settings.[25] This gradually became the norm for the brand after 1983 (prior to this, black characters were completely excluded from English-language Castle Lager commercials). The brewer "made a conscious decision in the mid-1980s to shoot multiracial advertisements after market research suggested that consumers would view such advertising in a favorable light."[26] As Holt argues, "these commercials are quite remarkable in how they echo the unfolding political drama of the final collapse of the apartheid system." By the early 1990s, he writes, "Black depiction [in Castle Lager ads] becomes more reformist to the point of representing an integrated South African middle class, consistent with a unitary state (rather than the separatist ethnic middle classes that were still being advocated by the [P. W.] Botha government)."[27] Not surprisingly, a few weeks after Mandela's liberation from prison in 1990, a leading advertising executive was quoted as saying that his release was "a move toward creating a market of 35 million people of all races instead of focusing only on the 5 million whites."[28] And in the wake of South Africa's first democratic elections in 1994, another executive remarked, "There has been a sort of shift in attitudes. We've started saying, 'We're facing a new era, and how are we in the advertising community going to adapt to it?'"[29] Though brands retained segmentation in how they marketed to prospective customers, the South African ad industry began seeing the nation as a larger market; the focus would no longer be on just the tiny slice that until then had access to television sets and purchasing power.[30]

Since the early 1990s, researchers and consumer analysts have been obsessed with quantifying the black consumer market. For example, the Unilever Institute of Strategic Marketing, established in 1999 and based at the University of

Cape Town, conducts research and produces annual reports on "the unique and evolving South African marketplace."[31] Among others, the Unilever Institute produced a longitudinal study of South Africa's growing black middle class titled "Black Diamond," which is what advertisers dub the emerging black middle class. But more than just seeing the nation as a market, South Africa's advertising industry began seeing the nation—or the idea of the nation—as perhaps its most valuable marketing tool, especially within the framework of the country's political transition.

Simunye Is Heritage

Advertising firms were among the first to catch on to the new zeitgeist. A number of South African print advertisements began to openly employ phrases or metaphors from constitutional negotiations.[32] These included car manufacturer Volkswagen, which lined up cars in formation to resemble the new South African flag's layout (accompanied by the slogan "For the people, by the people"), or oil company BP, which added the tagline "The future of South Africa is written with one letter X" to commercials promoting its range of products. (The X referenced the mark made by voters on their ballots in the historic 1994 election.) Candy company Beacon offered up an obvious pun on South Africa's diverse cultural heritage in promoting Allsorts, a popular candy: "It takes Allsorts to make a new South Africa." Of all these, however, a print ad for the popular milk brand Bonnita best illustrates the close relationship then evolving between advertising messages and larger political discourses at the time: a spill from an open milk carton forms the shape of a white cross with the slogan, "Why cry over spilt milk when we can build a healthy nation. The past is that . . . past. It's the future that's important." The message was explicit: "Four decades of apartheid are written off in a mollifying cliché as an unfortunate mistake, which is best forgotten, followed up with the promise that all the spilt milk of our past will be effectively mopped up by market forces."[33]

The first television commercials produced after 1990 clumsily attempted to reflect and comment on political changes. In an ad for Kit Kat chocolate bars, first aired on television in 1992, two men on horseback—one black, one white—meet on a narrow mountain trail. The black man is dressed in a straw hat and woven blanket and plays a thumb piano (to represent a catch-all black culture), while the white man is dressed in khakis and plays a small concertina. Both men's costumes are designed to evoke associations with viewers: the black traveler's garb references migrant labor and rural black people, while the white traveler's costume connects him to Afrikaners and Afrikaner culture. Since neither man can pass the other, we are left to wonder who will retreat. At this point, predictably, the white man takes the initiative, gets off his horse, and pulls out a Kit Kat that he shares with the black man. The commercial ends with the two men riding away in different directions, having exchanged horses, clothes, and musical instruments.[34]

The ad had done its work: a dominant trope of television commercials during South Africa's political transition was to engage with national identity and reconciliation without necessarily confronting the unequal relations embedded in South Africa's political economy. In the process, the advertising industry and its clients were merely reflecting dominant discourses about constructing new identities, markets, and histories in South Africa. Since the early 1990s, political, business, and media elites have been active in promoting various frameworks to understand as well as will into being the "new South African nation." These frameworks often fell into advertisers' and marketers' laps. The earliest of these frameworks was the "the Rainbow Nation."

Desmond Tutu first referred to South Africa as "the rainbow children of God"[35] in May 1994 as Mandela was about to be inaugurated as the country's first democratic president. Tutu extended this metaphor by referring to the country as "the rainbow nation." Mandela's new government quickly adopted Tutu's concept as official state policy, and Mandela made frequent references to the rainbow nation in his official speeches and public statements. For example, in his inaugural speech as president in May 1994, Mandela said, "We have triumphed in the effort to implant hope in the breasts of the millions of our people. We enter into a covenant that we shall build the society in which all South Africans, both black and white, will be able to walk tall, without any fear in their hearts, assured of their inalienable right to human dignity—a rainbow nation at peace with itself and the world."[36]

The idea of South Africans as a patchwork of identities united in their quest to craft a new collective identity was also present in Thabo Mbeki's formulations. Mbeki gained a reputation in the media—particularly among white commentators—as distancing himself from the rainbow metaphor. Rather, Mbeki emphasized the existence of "two nations" (one rich and white, another poor and black) in South Africa and went further by promoting the primacy of black interests (through his "African Renaissance" philosophy and BEE policies). However, at some level, Mbeki's reformulation of South African national identity also amounted to an affirmation of the rainbow: in his most explicit statement on the topic, Mbeki celebrated the existence of a diverse South African identity that was at once African as well as multicultural—one that whites as well as blacks could share.[37] When Jacob Zuma replaced Mbeki as president in 2009, his formulation of South African national identity explicitly played on primordial notions of ethnicity. Yet Zuma saw no contradiction between such notions of South African identity and celebrating the supposed "unity in diversity" formulation of the rainbow nation.[38]

The new SABC was one of the first South African corporations to incorporate the idea of national-identity-as-resource into its branding. From the moment SABC1 was launched, the station's managers and marketing staff insisted it develop its own "channel identity." It went for *Simunye*, a Zulu word that means "We are one." Simunye commercials and jingles—shown during breaks between television programs in the early years of democratic rule—celebrated unity, reconciliation, renewal, and the democratic transition and, predictably, invoked the rainbow nation.[39] The faces of the campaign were youthful and exuberant, mostly black (but with one or two white faces also), and aspirant. A major criticism of Simunye, however, was that it contained few if any images of the townships (the segregated, mostly poor and working-class areas where urban blacks were confined under apartheid and where most still live). Indeed, Simunye was a terrible campaign: the ads were clumsy, the jingles were annoying, and the project was widely criticized by scholars and other observers.[40] One researcher even asserted that Simunye amounted to a new "hegemonic nation-building language." As such, Simunye's creators were guilty of submerging conflict.[41] In a testament to its appeal among a broader public, the campaign endured for another six years and made an indelible mark on the national consciousness.

For a significantly long time, Castle Lager was the only other brand campaign to gain a similar kind of notoriety in South Africa as Simunye. While SAB produces a portfolio of beers, it is with Castle Lager that it has built its beer monopoly and reputation as a market leader in South Africa and the Southern African region. Today, Castle Lager's brand campaigns foreground South Africa's multiracial campaigns, but that was not always the case: during colonialism and under apartheid, SAB's marketing related to black consumers and white consumers as two separate groups, which meant producing and promoting different beer brands to the two markets. Still, white consumers were the priority in SAB's public campaigns. As a result, historian Robert Ross has suggested that South Africa's modern history "can be written through its drinking habits and [the] regulation [of drinking]" and that SAB's branding is an ideal place to interrogate the relationship between advertising and political change in the country.[42] (That beer is an ideal marker of a nation's identity is not unique to South Africa, of course. For example, Martin Lindstrom, a brand strategist from Denmark, has argued, "When it comes to identifying with a country, after flags, national anthems and national airlines comes beer. . . . The advantages are very clear. It is what you would call free branding—leveraging a country's brand rather than building your own."[43])

Castle Lager's brand was firmly identified with white South African masculinity and thus deeply bound up with apartheid. It is therefore striking how quickly Castle Lager adopted Simunye themes in the 1990s. In 1998, two years after SABC1 launched the Simunye campaign, Castle Lager floated the first of a series of commercials that explicitly celebrated the new South Africa. The commercial, set in New York City, opens with a caption, "New York, USA." The beat of the pop song "Africa" by the American group Toto kicks in. We see a young white man dressed casually—with the insignia of the new South African flag clearly visible on his shorts—pushing a cart covered with a dark sheet on a busy downtown New York City street. He enters a high-rise building. The scene cuts to a rooftop where a multiracial group of men awaits him. When he arrives, he reveals the contents of the cart: cases of Castle Lager beer. The group on the roof congratulates the young man. The camera cuts to the men who start drinking beer. Several hands (both black and white) reach for beers. "Africa" plays on in the background. Then the men pose for a portrait, lining up in a way that is reminiscent of old colonial photographs. The commercial ends with a wide-angle camera shot of the men holding beers, followed by a close-up of sausages on a grill with the men saluting Castle Lager as a half-visible new South African flag waves in the breeze. A male voice-over notes: "All over the world, a South African's home is his Castle." The tagline at the end of the commercial reads: "Castle Lager. The taste that stood the test of time."[44]

Some observers wondered why the commercial was set in New York City. One explanation could be that SAB was reacting to criticisms about its early 1990s ads, which depicted wholly unrealistic scenarios of mixed black and white social scenes. It made sense to imagine such common social spaces only outside South Africa. A second explanation could be that the commercial reflected the new worldliness among South African elites, especially white elites, who were no longer the pariahs they'd been toward the end of apartheid but were now mobile, free to travel all over the world and to expand the large expatriate communities of white South Africans already settled in places like the United Kingdom, Canada, Australia, and New Zealand.

The commercial also referenced familiar symbols of South African masculinity: *braai* (barbeque) and the replica sports shirts of South Africa's national rugby and soccer teams worn by some of the men. The difference was that now black men could help shape an identity previously limited to their white counterparts. That the group was multiracial and the new South African flag featured prominently also mattered. So did the impression that the men were united in their patriotism. But the continuities with apartheid commercials were also obvious: white men and what passed for white culture remained at the center of this commercial. The theme song by Toto was titled "Africa" but in the vernacular of 1980s American pop music was replete with patronizing and outmoded references to the continent. Not surprisingly, the song had been very popular with white South Africans when it first came out in the early 1980s and continued to be so long after the 1998 commercial was first aired.

Inevitably, Castle Lager and SAB would catch up with the times: in 2007 the company updated the 1998 commercial. The new version featured a globe-trotting black South African who (in voice-over mode) highlights his exploits during a multicountry vacation.[45] In the frenetic ad (all of 1 minute and 16 seconds), viewers follow the lead character as he travels—mostly by plane—to Buenos Aires, Rio de Janeiro, Mexico City, New York City, Los Angeles, "the desert" (presumably in Nevada), parts of Asia (Japan and China), Athens, Newcastle (in the United Kingdom), and finally Cairo. On the way, the young man expresses faint interest (often confirming outdated stereotypes) but mostly annoyance with local customs. In each of these cities, the protagonist pronounces on the deficiencies of the local beer: "tastes like lemonade" (in Buenos Aires), "green tea" (China), and "warm, flat beer" (Newcastle). This leads to the punch line at the end of the commercial as he stands on a busy street in Cairo, looks up, and muses aloud, "I am hot. I am thirsty. Then it hits me: I am South African and only one thing can satisfy my thirst." The camera cuts to the Castle Lager logo and the tagline: "Perfectly balanced to satisfy a South African thirst." Like in the 1998 version, by the end of the commercial the protagonist rediscovers his national identity through his thirst for South African beer.

Most obviously, this commercial arrives at the same conclusions as the earlier Castle Lager commercial, especially in the way it taps into discourses of nationalist belonging (and stereotypes of others). But it also differs in remarkable ways from its previous iteration: a black lead has replaced the ubiquitous central white character. The music is also more diverse, more attuned to the taste of the new multiracial middle class. The lead character is cosmopolitan. There is also an interplay of languages: the lead character speaks primarily in English but uses colloquial terms from Zulu/Xhosa (for example, *bafethu* as a nonspecific noun for "guys" and *u-beer* for the noun "beer"). However, both commercials have something striking in common: they displace their subjects. Both characters are physically outside South Africa, and they long for home. But what would happen if they were home? What if the commercials confronted the history of Castle Lager/SAB as well as South African history, especially the history of violence, racism, capitalism, colonialism, and apartheid?

The Idea of Heritage

The concept of heritage has been central to SAB's advertising campaigns both under apartheid and after 1994, argues historian Anne Kelk Mager. "Heritage," notes Mager, refers to "the reconstruction or invention of a past" and "reinforces the knowledge and expertise of prior success; . . . builds on nostalgia and relies on a mystique bigger than personality." Crucially, heritage enables a brand "to move beyond the parochial to claim universal values." Furthermore, Mager argues, "in providing a past it created reliability, something to hold on to in a rapidly changing consumer world. Heritage suggested permanence and security, the timelessness of a mythical . . . fantasy of the past."[46]

Under apartheid, heritage was connected to ideas and values about masculinity and the character of the white South African nation. Of all SAB's brands,

Castle Lager was most consistently connected with heritage. Castle Lager was marketed (both under apartheid and from 1994 on) as "the beer with the longest and proudest heritage in South Africa."[47] To make this connection, SAB invented a heritage for the product. The commercials centered on one "Charles Glass," a white beer brewer who, SAB claimed, lived and worked in Johannesburg in the second half of the nineteenth century, the period of the gold rush in Johannesburg and its surrounds. (This was also a period of great upheaval for black South Africa; it introduced the migrant labor system, for example, but viewers would be hard-pressed to make these connections.) In the commercials for the campaign introduced in the mid-1980s, Glass was "a genius, a master of the craft of brewing, and [had a] deep commitment to the country and its people." Glass was credited with starting his "Castle Brewery" in Johannesburg and teaching white men how to appreciate good beer and drink respectfully.[48] The actor who played Glass was the stereotype of a British emigrant: exemplifying hard work and British values like fair play. The campaign implied that men who identified with Castle Lager did the same.

In real life, Charles Glass was a minor brewer who abused his wife. She did the actual brewing of the beer, as it turns out. He failed at his business and returned to England not long after immigrating to South Africa.[49] These revelations, however, had little effect on the Charles Glass myth. In fact, well into the late 1990s, Castle Lager commercials would usually end with a multiracial mix of men downing Castle Lager beers while lifting their glasses together in a toast: "To Charles!"[50] They would then break into collective song as members of the fictional "Charles Glass Society":

> When we drink Castle
> We fill with admiration
> For Charles whose brewing class
> Won fame across the nation
> When we drink Castle
> We draw our inspiration
> From Charles' brew and
> How it grew upon our reputation!

Strikingly, the early Charles Glass commercials made little or no reference to South African iconography or showed any semblance of being grounded in a South African space. There was no mention of migrant labor, mining capital, or the black labor central to mines—nor, in this case, breweries. The music sounded "English" (meaning white English-speaking South African culture), the language did not stray from a formal British style, and the men's dress was fairly generic. Partly in response to political changes and economic imperatives (because SAB and those in charge of its advertising and branding budget took notice of such things), Charles Glass fell out of favor and mostly disappeared from commercials. Instead, SAB commercials began to celebrate multiculturalism, the rainbow nation, and democracy. But Charles Glass would make one final comeback.

In 2005 SAB decided to rebrand Castle Lager via a new campaign named "9644" for a short message service (SMS) code. The campaign's goal was to attract the newly emerging young, black, urban-based beer-drinking market, which saw Castle Lager as the drink of mostly older white men. As a designer on the print campaign for 9644 explained three years later, "Castle Lager was the big beer brand in the South African market. It started rapidly losing market share as South Africa's political landscape changed. The brand was struggling. The cool crowd, the young progressive black urban market, saw Castle as a dated brand drunk by older [mostly white] men. The challenge was to get it back into the hearts and minds of the identified target market, 25–34 [year-old] city living black males."[51] The television commercial for the campaign opens with a young black man coming into view. We hear the refrain of a Zulu phrase that means "We must not forget those who led the way." Kwaito—a local pop music form that emerged after 1994 and was at the time the soundtrack for postapartheid black youth—provides the background music as a voice actor solemnly notes:

> For their resilience,
> For their determination,
> For never giving up,
> Pay your respects.

Viewers watch as the background scene behind the young man transforms from a farm to a township council house and finally ends in front of a group of highrises. He also changes his outfits, which correspond to the changes in his location: from smart-casual (in front of the farmhouse and council house) to a suit (in front of the skyscraper). At the end of the commercial, the young man pours libations (beer), seemingly for comrades lost to political struggle as we soon find out when the words "June 16" flash on the screen.[52] The idea was to evoke a connection to June 16, 1976, when a student uprising by black youth in Soweto spread to the rest of the country. That protest also marked the beginning of the final phase of resistance to apartheid.[53]

What's going on here? The music soundtrack is different from previous Castle Lager ads. The American pop band Toto and house music has been supplanted by Kwaito. New York and other foreign locations have been replaced by three iconic (or stereotypical) South African settings (the farm, the township, and the city), and the thirst for beer is connected to remembrance and respect for South Africa's heroic liberation past. But there is one other subtle reference when the young man tips the bottle to pour libations: in that moment the viewer catches a faint glimpse of the name "Charles Glass" on the label. The connection to the mythical founder of Castle Lager is cemented; the brand's heritage is being celebrated and reproduced. Overall, a number of disparate, seemingly contradictory markers are connected: the farmhouse, representing white masculinity and heritage (that of Charles Glass) contributes the white apartheid identity; the references to Soweto 1976, evoking struggle and liberation, contribute the black antiapartheid identity; and Kwaito music from popular culture contributes black postapartheid identity.

This strategy of bringing together discordant bits of South African identity was ubiquitous in beer commercials that made use of sports as a metaphor or focus. In 2007 SAB unveiled its "War Cry" commercial. The members of the South African national football (or soccer), rugby, and cricket teams were the stars of the commercial. Each team was riding high at the time: the cricket and rugby teams were participating in global championships while the soccer team was building toward hosting the World Cup three years later. In the commercial, the players are shown vigorously singing a popular hymn, "Hamba nathi mkhululu wethu" (Go with us, our redeemer), before a match.[54] A member of each team, usually a black player, leads his teammates in song. Through clever editing, the teams merge to form, in effect, one team. Though each team was filmed in its respective dressing room, the commercial was shot in such a way as to make the three teams indistinguishable, creating the appearance of the men singing together. The commercial ends as the teams walk out onto the field to the deafening screams and cheers of South African supporters, and the slogan "Castle Lager. Satisfying South Africa's Thirst" flashes on the screen.

While soccer was viewed as a black sport, both rugby and cricket were associated with white South African sports. Since the end of apartheid, active policies to transform these sports increased the number of black players in rugby and cricket's professional leagues, but their connection with white popular culture has persisted. These associations were, of course, a direct result of colonial and apartheid state policy, which promoted certain sports for different races.[55] Television commercials during apartheid diligently followed this script. "War Cry" worked against this separation, but the commercial also wanted to blunt criticism about the lack of representation of black players in cricket and rugby by creating the impression of "one team." The teams were thus more representative in the commercial than in reality. But "War Cry" did more than merely merge or unite all beer-drinking sports fans. The choice of language and song was deliberate. *Hamba nathi* was generally associated with antiapartheid protest: some protesters interpreted *mkhululu* as "liberator." As a hymn, it was usually sung communally as a dirge. SAB, however, was not too keen on linking "War Cry" with liberation history. Senior brand manager Mike Middleton suggested the "war cry" only reflected some vague ideal, "the summoning up of the courage, inspiration and strength required to conquer the team they are about to face."[56]

Nevertheless, the effect was clear to viewers: liberation history was merged with Christianity and sport—both powerful symbols of South African national identity—to sell beer. As effective as all this celebration was, however, sports teams were not the only way that politics and national identity appeared in South African ads. Returning to the fate of the Simunye campaign is very instructive in this regard.

Pipe Dreams and Unsubstantiated Hopes

By August 2003, SABC1's managers were questioning the "glossy, metallic look and neon lights" of Simunye. The marketing manager of SABC1, Jerry Mpufane, argued that the channel brand needed "a more toned-down, earthy feel."[57] SABC's marketers thus came up with a new rebranding slogan: "Ya Mampela" (The real thing). The centerpiece of the new brand was a 2004 television commercial, "Take Another Look at Msanzi [translation: South Africa]."

It is morning, and viewers see a young man waking up. Dogs are barking. When he steps outside, viewers recognize the township milieu. When the camera films him from the front, we notice that he is white and dressed in the fashions usually associated with working-class young men in South Africa's black townships. A pulsating Kwaito beat kicks in. It is the song "Kleva Kasi lam" (My township clever) by popular Kwaito performer and producer Mapaputsi.[58] The "kleva," meaning "clever," of the song title equates the township tough with an American wiseguy, someone who is admired for hustling or who is considered entrepreneurial.[59]

The street quickly fills up with people going about their day: children head off to school; traders transact business informally. All these people are white. This should be jarring for anyone watching who is familiar with South Africa's racial political economy. A tour bus—the signage on the side of the bus identifies it as "Township Tours"—comes into view, and young white boys ham it up for those inside the bus; the "tourists" are black. This is the first time in the commercial viewers are introduced to any black characters.

The commercial then cuts to a busy and chaotic township taxi stand. The protagonist jumps into a minibus taxi and heads for the mostly white suburbs to the north of Johannesburg. As the taxi ambles through the city's northern suburbs, he notices two (white) domestic workers sitting at the side of the road. They are taking a break from cleaning houses or caring for children. The camera lingers on a scene in the driveway of a large, opulent house, and we observe two black schoolchildren dressed in school uniforms associated with expensive private schools getting into a car while the white maid (or servant) in full uniform runs after them with a school bag. The children ignore the maid. The camera cuts back to the young man, who appears to recognize and empathize with the resignation on the maid's face.

The locale shifts again. The young man gets out of the taxi and finds himself in a part of downtown Johannesburg usually populated by working-class black people but now is filled with poor, working-class white people. In contrast to the sterile suburbs we were introduced to earlier, this world is like the township: it is portrayed as joyful and enterprising. The camera cuts quickly to scenes of buoyant street life: young male dancers put on a street performance of township (*pantsula*) dance, and young women braid hair. But this idyllic scene is soon ruptured when the main character comes into contact with black people. When he walks past a parking lot, the black woman driver exiting the lot notices him and locks her doors. He walks into a grocery store only for the black store owner to eye him suspiciously, gesture at a wanted poster, and call the police. When the police officers—who are both white—arrive, the shop owner says, "This is him. Him," and points to the poster. The police officers are not convinced, and the shop owner responds despondently, "You all look the same." As the young man leaves the store, he asks for a ride back to the township from a group of people in a car. The scene cuts to his cramped bedroom where the young man sits on his bed and switches on the television. The screen goes black, and first the slogan "Take another look at Mzansi" appears and then in the next frame, "SABC1. "Ya Mampela" appears on the screen to close the commercial.

This commercial is striking for the ways in which it appeared to reflect realistic scenes of racial inequality in South Africa (of Mbeki's "two nations"), but with a twist. White people were now living in townships and black people employed uniformed maids, locked their car doors when whites walked past, or gawked at whites from inside township tour bus windows. Although some of the depictions of race and class inequalities were over the top (and in most cases gross stereotypes), the commercial reflected local realities in a sober, visual style. Moreover, it suggested that who ended up living in overcrowded townships and who lived in big houses in expansive suburbs was in a sense arbitrary rather than a product of some natural order. Finally, it drew attention to a world divided into haves and have-nots—a world of ongoing social and material inequity, even though it, jarringly, created the impression that this inequality could be remedied by the purchasing power of the free-market economy.

The commercial polled well with SABC1 viewers, and the channel won a Silver Apex Award from the Association of Communication and Advertising.[60] Yet despite all this support, the Ya Mampela theme had a relatively short shelf life compared to Simunye. In 2005, one year after the campaign was first introduced, SABC1 announced that it was rebranding away from Ya Mampela. Its new slogan would be "Mzansi fo sho" (slang for "South Africa for sure"). In explaining the shift away from Ya Mampela, SABC1 executives argued that "some of the values inherent in the Ya Mampela positioning, though relevant at the time [when it first came out], were no longer so in a post-2005 South Africa." Ya Mampela was too "gritty and rebellious." What was needed now, according to the SABC, was "real 'tell it like it is' content." Mzansi fo sho would teach young people how to "engage with their reality . . . for survival [and] prosperity and the construction of their identities in an uncertain environment." It is significant that in late 2017, Mzansi fo sho retained its position as the SABC's overarching marketing slogan.

Although the campaign was soon discarded, one of the more lasting legacies of Ya Mampela was that it inspired a genre of commercials that paired the racial reversal genre with the politics of reconciliation and the rainbow nation and in the process achieved what I term ironic pragmatism.

The most obvious candidate for the genre of ironic pragmatism was a 2007 campaign for Ford Bantam, a popular small pickup truck, what South Africans call a "bakkie." The model was a holdover from the 1980s, when the American-owned Ford Motor Company withdrew from South Africa under pressure from antiapartheid groups. Ford sold off its plants and equipment and licensed the name to a local manufacturer. The new company, Ford South Africa, began manufacturing the Bantam in 1983. Apartheid's leaders regarded the Bantam as part of white South Africa's resolve in the face of growing resistance to apartheid—that the political pressure and sanctions were not effective and that apartheid South Africa could make what it needed regardless of boycotts. Ford Bantam thus took on folk status under apartheid, and its advertising campaigns privileged white citizens, especially the stereotype of white farmers and their bakkies. In fact, the takeaway line from its earliest commercial campaigns employed a term of endearment associated with white Afrikaners: "Boet [brother], you need a Bantam."

Despite this history, Ford Bantam retained its popularity after apartheid. The one continuity in Bantam marketing campaigns was that Ford South Africa still emphasized the bakkie's usefulness to small businesses. What was striking was now Ford linked the bakkie's versatility and usefulness to the new democratic government's economic program: "As the workhorse for so many of the small businesses that are the lifeblood of our economy, the Ford Bantam really does contribute to creating the jobs and wealth that South Africa needs to be successful."[61] Given this background, the tropes employed in Ford Bantam's 2007 campaign were quite memorable.

The scene opens in a nondescript suburb. A bakkie pulls up at a house. Viewers' attention is immediately drawn to Afrikaans signage above the image of an electrical current on the side of the truck: "Monument Elektries: 24 Uur Diens" (Monument Electrical: 24 Hour Service). The camera pans out to reveal that a white man is driving the bakkie. Both the signage and who is driving will turn out to be significant. We notice a second man getting out of the bakkie: he is black. The camera lingers on the contrast between the two men's attire. The white man is dressed in casual clothes, the black man in a blue work shirt and jeans.

The white man is clearly in charge. He claps his hands, ordering the black man—in a mixture of English and Afrikaans phrases—to unload the electrical equipment. The white man is also the one who greets the white homeowner. The scene cuts to the two white men relaxing on the porch, drinking tea and eating while the black man works. The scene is obviously deliberate and meant to recall for the viewer the work relations normalized during apartheid. The two Monument Elektries employees get back into the pickup and drive off.

Next, we see them driving on a roadway when the cell phone rings. The black man, still in his blue work clothes, answers. Abruptly, the bakkie stops; the men get out on the side of the road and start to undress. One of them removes the company sign from the truck's doors. The commercial cuts to the bakkie pulling up at a different suburban house. The earlier scenes replay themselves. This time, however, the company sign on the bakkie reads "Ubuntu Electrical: 24 Hour Service." It is in Zulu and English, and the design of this logo incorporates an ethnic motif. We also notice a change of tasks: the black electrician now drives the truck and is dressed in casual clothes. He is the one who gets out and greets the homeowner, another black man. The white man, now dressed in a blue work shirt, is ordered in Zulu to gather the tools. The commercial closes with a voice-over by a (presumably white) narrator: "Ford Bantam. The bakkie that helps build the nation."

The commercial was quite popular at the time and the subject of much media debate. Years later, different versions posted on social media video sites like YouTube still rack up millions of views. Like the Ya Mampela commercial before it, this commercial directly commented on public discourses about the new South Africa. Most obvious was how it indicated the continued existence of racism. Somewhat more subtly, the commercial also evoked the government's affirmative action policies (BEE), particularly around accusations (from both Left and Right critics) that some black businesspeople served as fronts for cynical white companies taking advantage of these initiatives. The commercial appeared to slyly critique these policies.

More significant was the commercial's tagline and its implication—that Ford Bantam was helping to "build the nation" through some form of subterfuge. It combined two seemingly contrary messages: South Africans (given the historical white target market of Bantam bakkies) must accommodate the continuities inherited from apartheid (some form of white privilege) but at the same time must accommodate some form of affirmative action and black economic empowerment. Fundamentally, the Ford Bantam commercial presented the idea of things as they are as an acceptable settlement between the past and present. This was not a far-fetched view and reflected the reconciliatory politics of the first decade of South African democracy, manifested in public institutions like the TRC and campaigns like the Rainbow Nation.

Rebranding the Nation

In August 2002, the South African government launched the International Marketing Council of South Africa (IMC). Representatives of South Africa's biggest corporations along with senior government ministers were appointed to serve on the board by then South African president Mbeki. The IMC opened a main office in Sandton (an upscale suburb in the north of Johannesburg) and three country offices in London, Washington, DC, and Mumbai. They hired three prominent, mainstream South African journalists to run the international country offices.[62] The IMC's primary goal was to develop a singular message to market the country to South Africans and outsiders. From the outset, the IMC board made it clear which countries it considered its main targets for investment and trade: the United States, Great Britain, countries of the European Union, China, India, the United Arab Emirates, Brazil, and Russia. It also added "global South Africans" living outside South Africa to the list. Though it was less specific about the makeup of this latter group, it is significant to notice that one of the IMC's first major campaigns was a "Homecoming Revolution" aimed at expatriate, mostly white South Africans living in the United Kingdom.[63] In time, the IMC came up with a brand identity, "Brand South Africa," and a brand slogan, "South Africa. Alive with Possibility."[64] For the IMC, Brand South Africa "rolls together both the tangibles and intangibles [of South African identity] and highlights the touch-and-feel components of branding" that included "the diversity, warmth, and generosity of the people—the 'ubuntu.'"[65]

Brand South Africa's mission was to ensure equal billing for the country's musical traditions and sounds—the "rhythm of the nation"—with its wildlife, mountains, and beaches usually foregrounded in global marketing campaigns. The IMC concluded that "the brand that emerges is as tangible as Coca-Cola or Nike and it is the sum of all its parts—tourism, economic potential, and human diversity and togetherness."[66] Finally, Brand South Africa reflected the country's "collective confidence as people, and our fervent belief that tomorrow can be, and should be, better than yesterday."[67]

The centerpiece of the advertising campaign (produced by local advertising agency TBWA/Hunt/Lascaris) was a series of four television commercials under the title "Alive with Possibility."[68] The commercials blanketed local television, were featured on global news networks like CNN, and were shown to travelers on long-distance flights between South Africa and Asian, North American, and European destinations.

The first of the Alive with Possibility commercials was entitled "Invest in South Africa."[69] The public relations company employed by the IMC summarized the commercial's content: "A high wide camera shot of a line of models, an applauding audience, flashing cameras—Milan? No, it is South Africa. A close-up of red wine being poured into a glass, a couple having a picnic in a beautiful wine estate—Bordeaux? No, South Africa. Is that high-angled shot of lines of luxury cars filmed in Bavaria? No again. It's BMW's plant in Rosslyn, Pretoria."[70] At the climax of the commercial, a camera pans over footage of yachts and luxury apartments. A (presumably black) voice actor notes: "And if you think this is Monaco, think again. It's South Africa. Invest in a country alive with possibility."[71] For Brand South Africa, the commercial came with "an interesting twist": it is "infused with the sophistication and industry of the global world, but is intrinsically South African."[72]

The second commercial focused on "ordinary" South Africans going about their daily lives while joining in the "rhythm of the nation." They include a group of senior citizens sitting around knitting, office workers typing on computers, and a trader selling his wares. The characters collectively tap out a beat, amounting to an orchestra of beats. At the heart of the commercial is a ten-year-old black girl named Tlotlego Tsagae, who acts as conductor of the orchestra. Her presence is significant: Tlotlego was born on April 27, 1994, the date of South Africa's first democratic elections.[73]

In the third commercial, a range of well-known South African personalities—politicians, entertainers, and sports people—each complete a sentence that begins with the phrase, "Today, I woke up. . . ."[74] Those featured include Nelson Mandela, Thabo Mbeki, Desmond Tutu, jazz musician Abdullah Ibrahim, and Kwaito music star Zola. They each proceed to extol the virtues of South Africa, which are mostly symbolic. All speak of the possibilities of the new South Africa, endorsing the country's political transition. Mandela is up first, filmed on a soundstage with Robben Island projected behind him: "Today, I woke in a place that said to me, be free." Tutu, filmed in his signature purple tunic, opines: "All I need is to believe." Zola, who is also an actor and reality television star, points a microphone at the viewer, saying "I don't need a gun to make you listen," while Mbeki, who was very unpopular at the time (because of his views on HIV and AIDS, discussed in chapter 5, and the government's economic policies), concludes: "Today, I woke up and I smiled because South Africans are creating a new dawn, every day." In between these testimonies, actress Pamela Nomvete reads inspirational lines as images of a number of local sports stars and a few images of mostly poor black people—identifiable people or actors dressed as poor black people—flash on-screen. Most of the athletes in these scenes are recognizable for having overcome some physical disability or challenge. They include Zanele Situ, a Paralympian; Jacob Matlala, the shortest world boxing champion; and swimmer Natalie du Toit, who competed with one leg against able-bodied athletes in the 2008 Summer Olympic Games in Beijing. The football coach and club owner Ephraim "Jomo" Sono and rugby player Joel Stransky also make up the numbers. The commercial seems to imply that being South African is the special quality these athletes possess that allows them to be successful.[75]

The exception among those profiled is Josia Thugwane, a runner who won the Gold Medal in the men's marathon race at the 1996 Olympic Games in Atlanta, Georgia. Thugwane was a mineworker, and the reference to his employment is the only time the commercial explicitly points out South Africa's past and present political economy. We see Thugwane running along a road with a mineshaft visible in the background and hear Nomvete reciting his thoughts: "Yesterday, I was digging for gold and today I am wearing it." But that's as far as it goes. The only other explicit reference to South Africa's past is a quick cut to the mother of Hector Pietersen, the first known victim of the June 16, 1976, student uprising. Pietersen's mother is standing next to his gravestone close to where he was gunned down by police. The commercial ends with rousing music as a choir sings the brand slogan ("Alive with Possibility") in time for Nomvete to conclude: "Today, I woke up in South Africa."[76]

The final commercial, "We've Done It Again," is the most stirring and is the one ad in the series that explicitly references political events, though very clumsily.[77] It revolves around the memory and symbolism of the 1994 democratic elections. The commercial opens with a black screen and the sounds of gunshots, screams, helicopters, and sirens. The next few frames consist of aerial shots of long lines of people snaking through an open field. We can hear the voice of a narrator (recognizable as that of a well-known black South African actor) kicking in: "Of all the challenges we have yet to overcome, none is greater than we have already overcome." The actor continues: "On the twenty-seventh of April 1994, we shifted our world and we shifted the perceptions of the world." Viewers are carried along as long lines of mostly black first-time voters are seen ready to cast their ballots. The camera closes in on three characters: a young black mother, a black child resting on the mother's back, and a middle-aged white woman. The white woman gets the child's attention and strokes her hair. Finally, we watch the young mother enter and leave the polling booth. As rousing music plays (by then a standard in these commercials), the voice-over concludes: "We've done it before, let's do it again." The brand logo then flashes on the screen; end commercial.

These commercials had a clear agenda. They attempted to promote foreign and domestic investment—the IMC's mandate—by selling the country's recent history and adversity as a resource. In essence, they were marketing the rainbow nation. The aim, of course, was to sell the idea of a stable South Africa, the most important criteria for potential investors. It also sold a vision of South Africa to South Africans themselves and, crucially, to the country's substantial white expatriate population. More than that, it invited those outside (non-South Africans) to become part of the "we"; we who have done it before and can do it again.[78]

Not surprisingly, similar processes played out in the lead-up to the 2010 World Cup, a football tournament that turned out to be a marketer's dream. Coca-Cola, Pepsi, and Brand South Africa this time introduced a series of commercials celebrating a local brand of street football. They latched onto the tournament, placing full-page color advertisements in national newspapers at the end of the tournament and running television ads on a loop between news or dramas. At the same time, some banks, like First National Bank (FNB), had explicit messages for South African fans to not jeopardize the security and safety of visiting fans. In some television commercials, criticism of conditions in South Africa was equated with lack of patriotism.[79]

As football scholars Peter Alegi and Chris Bolsmann have pointed out, banks and grocery chains were quick to congratulate South Africa on hosting a "World Class event," and corporations ran a number of successful campaigns tying the nation to the World Cup.[80] One of these was "Football Fridays," begun as a corporate initiative by the Southern Sun hotel group, which encouraged its employees to wear football shirts on Fridays. The campaign was also later adopted by the World Cup Local Organizing Committee (LOC) and by government departments and ministries. At the end of the World Cup, "Football Fridays" became "Fly the Flag Fridays." For Brand South Africa, Football Fridays was "a meaningful collective experience of a lifetime" and South Africans, not just football fans, were exhorted by President Zuma to continue the tradition as "national duty still calls."[81] Fans were asked to wear replica jerseys of the national football, rugby, and cricket teams; fly the country's flag at home or at their office; buy South African goods "to help create jobs and grow the economy"; and volunteer.[82] It was clear that local history and conflicts were being foregrounded, worked out, and repackaged for local and external consumers in the service of brands, corporations, and a new politics. But it was not all plain sailing.

While South African corporations and the state largely controlled the local reception of Brand South Africa during the 2010 World Cup, it had a more difficult time globally. Global brands were more prone to repeat and recycle outdated and fantastical images of South Africa and Africa.[83] The most visible were the campaigns for Pepsi and Coca-Cola soft drink companies: "Quest—Longest Celebration," one of Coca-Cola's feature commercials for the 2010 World Cup (first broadcast in April 2010), for example, revolved around an animated "African Boy" battling giant Transformer-like machines ("robots" in the commercial) so he could play football. The soundtrack to the commercial, "Wavin' Flag," is a song about refugees by the Somali-Canadian rapper K'Nnaan. The original lyrics critiqued refugee and migrant policy, described the difficult world of new arrivals, and lamented the political instability and conflict in his homeland.[84] For the Coca-Cola commercial, the song was stripped of any political meaning and the words were replaced with bromides about celebration for "the beautiful game."

Similarly, Pepsi made a commercial ("Oh Africa") for the 2010 World Cup that featured football stars Didier Drogba, Kaká, Lionel Messi, Thierry Henry, and Frank Lampard, in which they play against a group of "African children" in an "African bush" complete with all the stereotypical props: a moving dry-grass pitch, star players in colorful shirts, lion noises, and baobab trees.[85]

Nevertheless, as historian Derek Catsam has pointed out, hosting the World Cup had the desired effect: "Few can doubt that, in the quest for narrative, the true winners were the South African boosters, the LOC and the tourist board, the millions with their painted faces and their South African flags, the supporters of South Africa's *Bafana Bafana* ("The Boys," South Africa's national squad) who embraced the world, and who in turn were embraced by the world."[86] Catsam continues:

> For all of the boosterism and naked appeals to consumerism, for a month South Africa presented its best face, painted and ebullient, joyous and friendly, defiantly proud and desperate for approval. July 12 [the day after the final] rolled around and South Africans were left to deal with the hangover. Unemployment and AIDS and crime and corruption and the hand-to-hand combat that characterizes South African politics (but that also make those politics more vibrant than most critical observers seem to grasp) would return to the fore almost immediately. But in the ongoing process of nation-building the World Cup proved to be a central pillar.[87]

Conclusion

What all this shows is that South African elites have understood the mystique of liberation and packaged the transition to be, among other things, a commercial resource, something that people want to be associated with. That said, most observers might not be surprised that the South African state and advertisers would embark on such a strategy. The growing literature on nation branding suggests this is a given.[88] The only difference is that most nations do not sell their violent histories as moral virtue.

What makes the South African case study more striking is that in South Africa, corporations, despite their seemingly public differences with the state, share this philosophy and reflect these political values in how they promote their brands. This type of branding forms part of the neoliberal settlement in South Africa, and both the state and corporations draw on these signifiers for a variety of purposes. But in the process, these signifiers get emptied or retain very little content in relation to their original meanings. The story of liberation becomes a series of past events rather than an ongoing struggle for economic and social justice. The result is a paradox in which nations like South Africa participate in the branding of globalization while simultaneously emphasizing the local and the particular and transforming those branding signifiers into commodities that can be enjoyed universally.

Notes

1. See Xin Zhou and Russell Belk, "Politicizing Consumer Culture: Advertising's Appropriation of Political Ideology in China's Social Transition," *Journal of Consumer Research* 35, no. 2 (2008): 231–244; Charles McGovern, *Sold American: Consumption and Citizenship, 1890–1945* (Chapel Hill: University of North Carolina Press, 2006); and Lizabeth Cohen, "A Consumer's Republic: The Politics of Mass Consumption in Postwar America," *Journal of Consumer Research* 31 (2004): 236–239.

2. South African advertising is dominated by four large, foreign-owned corporations: WPP (UK), Omnicom (US), Publicis (France), and Interpublic (US). In 2011 *AdVantage Magazine* (focused on the advertising industry) surveyed firms for "which agencies, agency bosses and creative directors other Cape Town agency execs most admire." The results revealed exclusively white candidates and winners (see "AdVantage Magazine's Execs Cape Town's Execs Most Admire," MarkLives.com, July 20, 2011, http://www.marklives.com/2011/07/the-execs-cape-towns-execs-most-admire/.

3. Adesegun Oyedele and Michael Minor, "Consumer Culture Plots in Television Advertising from Nigeria and South Africa," *Journal of Advertising* 41, no. 1 (2012), 99.

4. Carla Lewis-Balden, "Maatskappye nuwe ligdraers" [Translation: Companies New Torchbearers], *Rapport*, July 22, 2013, 4. Unless otherwise noted, all translations from Afrikaans are mine. For a similar argument, see Masingita Mazibuko, "Africa Style: Social Context and Your Brand," MarkLives.com, March 5, 2013, http://www.marklives.com/2013/03/social-context-and-your-brand/.

5. Alexander Robert Holt, "Political Economy of Racial Stereotyping in Advertising," in *Political Economy of Media Transformation in South Africa*, edited by Anthony Olorunnisola and Keyan Tomaselli (New York: Hampton Press, 2011), 65.

6. The "book" by Michael Morris, Bill Krige, Charmaine Koppehel, et al., *From Groot Constantia to Google: 1685 to 2010: A Colourful History of Brands and Branding in South Africa* (Johannesburg: Affinity Advertising and Publishing, 2011), is a case in point of the uncritical tone in the industry to its own history. Oyedele and Minor point to the dearth of scholarship on advertising in "emerging markets" ("Consumer Culture Plots," 91). In the South African case, the exceptions include the work of Eve Bertelsen (referenced later in this chapter); Rehana Ebrahim-Vally and Denis-Constant Martin, *Viewing the "New" South Africa: Representations of South Africa in Television Commercials: An Experiment in Non-directive Methods* (Newtown: IFAS, 2006); Anne Kelk Mager, *Beer, Sociability and Masculinity in South Africa* (Bloomington: Indiana University Press, 2010); Alexander Holt's work (referenced in this chapter); and marketing professional Sarah Britten's unpublished PhD dissertation, "One Nation, One Beer: The Mythology of the New South Africa in Advertising" (University of Witswatersrand, Johannesburg, 2005).

7. Oyedele and Minor, "Consumer Culture Plots," 95.

8. Molson and Coors merged to form MCBC in 2005.

9. The Molson "I Am . . ." commercial can be seen at Pat P, "Molson I Am Canadian," YouTube, May 18, 2006, http://www.youtube.com/watch?v=pXtVrDPhHBg. For a discussion of the campaign and its "fallout," see Robert M. MacGregor, "I Am Canadian: National Identity in Beer Commercials," *Journal of Popular Culture* 37, no. 2 (2003): 276–286; Chris Daniels, "Molson Canadian," *Marketing* 113, no. 19 (2008): 48; and Ira Wagman, "Wheat, Barley, Hops, Citizenship: Molson's 'I Am [Canadian]' Campaign and the Defense of Canadian National Identity through Advertising," *Velvet Light Trap*, no. 50 (Fall 2002): 77–90.

10. For similar discussions about the relationship between nationalism and commercials in the United States, see the following articles by Stuart Elliot: "Close Super Bowl Helps Late-Game

Spots," *New York Times*, February 2, 2009, https://www.nytimes.com/2009/02/03/business/media/03adco.html; "Upbeat But Sympathetic: A Fine Line for Super Bowl Ads," *New York Times*, January 29, 2009, https://www.nytimes.com/2009/01/30/business/media/30adco.html; and "Ads That Pushed Our Usual (Well-Worn) Buttons," *New York Times*, February 2, 2009, https://www.nytimes.com/2009/02/02/business/worldbusiness/02iht-02adco.19855100.html. See also Patricia Cohen, "Energetic Rabbits, Melt-Proof Candies and Other Advertising Coups," *New York Times*, July 8, 2008, https://www.nytimes.com/2008/07/08/arts/design/08mad.html.

11. James B. Stewart, "When Cars Meet Politics, a Clash," *New York Times*, February 10, 2012, https://www.nytimes.com/2012/02/11/business/how-clint-eastwoods-chrysler-ad-stirred-politics-common-sense.html; Charles M. Blow, "It's Halftime in America," *New York Times*, February 6, 2012, https://campaignstops.blogs.nytimes.com/2012/02/06/its-halftime-in-america/; "Sergio Marchionne: Resurrecting Chrysler," *60 Minutes*, CBS, March 25, 2012.

12. Jeremy Peters and Jim Rutenberg, "Republicans See Politics in Chrysler Super Bowl Ad," *New York Times*, February 6, 2012, https://www.nytimes.com/2012/02/07/us/politics/republicans-see-politics-in-chrysler-super-bowl-ad.html.

13. Ibid.

14. Solly Maphumulo, "Malema: Nando's Must Pay to Use Me," Independent Online, April 22, 2009, http://www.iol.co.za/news/politics/malema-nandos-must-pay-to-use-me-440729.

15. Holt, "Political Economy," 55.

16. For example, YouTube user briantw1 compiled a playlist of thirty-one commercials from the 1980s. It is striking how exclusively white these commercials were. View the complete playlist at Old News, "Linctifed [1985]," YouTube, May 3, 2011, http://www.youtube.com/watch?v=FG1ovFgPq5c&list=PLAFC79BA59C415CAC.

17. See Roluxmagnum, "Rolux Magnum Cape to Cairo," YouTube, January 26, 2012, https://www.youtube.com/watch?v=JrksVIrSblk.

18. Holt, "Political Economy," 57.

19. Ibid., 56.

20. See Old News, "Ford Sierra XR6 ad (1984)," YouTube, November 29, 2010, http://www.youtube.com/watch?v=UiXNGz7Akbg.

21. See Old News, "Toyota Corolla Ad (1984)," YouTube, November 29, 2010, http://www.youtube.com/watch?v=JEUC_5SUU7I.

22. See Old News, "Standard Bank Ad (1984)," YouTube, November 29, 2010, http://www.youtube.com/watch?v=wos3CoDOlpk.

23. Steven A. Holmes, "South African TV Ads Switch to Black and White," *New York Times*, June 19, 1994, 4.

24. Holt, "Political Economy," 59.

25. See Mager, *Beer, Sociability, and Masculinity*.

26. Britten, "One Nation," 147.

27. Holt, "Political Economy," 62.

28. Tony Koenderman and Gary Levin, "S Africa Shops Upbeat," *Advertising Age*, February 1990, 2.

29. Holmes, "South African TV Ads," 4.

30. Alexander Holt, "Structural Processes of Reform as an Influence on Advertising," in Olorunnisola and Tomaselli, *Political Economy of Media Transformation*. See also Britten, "One Nation," 147–149.

31. Unilever Institute of Strategic Marketing, "About Us," accessed July 2, 2018, http://www.unileverinstitute.co.za/about-us/. Other private research firms and consultants include Freshly Ground Insights (http://www.fgi.co.za) and Ipsos (https://www.ipsos.com/en-za), which compiles an annual list of the "Top Brands" in South Africa.

32. Eve Bertelsen, "Ads and Amnesia: Black Advertising in the New South Africa," in *Negotiating the Past: The Making of Memory in South Africa*, edited by Sarah Nuttall and Carli Coetzee, 221–241 (Oxford: Oxford University Press, 1998).

33. Bertelsen, "Ads and Amnesia," 226.

34. Holmes, "South African TV Ads," 4.

35. Desmond Tutu, *The Rainbow People of God: The Making of a Peaceful Revolution* (New York: Doubleday, 1996).

36. Nelson Mandela, "Statement at Inauguration as President of the Republic of South Africa" (inaugural speech, Pretoria, May 10, 1994), https://www.africa.upenn.edu/Articles_Gen/Inaugural_Speech_17984.html.

37. Thabo Mbeki, "I Am an African" (speech delivered to South African Parliament, Cape Town, May 8, 1996), http://www.mbeki.org/2016/06/06/statement-on-behalf-of-the-anc-on-the-occasion-of-the-adoption-by-the-constitutional-assembly-of-the-republic-of-south-africa-constitution-bill-1996-cape-town-19960508/.

38. Jacob Zuma, "'South Africa Is Not a Xenophobic Nation': A Letter from Jacob Zuma," *The Guardian*, April 28, 2015, https://www.theguardian.com/world/2015/apr/28/south-africa-is-not-a-xenophobic-nation-a-letter-from-jacob-zuma.

39. An example of the Simunye jingle from 1996 can be viewed at Brisbane History Geek, "SABC1 'Simunye' Ident 1996," YouTube, December 29, 2008, http://www.youtube.com/watch?v=gE4PIsKIjDY.

40. See Gugu Hlongwane, "Simunye (We Are One!): Discourses of Nation-Building in South African Texts" (PhD diss., York University, Toronto, 2003); and Lee Watkins, "'Simunye, We Are Not One': Ethnicity, Difference and the Hip-Hoppers of Cape Town," *Race and Class* 43, no. 1: 29–44.

41. Hlongwane, iv.

42. Robert Ross, quoted in Mager, *Beer, Sociability and Masculinity*," 164.

43. Martin Lindstrom, *Brand Building on the Internet* (Kogan Page, 2000), quoted in Nnamdi Madichie, "'Made-in' Nigeria or 'Owned-by' Ireland," *Management Decision*, 49 (10), 2011, 1616.

44. Though Toto's "Africa" would be scratched from Castle Lager ads for a while, it returned as the brand's soundtrack for a television commercial in the run-up to the 2013 African Cup of Nations soccer tournament that was held in South Africa. That commercial employed all sorts of stereotypes about Africa that are common in Western popular media. See Olgilvy and Mather South Africa, "Castle Lager—Africa United," Vimeo, accessed October 31, 2016, https://vimeo.com/54019424.

45. "Whirlwind," dir. Kim Geldenhuys (Egg Films, 2006), http://www.moonwalk-films.com/movies/castle-whirlwind.

46. Mager, *Beer, Sociability and Masculinity*, 166.

47. Ibid., 168.

48. Ibid., 178.

49. Mager, *Beer, Sociability and Masculinity*; cited in *Business Report*, "Legality Still a Mystery at Brewer of Myths SAB," Independent Online, April 13, 2011, https://www.iol.co.za/business-report/opinion/legality-still-a-mystery-at-brewer-of-myths-sab-1056064.

50. See, for example, Eastrand, "Castle Lager Advert," YouTube, March 21, 2007, http://www.youtube.com/watch?v=BvkJs2E7iIQ.

51. Torgny Hylen, "Castle Lager 9644," *Torgny Hylen* (blog), January 14, 2008, http://torgnyhylen.wordpress.com/2008/01/14/castle-lager-9644/.

52. Madodasifiso, "Castle Lager—June 16 Tribute.mpg," YouTube, July 24, 2010, https://www.youtube.com/watch?v=BUQZA-hGSms.

53. In 1976 black high school students, first in Soweto and then countrywide, protested lower standards of education and the introduction of Afrikaans as the language for instruction in schools. See Thomas G. Karis and Gail M. Gerhart, *From Protest to Challenge: A Documentary History of African Politics in South Africa, 1882–1990*, vol. 5, *Nadir and Resurgence, 1964–1979* (Bloomington: Indiana University Press, 1997); and Helena Pohlandt-McCormick, *"I Saw a Nightmare . . .": Doing Violence to Memory: The Soweto Uprising, June 16, 1976* (New York: Columbia University Press, 2008).

54. Eastrand, "Castle Lager Advert—War Cry" [Creative Circle], YouTube, August 30, 2006, http://www.youtube.com/watch?v=tcpgO_Hpb4k&feature=related.

55. David Black and John Naurigh, *Rugby and the South African Nation: Sport, Culture, Politics and Power in the Old and New South Africa* (Manchester: Manchester University Press, 1998); Bruce Murray and Christopher Merrit, *Caught Behind: Race and Politics in Springbok Cricket* (Pietermaritzburg: University of KwaZulu-Natal Press, 2004); Peter Alegi, *Laduma! Soccer, Politics and Society in South Africa* (Pietermaritzburg: University of KwaZulu-Natal Press, 2004).

56. "Castle Provokes a War Cry," *Bizcommunity*, August 3, 2005, http://www.bizcommunity.com/Article/196/12/7355.html.

57. Christelle de Jager, "South Africa: The New Look Is 'The Real Thing' for SABC1," *Variety*, August 28, 2003, 28.

58. Panique2, "Mapaputsi—Kleva Kasilam.flv," YouTube, November 23, 2008, http://www.youtube.com/watch?v=DT2gzxi12Vw.

59. Don Mattera, *Memory Is the Weapon* (Johannesburg: African Perspectives, 2007); Clive Glaser, *Bo-Tsotsi: The Youth Gangs of Soweto* (Oxford: James Currey, 2000).

60. SABC, *Annual Report and Financial Statements* (Johannesburg: SABC, 2007), 94.

61. "The Bakkie That Helped Build the Nation—The New FordBantam Ad Campaign," Ford.co.za, May 2007, accessed August 1, 2014. For the commercial, see SoulProviders, "Ford Bantam BEE Ad," YouTube, March 29, 2007, https://www.youtube.com/watch?v=IHbs0Yy8gP4.

62. These journalists were John Battersby (London), Simon Barber (Washington, DC), and Govin Reddy (Mumbai).

63. See Morris Jones and Co., "Our Story Video," accessed November 15, 2016, http://homecomingrevolution.com/our-story-video/. Also see Rory Carroll, "South Africa Hopes to Reverse the 'Chicken Run,'" *The Guardian*, January 7, 2005, https://www.theguardian.com/world/2005/jan/07/southafrica.rorycarroll1.

64. Brand South Africa, "About Us," BrandSouthAfrica.com, accessed November 16, 2016, http://www.brandsouthafrica.com/what-we-do.

65. John Battersby, UK country manager for the IMC, quoted in an interview with Melissa Davis, "Is Africa Misbranded?" Brandchannel.com, August 21, 2007, https://www.brandsouthafrica.com/investments-immigration/africa-gateway/branding-210807.

66. Ibid.

67. Brand South Africa, "Talking Points," BrandSouthAfrica.com, October 2008, http://www.brandsouthafrica.com/content/talking-points_10oct08.pdf.

68. IMC-Brand South Africa, "Alive with Possibility." All the videos are archived in a playlist at Southafricainfo, YouTube, accessed August 1, 2016, http://www.youtube.com/user/southafricainfo.

69. Southafricainfo, "Invest in South Africa" [IMC-Brand South Africa], YouTube, April 7, 2008, http://www.youtube.com/watch?v=uqryZJ_Z57Y.

70. Statement by Meropa Communications on behalf of the International Marketing Council of South Africa, December 7, 2007, in author's possession.

71. Brand South Africa, "Ad with a Twist Urges Global Business 'Invest in South Africa,'" BrandSouthAfrica.com, February 13, 2008, http://www.brandsouthafrica.com/news/173-ad-with-a-twist-urges-global-business-qinvest-in-south-africaq.

72. Ibid.

73. Southafricainfo, "Rhythm of the Nation" [IMC-Brand South Africa], YouTube, February 8, 2007, http://www.youtube.com/watch?v=bi4UlkegLPg.

74. Southafricainfo, "Today I Woke Up . . ." [The Jupiter Drawing Room], YouTube, http://www.youtube.com/watch?v=owEYKyK9z64.

75. A similar trope is employed in a March 2013 television ad created by The Jupiter Drawing Room in Johannesburg for a local bank, ABSA, which emphasizes investing in the "human spirit" of South Africans: ThePendoringAwards, "The Jupiter Drawing Room, Johannesburg – Absa – Human Spirit," February 10, 2014, YouTube, https://www.youtube.com/watch?v=wD35letRdcU.

76. In 2012 Brand South Africa introduced what amounted to an updated version of this television commercial. Its "Inspiring New Ways" ad featured "prominent South African celebrities, sports stars, entrepreneurs and entertainers." Brand South Africa, "Inspiring New Ways," July 4, 2012, https://www.youtube.com/watch?v=TUCwaAmvu8o.

77. Southafricainfo, "We've Done It Before . . ." [IMC-Brand South Africa], YouTube, June 22, 2007, http://www.youtube.com/watch?v=_w_ZksXtmrw.

78. By 2011, Brand South Africa was extending its reach to "Brand Africa" with an advisory council consisting mostly of representatives of South African capital and former employers of Brand South Africa. See http://brandafrica.net/.

79. This theme was a constant in pre–World Cup ads made for FNB. See South African Magazine, "2010 FIFA World Cup FNB TV Commercial" [Foote, Cone, and Belding (FCB)], YouTube, February 8, 2008, http://www.youtube.com/watch?v=hjPazSFQrwA.

80. Peter Alegi and Chris Bolsmann, interview by the author, Email, July 4, 2013.

81. Brand South Africa, "South Africa: Keep Flying!" July 13, 2010, https://www.brandsouthafrica.com/people-culture/sport/2010/flytheflagfridays.

82. Ibid. See also Derek Charles Catsam, "*Ayoba!* Reflections from South Africa's World Cup," *Impumelelo* 6 (2010), https://www.ohio.edu/sportsafrica/journal/catsamreflection.htm.

83. Tony Koenderman, "Close-up: How Selling South Africa 2010 Is an Uphill Task," *PRWeek*, February 5, 2010, 14. One striking exception was Puma's "Journey of Football" commercial shot largely in Côte d'Ivoire, Ghana, and Cameroon, which intercut between the players (in dressing rooms, on the team bus, and in stadiums) and the fans (in the stands or playing football on rooftops and in dusty streets) to present a visual image more rooted in the reality of African football's underdevelopment. See Gui Borchert, "Puma Journey of Football," Vimeo, accessed August 1, 2014, https://vimeo.com/11207120.

84. Q on CBC, "Exclusive Feature Interview with K'naan on Q TV," YouTube, April 23, 2010, https://www.youtube.com/watch?v=rzL9Ztnb2fw.

85. Tvspotblog1, "New Pepsi Advert—'Oh África' Feat. Akon—Henry, Messi, Drogba, Arshavin, Lampard and Kaká," YouTube, February 28, 2010, http://www.youtube.com/watch?v=eQmu48sZohc.

86. Catsam, "*Ayoba!*"

87. Ibid.

88. See Wally Olins, *The Brand Handbook* (Thames and Hudson, 2008); and Fiona Gilmore, "A Country—Can It Be Repositioned? Spain—The Success Story of Country Branding," *Journal of Brand Management* 9 (2002): 281–293.

CHAPTER 3

The Aspirational Viewer

FOR AT LEAST for a decade and a half after 1994, soap operas broadcast on the SABC served as key sites for the production of national identities and political values and for reflecting on or making sense of the changes brought into being by the end of apartheid, the negotiation of a new political deal, the advent of liberal democracy, and a new constitutional order, among others. The plotlines of these soap operas, which were the most-watched shows on local television, provided models for changing racial attitudes and, among black South Africans in particular, for cultivating aspirational politics. A socially driven understanding of media, especially television, facilitated this shift. As a result, the two groups with the most influence over the production of soap operas—the drama commissioning editors of the SABC and production companies—have been encouraged to explicitly engage with the political transition as well as imagine or create new values for a "new" South Africa.

This chapter discusses two of the longest-running, top-rated soap operas on South African television that dominated television schedules on the SABC for the first two generations or so of South African freedom: *Generations*, broadcast between 1994 and 2014, and *Isidingo*, which made its debut in 1998 and is still on the air. Both *Generations* and *Isidingo* are seminal television shows that are widely associated with the political changes in South Africa in the two decades since the end of apartheid. *Generations* was set in an all-black media company based in Johannesburg and was explicitly geared toward upwardly mobile black viewers. *Isidingo* first revolved around the happenings in a mining town and later moved to events centered on a television studio. *Generations*' plotlines and characters reflected the aspirational politics associated with South Africa's black middle and working classes. It also highlighted discourses of black economic empowerment favored by Nelson Mandela's successor, Thabo Mbeki. *Isidingo*, with its mixed cast, reflected the compromises and reconciliatory politics of the political and economic transition. *Isidingo* marketed itself as "one-nation viewing"—a show equally for black and white viewers.[1] Overall, the idea with both programs—and with soap operas on the SABC in general—was to cultivate a particular kind of viewer, the "aspirational viewer,"[2] one who was open to the promises of capitalism and the market economy and thus would thrive under the new conditions of political and, presumably, economic freedom.

Ratings Juggernaut

Homegrown soap operas dominated postapartheid television ratings for long, uninterrupted periods. They also occupied the prime-time slots on the most popular television channels in South Africa, those of the SABC. As recently as 2015, it was estimated that at least 80 percent of weeknight prime-time television audiences were tuned into one of the SABC's soap operas. This figure cut across generations, race, and class. Locally produced soap operas also consistently topped the "most popular" rankings of television programs.[3] Opinion surveys often quizzed young people about their "current favorite TV program." Local soap operas like *Generations*, broadcast on SABC1, regularly came out on top, in the process significantly beating out US and British shows for viewers' loyalties. This was not just the case on terrestrial channels; viewers and subscribers of satellite and cable television were no different. A 2015 survey by a local newspaper group reported that while young people, especially teenagers, preferred paid channels such as DStv (the satellite broadcaster) and M-Net (a cable television monopoly) over analog ones, they, like their older compatriots, preferred locally produced content over American productions.[4]

The appeal of soap operas made business sense. The primary function of soap operas for broadcasters is to deliver audiences for advertisers.[5] But apart from being good for business, in a context of declining state investment in public broadcasting, soap operas became a means with which to square the SABC's competing commercial and public broadcasting mandates. For public broadcasters, soap operas assist "in fulfilling [broadcasters'] public service remit by appealing to the largest number of viewers."[6]

The SABC soaps *Generations* and *Isidingo* stood out for their attempts to, unlike their American counterparts, engage directly with the country's political economy in their plotlines, whether incorporating routine postapartheid lives into story lines or engaging in complex ways with the country's political, social, and economic transition. In the process, soap operas have proven to be key sites for the production of South African national identities, including class politics, and have become public forums for debating important social and political changes in the country. In some cases, they have also provided models for how South Africans could imagine and bring into life changing racial and political attitudes among other South Africans.

I argue that decision makers involved in broadcasting (whether at the SABC or private producers) took note of the popular political and media discourses about the rainbow nation, reconciliation, and black economic empowerment and injected these concepts into and engaged with them in soap opera story lines. These producers and commissioning editors were guided by a socially driven understanding of media, one shared with the public broadcaster's board: they would be tasked with creating new values for a new South Africa. Specifically, they focused on cultivating aspirational viewers and encouraged what the producers of *Isidingo* referred to as "one-nation viewing."

The success of television soap operas in South Africa (and elsewhere in Africa and the developing world) contrasts sharply with their decline in advanced capitalist countries, where they have been mostly eclipsed by reality television programs.[7] In the United States, for example, where the genre was invented, soap operas have steadily lost audiences and advertisers.[8] This is not the case in South Africa. A 2012 study of editorial content on the SABC concluded that the soap opera genre dominated the airwaves, filling 16 percent of all broadcasting time, with educational programming second (at 12 percent), followed by current affairs (10 percent), and drama programs (9 percent).[9] It is also telling that while elsewhere soap operas have been marketed as a female television genre,[10] thus limiting their appeal, in places like South Africa, soaps enjoy massive cross-gender appeal.

Soap operas in South Africa thrive on public channels at a time when public broadcasters are being pressured to deregulate—that is, abandon public mandates in favor of programming funded overwhelmingly by advertising. In the last two decades, a large number of governments and public television regulators—both in the West and industrialized north as well as in the developing world—have cut or withdrawn public financing and subsidies earmarked for public television, in the process compromising these channels' ability to produce local content.[11] The SABC is no exception. In 2010 a senior manager for the Independent Communications Authority of South Africa (ICASA), which regulates the country's broadcasting sector, summarized the SABC's quandary: "The public service broadcasting market across the globe has been negatively affected by a lethal combination of recent economic downturn and recession caused by global financial woes, changing audience behavior and needs, growth of competition and consolidation, dramatic decline in advertising revenues, shrinking government funding support, and the change and growth of new digital technological media. Most broadcasters are struggling and teetering on the edge of bankruptcy due to heavy burden and costs, and are shedding jobs and assets, considering and looking at new partners that can help these corporations deal with or reverse their consistent losses."[12]

The SABC entered this business environment saddled with two seemingly intractable mandates: (1) to operate and manage the corporation as a business based on market principles while (2) fulfilling its public service function in a rapidly transforming society. In publicity materials, the SABC stated that it would not shy away from this double mandate: it was "obliged to provide a comprehensive range of distinctive programs and services"; would "inform, educate, entertain, support and develop culture and education"; and "secure fair and equal treatment for the various groupings in the nation and country." The SABC would also strive to offer "world-class programming on television."[13]

How did the SABC plan to fulfill this public mandate, and what kinds of revenue streams would it pursue in the process? One of the three public channels, SABC1—the SABC's flagship channel aimed at young black viewers—gave a clue in an undated memo from the early 2000s:

> SABC1 has to simultaneously deliver a public service while earning all our revenue from selling airtime commercially. Advertising is our only revenue stream at present. Our substantial obligation for local content drives very high costs. We commission the most local drama, the most local documentaries, the most children's programs, the most local culture and music programs, and we are the biggest investor in local soccer. The news and sport [divisions] alone account for about 50% of our costs. SABC1 earns the biggest share of the revenue available. [In contrast, the rival subscription-based network] M-Net is more profitable, but has fewer obligations, offers far less local content, and therefore, has less costs.[14]

It is telling that more than two decades into the transition to the new South Africa, the successes of SABC's soap operas as a project of public broadcasting are mostly forgotten. By 2017, the SABC was largely associated with failure, waste, government interference, corruption, and crisis. The corporation seemed unable to settle its bills or pay its creditors. Massive marches and protests outside SABC's Johannesburg headquarters were periodically staged by producers and actors, including those from *Generations* and *Isidingo*. Large numbers of white viewers and a growing number of black middle-class viewers as well as advertisers abandoned the SABC for commercial satellite television channels and private free-to-air stations that projected more "cosmopolitan, worldly" outlooks.[15] But it does not negate what the SABC achieved with *Generations* and *Isidingo* or the impacts of those shows in shaping the national discourse. Before we can engage more closely with the kinds of politics advanced in these soap operas, however, we must first revisit the institutional history of public broadcasting, especially of television, in South Africa.

Restructuring Public Television

In 1934 the South African government commissioned the director-general of the BBC, John Reith, to write a charter for a national broadcaster (meaning radio). The SABC was established two years later. However, this commitment to public broadcasting barely got underway before the SABC transformed into a full-fledged propaganda arm of white supremacy. To make this happen, members of the Broederbond (Brotherhood), a secret Afrikaner nationalist organization, took over the SABC's board and management structures. This ideological dominance would last until nearly the end of apartheid. When South Africa reluctantly introduced its first television channel in 1976, the new service was wholly state-owned. SABC TV would go to enjoy an unrivaled monopoly for more than a decade and a half.

As discussed in the introduction and chapter 1, for most of the twentieth century, South Africans were subjected to racist, white minority rule, and SABC TV was in service to the apartheid government. In 1978 the SABC's director-general told a journalist about the broadcaster's political role: "We [white people] are involved in the politics of survival. The SABC cannot stand aside.... We cannot cast doubt on the rulers of the country. No useful purpose can be served by causing the public distrust of our leaders' policies."[16]

While the SABC did compete for the television audience with two private stations—BopTV (broadcasting from the Bophuthatswana homeland and reaching some of the urban areas around Johannesburg) from 1983 and the cable service M-Net from 1986—rival broadcasters could not make serious inroads into the SABC's monopoly over audiences or its dominance of the local television market.[17] The apartheid SABC TV spent the bulk of its commissioning budgets on television drama with productions aimed at white audiences. These shows featured white actors or employed whites-only production crews, with their bidding processes open to wild abuse. In the wake of Mandela's release from prison in 1990, the emphasis shifted to restructuring and transforming the SABC from a state broadcaster to a public broadcasting service (PBS). Though racial deficits in SABC TV's coverage and content was high on the agenda, business considerations dominated, with "finance as the dominant organizing principle."[18] Yet questions of representation did not go away. Social movements and civil society groupings focused on the composition of the SABC board, representation onscreen, and the corporation's public mandate.

In 1993 the outgoing government of F. W. de Klerk announced that it was taking nominations for a new board. Technically, De Klerk's government was in charge, but it had to consult with a transitional authority made up of representatives of all political parties privy to constitutional negotiations between the government and the ANC. Following public hearings, a new board was appointed.

Njabulo Ndebele, a novelist, critic of apartheid, and former exile became the new chairperson. He was also the first black person to be appointed to the post. A sense of what the new SABC board had to reform was reflected in the nature of De Klerk's objections to Ndebele as chairperson. He claimed Ndebele was "not bilingual." By this he meant Ndebele did not speak Afrikaans. De Klerk was merely demonstrating how white South Africans understood bilingualism: that a person could speak Afrikaans and English, the two languages that the majority of white people knew. By contrast, most black South Africans could speak, read, and write Afrikaans and English as well as two or three African languages. As a fellow SABC board member pointed out, Ndebele "speaks and understands no less than nine of South Africa's official languages, while De Klerk is so linguistically challenged he can hardly say Molweni,'" referring to the Nguni word for "good morning."[19]

Nevertheless, despite these early setbacks, the SABC board was filled with optimism and declared a "new broadcast environment" to transform the SABC from a state propaganda machine into a full-fledged public broadcaster.[20] One of its biggest reforms was, fittingly, around language. While the old SABC privileged Afrikaans and English, the new public broadcaster worked hard to mainstream the country's other ten official languages per the new, postapartheid constitution.[21] This language requirement was built into news, drama, and entertainment programming. An SABC commissioner later judged the language policy as a success: "[It was] potentially one of the most empowering decisions [I've been involved with]. The state and the SABC language policy is essential to deepening mass democratic participation, education and development, intraAfrican communication, and Africanizing colonized minds in this country."[22] The new language policy was not without its critics, however. They claimed the SABC did not go far enough. A 2012 report on the SABC's language policy seemed to bear the critics out: "Although English is only spoken as a first language by 8% of the population and the SABC is required to broadcast in all official languages, English dominates SABC programming (76%). A massive 65% of all locally produced content on the SABC is in English. The next biggest languages trailing far behind are Afrikaans at only 6%, Zulu (5%) and Xhosa, Sotho and Tshivenda (3%). Half of the Afrikaans (50%) language broadcast on the SABC is accounted for by the soap *7de Laan* [Seventh Avenue] alone."[23]

Apart from language, the racial and class stratifications within and between the SABC's television services was also considered a priority. In South Africa, race and market categories overlap to a staggering extent. The stratification is unambiguous and profound: white South Africans, less than 10 percent of a population of more than fifty million people, enjoy the highest levels of income. Asian or Indian people (2.5 percent of the population) average the second highest incomes. Coloured people (those of mixed race), who number not quite 9 percent, and Africans, the majority of the population at 79 percent, make up the bulk of the poor.²⁴ To tackle this stratification, the SABC announced a reconfiguration of its three television channels: from now on they'd be known as SABC1, SABC2, and SABC3. Instead of race, the channels would target market segments. In reality, the market segments still coincided with racial divisions to a large extent, but at least formally and in principle, SABC audiences would cease to be defined by race. The new SABC1 and SABC2 really operated as public channels—meaning they served the black majority and other marginal groups. SABC1's target market was a young urban black audience.²⁵ SABC2 was aimed at white Afrikaners, working-class Afrikaans-speaking coloured people, and viewers from other so-called marginal language groups (Tswana, Pedi, Venda, etc.). As for SABC3, it operated like "a commercial channel."²⁶ Not surprisingly, SABC3 quickly became the advertising revenue powerhouse of the public broadcaster, largely for reasons related to the purchasing power of its mostly white audience. Not coincidentally, SABC3 also featured the nation's important nightly news bulletin.

The conventional strategy pursued by public broadcasters faced with shrinking profit margins and reduced state subsidies has been to flood viewers with popular programming: game shows, variety shows, and reality television.²⁷ The new SABC—investing heavily in and producing socially conscious television dramas—appeared to buck this trend, so much so that the early postapartheid period turned out to be the golden era for socially relevant television dramas in South Africa. The new shows were commissioned and coproduced by the SABC's education department. The output was exceptional and genre-bending: the dramas *Soul City* (1994–2015), *Tsha Tsha* [Cha Cha] (2003), *Yizo Yizo* [This Is It] (1998, 2001, and 2004), and *Gaz'lam* [My Friend] (2002–2005), to name a few, come to mind.²⁸ These dramas have been widely analyzed elsewhere, but in summary, they had a tendency to be educational and strength affirming as well as containing explicit moral lessons. The action in them revolved around health, sex, sexuality, AIDS, the state of public infrastructure like schools and hospitals, and attempts to build alternative social lives.²⁹

By 2004, however, appetites for socially relevant dramas were tempered by some of the public reaction. *Yizo Yizo*, in particular, was targeted. It ran afoul of political and religious authorities for its unflinching portrayal of the crises in South African township schools and for encouraging a perceived aimlessness of township youth.³⁰ When *Yizo Yizo* further depicted the unglamorous aspects of prison life (including male rape), conservative MPs and some media commentators objected and made spurious arguments that the show was glorifying violence and gangsterism and would have a negative and damaging effect on viewers.³¹ Although most studies could point to no correlation between television violence and real-life crime, the accusations stood. An exasperated SABC commissioning editor responded later to this fact in an interview: "I ask why when talking about SABC1 viewers—mostly young, black people—we assume that they're stupid and will copy what they see. After all, no South African has expressed any concern that middle class white women are in danger of gratuitously fucking firemen after watching *Sex and the City*.[32] Not long after, the SABC established new content hubs to organize its business units. One of these was a new drama hub, which observed the SABC education department. From now on, the SABC would be guided by "a socially-driven understanding" of media, especially as regards television's agenda-setting role.[33] The SABC quickly moved away from an education model for drama. As one SABC commissioning editor told me, "We understand that the reason why people want to watch any drama [is that] it helps them [to] understand [challenges] in their lives. So, in doing that within a fairly new democracy there are certain imperatives at play. And we understand [those imperatives] to [focus on] who we are as South Africans within a South African context."[34]

To make those imperatives reality, the SABC supplied its commissioning editors with a set of general guidelines and objectives organized under the titles "Personal Fulfillment," "Institutions," "Heritage," "Professional Advancement," and "African Renaissance." Commissioning editors also had to satisfy "stakeholder management" as well as produce programming that was "entertaining" and "ha[d] to sell." Together, these concepts added up to an endorsement of certain postapartheid politics—those observed in television commercials in which the struggle against apartheid and the country's racist legacy are presented as heritage, self-help (personal fulfillment), thrift, entrepreneurialism, the rainbow nation, and the politics of reconciliation combined. As a result, SABC commissioning editors developed self-conscious understandings of the activist nature of their job and what expectations they had of producers. As one of them put it, "[Producers pitching the SABC] couldn't just say 'I am telling a story.' Whatever you're saying [you could not deny that] you are making a comment about a society that is still really creating an identity of itself."[35]

The emphasis was on a singular identity for society. The editorial "line" was to "deliver stories in the context of a new democracy" and "to show how communities function." Content that was "positive and building" and "show[ed] competing interests" were welcomed. Finally, SABC commissioning editors understood that the function of television dramas was to create "new values" for South Africans. Apartheid and colonialism eradicated, even militated against whatever collective values South Africans could develop. The task ahead was to "instill new values in our audiences."[36] Nevertheless, commissioning editors were mindful of the pitfalls of didacticism: "We don't [install new values in audiences] by telling them exactly what to do, but by telling them stories you can open their minds to, to see the world in a different way."[37]

The Apartheid Soap Story

During apartheid, the SABC produced or commissioned a number of dramas and miniseries that profoundly influenced how the genre presented itself post-1990.³⁸ These programs were not classed as soap operas, however; that descriptor was reserved only for popular American soap operas like *Loving* and *The Bold and the Beautiful*, which had aired on South African television since the early 1980s.

The local apartheid dramas of the late 1970s and 1980s shared a number of characteristics associated with the soap opera genre in terms of form and story lines, with the only distinction that they were targeted specifically at local white audiences. In addition, the casts were often all-white and the plotlines reflected the imagined worlds of white South Africa. Initially, white characters even performed menial and unglamorous work—a depiction at odds with reality as these tasks were restricted to black people in South Africa. These shows did have black viewers, of course, but only because there was mostly nothing else to watch. And, with very little exception, characters in Afrikaans shows spoke Afrikaans and characters in English shows spoke English. The languages did not mix, and African languages were hardly present, mostly heard as instructions or orders to black characters doing housework or working in factories or in the mines. Finally, these shows lacked any overt political character. One South African producer described the shows on SABC as depicting a world "more folksy, more comfortable."³⁹ Whether he meant it or not, he was referring to how soothing they were for white audiences against the backdrop of apartheid's uncertainty and upheaval. By the late-1970s and throughout the 1980s, apartheid had reached a profound crisis: sanctions, a national uprising, states of emergency, and violent proxy wars that engaged South Africa's army in Angola and Mozambique and had it occupying Namibia. Inside South Africa, the army and police were occupying black townships. If the goal of these shows was to make viewers not notice the effects of apartheid, then they certainly succeeded. As some studies suggest, apartheid propaganda was so good that white South Africans, television viewers especially, mostly had no clue what was happening in the country.⁴⁰

The first and most culturally significant of the apartheid television dramas was *The Villagers*, which ran for three seasons on the SABC between 1976 and 1978. The intrigue in a small mining town outside Johannesburg revolved around a succession crisis at the local mine, Village Reef, after the mine's general manager dies suddenly. The expected successor, Buller Wilmot, is passed over for an outsider, Hilton McRae. The McRae family is from the big city and initially finds it hard to adjust to small-town life. The McRaes were presented as typical English-speaking white South Africans, and the plot dealt with manners and class politics among English white South Africans. As a sign of its diversity beyond that group, in its second season, *The Villagers* introduced a white Afrikaner family, the Van Wyks. *The Villagers* shied away from politics. Despite the fact that the majority of mine workers at the time, apart from managers and skilled technicians, were black people, *The Villagers* hardly showed any. Neil McCarthy, a scriptwriter for both *Generations* and *Isidingo*, told me, "They had a domestic servant in one of the houses [on *The Villagers*], and she was white. They weren't allowed to [write] a black domestic servant [into the plot]."[41]

As a sign of its lasting impact on white viewers, *The Villagers* is still fondly remembered by older white South Africans on fan sites, in user groups, and in blogs.[42] *The Villagers* was the brainchild of a young white producer, Gray Hofmeyr. He would play a crucial role in the development of a postapartheid soap opera aesthetic: he went on to produce *Isidingo*, one of the two shows at the heart of this chapter.

When *The Villagers* ended, Hofmeyr produced a new series, *Westgate*, for SABC, debuting in 1981. The new show was set amid the plotting and rivalries at an advertising agency in Johannesburg. As was very common in South African television, many of the leading actors from *The Villagers* ended up on *Westgate*. For example, Gordon Mulholland, the actor who portrayed Hilton McRae on *The Villagers*, played the main character on *Westgate*. *Westgate* went off the air in 1985. What is striking about both *The Villagers* and *Westgate* is how much of their basic plot structure would be replicated in shows like *Generations* and *Isidingo*: *Generations* was basically a black *Westgate*, whereas *Isidingo* was actually a multiracial version of *The Villagers*.

Given the SABC's function as an extension of Afrikaans cultural politics, Afrikaans dramas were abundant. The most popular of these was the series *Agter Elke Man* (Behind every man), which aired from 1985 to 1986 and focused on class politics among white Afrikaners in inner-city Johannesburg. *Agter Elke Man* had a gritty feel that contrasted heavily with the "folksy, more comfortable" feel of *The Villagers* and *Westgate*.[43] *Agter Elke Man*'s focus on class tensions among white people (especially Afrikaners) was, however, not unusual for SABC. For example, one of the most popular dramas of the mid-1980s was *1922*, a miniseries about the 1922 miner's strike in Johannesburg. That strike by white workers is memorable for exposing class differences between white workers and their employers but also, crucially, for uniting white workers against their black colleagues over labor protections (closed shops) and lower wages. But the creators or scriptwriters of *1922*, like those for *The Villagers* and *Agter Elke Man*, could not get themselves to engage with the racial character of South Africa's class structure or the intimacy of black and white relations.[44] The Afrikaans shows, like their English counterparts, were deliberately oblivious to the presence of black South Africans. As previously noted, all these shows recycled the same set of white actors and popular entertainers and provided work for a number of white producers and directors. Many of these same producers and directors would play central roles in the development of a soap opera industry after 1990.

However, none of these local dramas could rival the ratings of their American competitors, shows like *Loving*, *The Bold and the Beautiful*, and *Days of our Lives*.[45] In contrast to local dramas on SABC, American soap operas, despite their overwhelmingly white casts, had a broader appeal—especially among black South Africans. How South Africans, especially black citizens, viewed these imported American (and later Australian) soap operas has been widely debated. Micki Flockemann, a South African literary scholar, argues that television viewers, especially black viewers, actively and critically engaged with these American soap operas as texts and defined their own identities and agendas in the process.[46] Media scholar Larry Strelitz studied the viewing habits of young Zulu-speaking men who were fans of *Days of Our Lives*. Strelitz found his respondents were "anything but passive vessels" for the messages conveyed by American soap operas. He concluded that how these young male viewers "respond to these cultural imports depend[ed] on their existing cultural context." For example, Sipho—a self-described "very, very strong Zulu man"—reported to Strelitz that he drew lessons from watching *Days of Our Lives*, "especially relationship-wise," whether with a romantic partner or family members. *Days of Our Lives* "fortified [Sipho's] view that 'if a guy can tell a woman that he loves her, she should be able to do the same.' What's more, after watching the show, Sipho 'realized that I should be allowed to speak to my father. He should be my friend rather than just my father.'"[47]

Philosopher Anthony Appiah, citing Strelitz concludes that "it seems doubtful that that was the intended message of multinational capitalism's ruling sector."[48] The social function and general appeal of American soap operas were obviously not lost on SABC executives as they prepared to make the transition from state broadcaster to public broadcaster and were looking for programming to fulfill their new mission to inform, entertain, and educate—basically, combining a public mandate with making money.

Generations: Representing Postapartheid Realities and Aspirations

The SABC is usually credited with broadcasting the first postapartheid soap opera, *Generations*. That honor actually belongs to private cable channel M-Net, which debuted *Egoli* in April 1992. *Egoli* is the Nguni language word for "Johannesburg," and the show evoked the city's association with gold mining and glitter.[49]

Egoli revolved around the goings-on of both owners and employees at a wealthy car manufacturer. The key characters, with few exceptions, were white people. When *Egoli* tackled political issues, such as the transition from apartheid, crime, skills shortages, or even AIDS, these were usually viewed from white, middle-class perspectives and anxieties about the new South Africa. The show also featured guest appearances by American and British show business personalities such as Joan Collins (from the nighttime soap *Dynasty*), talk-show host Jerry Springer, and British glamor model Samantha Fox. The main languages used by characters on *Egoli* were English and Afrikaans. In later seasons, *Egoli* added other major South African languages, such as Sotho, Zulu, and Xhosa, in subtitles. From 1997 on, different local and international versions (to cater to new audiences in Southern Africa and, later, elsewhere in Africa) were shot entirely in English. However, the focus of *Egoli* remained very South African.

To watch *Egoli*, viewers needed to pay a subscription, but M-Net enjoyed an arrangement with the SABC called Open Time, during which the cable channel was available free of charge without a cable box to any viewer every night between 5:00 p.m. and 7:00 p.m. *Egoli* came on at 6:00 p.m. Open Time, which was supposed to last only for M-Net's first year of operations, ran for fifteen years, until 2007. *Egoli* finally went off the air in March 2010. Some observers cited declining audience ratings suffered after the end of Open Time.[50] *Egoli*'s legacy is also mixed. Typical reactions ranged from comments about it being a "one dimensional fantasy" despite the show's writers injecting contemporary politics into the script and that it amounted to "a wish list" of what South Africa could be—at least in the vision of the producers and writers.[51] In the end, *Egoli* struggled to break with apartheid television formats and, more importantly, with its predominant focus on white social life.

One of the key legacies of apartheid dramas was to leave in place an infrastructure, in terms of personnel, for postapartheid soap operas. The most noticeable example was Gray Hofmeyr, who directed *The Villagers* and both produced and directed *Isidingo*. White screenwriters, producers, and directors who had cut their teeth on apartheid dramas would, at least for the first decade of postapartheid soaps, be at the helm of the new shows. *Egoli*, for example, considered the first transitional soap opera of the 1990s, was primarily the work of a group of white producers, directors, and screenwriters who had made their careers creating apartheid-era melodramas. Even the wildly successful *Generations*—credited to Mfundi Vundla, a black South African producer and screenwriter who gained his experience working on US daytime soap operas—was a collaboration by Vundla with a white producer, Friedrich Stark, who built his career with Afrikaans feature films under apartheid.[52]

For a long time, *Generations* reflected the zeitgeist on South African television. It consistently delivered the highest audience ratings of any program on any television channel in South Africa, including private television stations. Throughout the 2000s, *Generations* averaged a viewership of four million people per day, 80 percent of whom were black viewers. More than half—52 percent—of all South African viewers between the ages of 16 and 34 (the most-desired television demographic) viewed the soap.[53]

Generations' main story line revolved around the adventures of a wealthy black family, the Morokas, at their advertising firm in Johannesburg appropriately named New Horizons. The SABC markets the story line as one "that celebrates the dreams and aspirations of South Africans" and that "stimulat[es] a conversation on the transfer of wealth, knowledge and culture."⁵⁴ The SABC emphasizes that *Generations* addresses these larger questions in "its own way . . . not in a didactic manner but in interesting narratives."⁵⁵ This connection between *Generations*, aspirational politics, and the new South Africa was also employed when the show was marketed to audiences outside South Africa: the majority of South Africans could now "fantasize about glamorous characters who share their skin color and speak the usual clichés in a variety of indigenous languages."⁵⁶ The story line "celebrat[ed] the aspirations of South Africans who dream of a better future" and the show's target audience was "unique: Born and bred in South Africa . . . unconventional in that it is cross-cultural, multi-lingual, combines humor with traditional 'soap opera' techniques, while at the same time incorporating relevant social issues."⁵⁷

For many viewers and critics, this world of wealthy, self-confident black people appeared at odds with the reality of most South Africans, where deracializing boardrooms and offices was still a slow-moving struggle. It was a fantasy that presented "an already-achieved world of commercial success beyond debates around affirmative action and black empowerment."⁵⁸ The show's producers, however, suggested there was a power in this fantasy. Vundla defends the choice of locale, characters, and plots as a deliberate political statement. He insists that the show's setting was "natural" and that he liked the "glitzy, glamorous" nature of the advertising world. He also claimed that he drew on his brother's experiences. Vundla's brother Peter was one of South Africa's first black advertising executives. *Generations* was merely reflecting real aspirations of black South Africans and "evolved in tandem with our nation from the birth of democracy in 1994 to the present time."⁵⁹ The reality that there were few major black-owned advertising firms in South Africa did not blunt the show's appeal. The premise was aspirational, something black South Africans were longing for.⁶⁰ As a newspaper columnist pointed out—making a tongue-in-cheek reference to a government-branding slogan—*Generations* "showed that South Africa is alive with possibilities."⁶¹ Reflecting the show's aspirational politics, the story line moved to a media empire after a few seasons. In 2003 New Horizons became Ezweni Communications—the change from English to Zulu expressing the "Africanization" of South Africa under Mbeki.

Aspirational politics was perhaps reflected in some of the show's main characters as well. One of the original characters was Queen, a receptionist at New Horizons who would eventually marry one of the Moroka sons. Queen was from Soweto, the vast black township to the south of Johannesburg's city center. The character is described as "always aspir[ing] to move to the [formerly white] northern suburbs" of the city, aiming to be "a wealthy respected woman with class and status."⁶² Starting out as "an opportunistic gold digger," she transformed herself into someone whose "passions in life are men and fashion" and whose "main aim in life is to marry well."⁶³ Part of the show for twenty years, Queen became one of the most recognizable characters on *Generations* and one of the viewers' favorites until the actress playing her left over a contract dispute. Another character, Ntombi, is described as "a feminist who believes that anything a man can do, a woman can do better" and "fights the stereotypical image that beautiful equals brainless, but isn't militant about standing up for women's rights, showing that actions speak louder than words by making a success of anything she tackles." Finally, Tau, a longtime business rival and occasional lover of the show's main character, is representative of crass "new wealth." He "tries to buy class, which often translates as an accumulation of sometimes tasteless, sterile and impersonal objects." However, he has since transformed into someone who "can handle himself in any conversation or situation."⁶⁴

Vundla believes *Generations* was "at the center of class mobility," saying that "South Africa right now is in an aspirational mode. South Africa is upwardly mobile."⁶⁵ He suggests that people struggling in squatter camps as well as new black elites who moved to formerly white suburbs shared this sentiment. Freed from decades of oppression ("fascist oppression"), with its depressing effects, black South Africans now had opportunities to construct new lives and new opportunities. *Generations* reflected this mood: "And our show is very aspirational. We are showing African [meaning black] people running media companies."⁶⁶

Research done by the producers and the SABC suggested some viewers took advice from *Generations* about home décor, manners, style, and self-actualization. One viewer told researchers, "*Generations* taught me to decorate my house," while for others *Generations* provided them with parenting tips and, more crucially, implanted ideas about class mobility and aspiration. *Generations* had a larger mission: "[During Apartheid] people were used to seeing Black people on television just shouting [incomprehensibly] in townships. . . . Black people on television were always caught in a quagmire, victims of circumstances beyond their control, depicted only in working class dramas in which life was just a maze of complications, with no solutions. . . . I brought them beautiful, stylist, upwardly mobile Black people who were confident and successful. . . . [My characters] are in complete control of their lives. . . . That is what people needed to see."⁶⁷ Vundla had a missionary zeal shared by advertisers, black commentators, popular weekly magazines like *Tribute*, *Bona*, and the reinvigorated *Drum*, and television like *Top Billing*, a lifestyle television show that portrayed new black South African wealth with a certain amount of gloss. Ideas about entrepreneurship, individual thrift, and achievement as well as capitalist reward permeated *Generations*. One long-running story line, for example, focused on a young singer breaking into the local music industry. The aspiring musician was advised "on managing his income, growing his wealth and becoming self-sustainable." Vundla was merely reflecting a shift in public opinion and popular culture: entertainers were seen more and more as drivers of class mobility and as role models. Vundla, however, was aware of the tensions around these ideas: "In society it is the state [that is tasked with creating conditions to make the economy grow and affect class mobility]. But in the show, the idea is that everybody is an entrepreneur now, so we'll teach people how to be entrepreneurs."[68] *Generations* was publicly lauded for giving black South Africans a sense of identity and pride.[69] Its growing cultural influence coincided with the SABC pressuring producers to "reposition the show towards the youth market that the [SABC1] channel appeals to—that is 16-to-34 year olds." Older cast members were jettisoned for younger actors. The SABC wanted *Generations* to "endorse a clear-cut aspirational model for young Black South Africans."[70] Over time, *Generations*' story line, setting, original cast, and racial composition underwent a number of changes, rendering the show unrecognizable to older viewers; nevertheless, its underlying thrust—that of aspiration—remained central. By 2010, "the plot, which initially centered on two rival advertising agencies run by feuding families . . . focuse[d] on two media empires; the two families originally depicted have all been wiped out, and only two of the original cast remain, played by original actresses."[71]

Isidingo: The New South African Soap Opera

In 1998 the SABC debuted a new soap opera, *Isidingo*. This would be the first soap opera to rival the success and mass appeal of *Generations*. Like *Generations*, it would also try to engage directly with the politics of the transition. In contrast to *Generations*' fantasy plot, however, *Isidingo* set out to make connections with the history of soap operas under apartheid and in the process tried to invent a new, local model for the genre that would not only fulfill the SABC's public mandate but would be commercially successful. Chiefly, *Isidingo* aimed to represent South Africa's political and social reality alongside the show's rainbow ideals (at any time, half the cast was made up of white actors, and the show emphasized Mandela's reconciliatory politics). It succeeded in that it had a wider appeal than *Generations*, also drawing a large viewership among white South Africans.

Isidingo was clearly in conversation with *The Villagers* not just in the setting (a mining town outside Johannesburg) but in parallels with the way the story was constructed. For example, the first episode of *The Villagers* (in 1976) opened with the death of the general manager of the Village Reef gold mine. The owners decide to hire a new general manager, and the drama revolves around the new white manager and his family's attempts to adapt to their new surroundings and their father's new job. Subsequent episodes incorporated labor unrest (over promotions), economic downturns, corruption, industrial sabotage, and "terrorism" (code for antiapartheid protest in the 1980s), alongside more familiar tropes (family intrigue and romance). All this action played out exclusively among white characters.

Viewers old enough could not help notice when season 1 of *Isidingo* also led with a crisis at a mine, Horizon Deep, described as "one of the rainbow nation's imagined communities."[72] The crisis is a pending strike by the mine's mostly black labor force. To solve this crisis, the white mine management decides not to opt for a white replacement but instead hires a black man, Derek Nyathi. In script notes, Nyathi is described as "Mandela-like." Over the next few episodes, Nyathi succeeds in convincing the workers to buy shares in the company as a tactic to end the industrial strife. Nyathi also later marries into the family that owns the mine (resulting in the first interracial wedding on a South African television drama). Nyathi's character was only written out of the soap when he and his new wife moved to London to take up a job there. (In truth the actor playing Nyathi found other work.)

Isidingo explored class politics not only between its white characters but, crucially, between its black characters. Nyathi was not the only major black character. The Matabanes were a working-class family whose economic fortunes improved over the course of the soap's first couple of seasons. The father, Zebedee, starts off as a stope worker[73] at the mine, and his son becomes a jewelry designer.

As discussed earlier, the usual soap opera plotlines were teamed along with subject matter deemed realistic—themes that reflected elements of the political and economic transition such as labor unrest, a declining mining industry, gay and interracial marriages, and new health crises such as HIV.[74] For example, when Zebedee's daughter, Nandipha Matabane, was first introduced in 2006, she was identified as the victim of an abduction and rape that left her HIV-positive. She then became a glamorous television presenter before the scriptwriters decided Nandipha would "succumb to full-blown AIDS and begin dying in public."[75] When the character was introduced in 2006, "the stigma attached to Aids is so great that millions shun[ned] treatment and testing. Families routinely cover[ed] up the cause of death when loved ones die[d] in the epidemic."[76] In an environment of denialism from South Africa's president Mbeki, the idea behind Nandipha's character was to show people living with HIV and receiving antiretroviral treatment going about their active lives.[77]

Similarly, *Isidingo* introduced an openly gay character (though, significantly, the character was white). This was deemed the first such portrayal on local television. A publicist for the show later explained the character's wider impact: "We had both positive and negative response [to the character, Steve Stethakis]. But never one to shy away from dealing with the real issues, *Isidingo* went on to develop various storylines for Steve, including him coming out to his parents and friends and having gay relationships, being wrongfully accused of sexual misconduct with one of his students and eventually marrying the love of his life, Luke."[78] After a few seasons, however, and perhaps as a way to indicate its adoption of the "aspirational mode," the central focus of *Isidingo* shifted to a series of more conventional soap opera plots and characters while the primary location for the show (Horizon Deep) had to compete with a television studio that the mine owners had bought and where the bulk of the show's characters now seemed to work. McCarthy, an *Isidingo* screenwriter, explains the change: "Advertising was an issue. Advertisers couldn't understand who was going to watch *Isidingo*. What types of products do you pitch to this audience? At the end of the second year of *Isidingo*, they had a big meeting and there was instruction to market a more aspirational version of the story.... [T]he way they explained it, was that SABC 3 [now had to be] more appealing to the higher classes, top end audience etc."[79] By the early 2010s, *Generations* and *Isidingo* lost their dominant market position when soap operas proliferated (not just shows with English as the main language but also shows in local languages), and the more manageable telenovela format (with its distinctive limited-run character, faster action, and more dramatic plotlines) became more ubiquitous. Yet *Generations* and *Isidingo* had an impact on the story lines and tone of local telenovelas and drama series that remains (telenovelas are not necessary nonpolitical),[80] and so does their influence on public television.

Postapartheid soap operas may not deviate much from the conventions of the genre, but they differ in one crucial way. While characters obsess over power, money, and sex, they do so while reflecting on or engaging with larger debates in the society about political, economic, and social changes since the end of legal apartheid.

The Question of Agency

When I first began this research in 2007, soap operas were turning away from the grittier, more political themes to what came to be known as the aspirational, a shorthand term for class mobility. "Aspirational" described an ideal viewer that the SABC could sell to advertisers. At the time, I assumed that this change in tone and focus could be explained by commercial pressure, largely from advertisers who did not want their products associated with negative or heavy themes. I still suspect there is a kernel of truth in that, but it was never the case entirely.

Interviews with producers, writers, and directors of these soap operas suggest that commissioning editors at the SABC actively promoted television serials and plotlines that emphasized racial and class mobility and glossed over racial and class conflicts as well as lingering inequalities. McCarthy, for example, repeated to me what he had once told a local journalist: "There is a clear message from the [SABC's commissioning editors] that television, and particularly television drama, has an important role to play in guiding viewers towards a more positive view of themselves and their country. 'Aspirational' is a word one hears repeated over and over."[81] And separately, in a group interview with commissioning editors at the SABC, I was expecting the editors to deny this charge. They confirmed that they wanted to do just that: "The identity we want to create [through the programs that we commission] is an identity that is positive, affirming, hopeful and is out to . . . conquer [the world]. We want to build a great nation, to be a global player [where our people] go out and achieve what they want to achieve."[82] Not surprisingly, they were pleased with how these soap operas punted class mobility and cultivated aspiration especially among black viewers. One commissioning editor put it this way: "Take the journey of Nandipha [Matabane, the HIV-positive character in *Generations*] who moves from being a domestic worker to a TV executive. . . . By showing that journey . . . not as a crazy, fantastical one . . . you show people that it is possible in their lives."[83]

Aspiration was also offered as a solution for a series of larger crises in the economy. One of the key themes explored in *Isidingo* was the decline of the mining industry and economic recession. On this, another SABC editor offered this political solution: "How do you get [those left unemployed by economic shifts as well as new entrants to the job market] employed? The state can't do it. Traditional employment does not work. The economy worked for four million people. Now it must work for 40 million people. The state can't and won't. [So] create an entrepreneurial class."[84] The SABC wants to do more than just provide parameters for producers: the public broadcaster actively takes on the mantle of voice of the nation, speaking for and representing its viewers. This was especially present in promotional material like "Simunye/We Are One," the tagline of SABC1. Then there's the message that greeted online visitors to the landing page of SABC.co.za around 2014. It emphasized "personal ownership and responsibility" and downplayed the role of the state or corporate sponsors."[85] On the basis of SABC publicity material, the use of a collective noun for its workers and viewers ("we"), and user instructions for how to navigate its website ("see how it changes to reflect your selected reality"), the scholar Sarah Ives concludes: "The SABC redefines the nation from [the] distinct spatially determined homelands (from Apartheid) into one coherent whole. In this context the SABC uses the notions of unity to market their products, combining the messages of equality through solidarity and neoliberal economic growth policies."[86]

Isidingo was always explicit about the kinds of politics it represented. Producer Hofmeyr suggests that "the gold mines are a microcosm of our society. There is a class system but it's divided along financial not race lines." Hofmeyr is, of course, articulating *Isidingo*'s tendency to downplay racial fissures in favor of class differences. Hofmeyr's comment reflects both aspiration as well as the reality of the new South Africa: black South Africans are joining white people in the middle class, but the poor still mainly consist of black people. Remarks by another *Isidingo* producer, Hilary Blecher, also reflect the tensions between aspiration and reality. Blecher suggests that *Isidingo* is "not a heavy-handed reflection of society" but a reflection nonetheless.[87] Endemol, the company that owns and produces *Isidingo*, summarizes the soap as covering "the trials, tribulations, romance and passions *of everyday South Africans* [emphasis added] working at the (Horizon Deep) mine, in the high-flying corporate world of Johannesburg and the glamorous surroundings of a television station."⁸⁸

Hofmeyr, however, wanted *Isidingo* to represent a vision of a new South African television aesthetic. For example, he deliberately set out to upend the racial politics of *The Villagers* with *Isidingo* by incorporating some of the elements of the earlier show. It was not just the setting that was the same (i.e., mining town, fraught industrial relations, crisis in the mine's leadership), but Hofmeyr also retained a few original characters and actors. The original Ted Dixon (played by well-known English actor Clive Scott) was a bumbling white miner in the original series. In *Isidingo* he is now retired and working as a bartender at the local establishment where mine workers, both black and white, hang out. Hilton McRae, *The Villagers*' former white mine manager (who along with his family were the focus of the original series), is now "a special consultant steeped in old school ways as the mine and its community go through the new South African transformation."⁸⁹

The audience profile bore it out. The critic Charl Blignaut has described the viewers of *Isidingo* as "a new kind of audience,"⁹⁰ equally white and black, crossing generational boundaries and from both genders. *Isidingo* deliberately downplayed the idea that soaps are geared toward women, instead targeting both genders equally. And at some level, the producers tried to run away from the soap opera tag, favoring the more random "daily drama." Viewers warmed to the new category of show: "in terms of storyline, life on *Isidingo* is at least plausible and not overly far-fetched."⁹¹ All this added up to the producers' insistence—in publicity material as well in interviews with journalists—that *Isidingo* was premised on "one-nation viewing."

What about one-nation viewing? It referred to *Isidingo*'s supposed ability to "bring together as viewers the Black and white people formerly separated by apartheid and now being joyously reunited by the rainbow nation."⁹² This prompted *Isidingo*'s writers to use television not just to provide entertainment but also as a "memory box."⁹³ The idea was to "reproduce the matters that need resolution in society and to articulate their concerns and deep-seated fears about threats to the rainbow nation."⁹⁴ In this way, postapartheid South Africa, as represented in *Isidingo*, is a place where middle-class people of all colors are guaranteed a rollicking good time, provided there is an acceptance of certain truths: that crime and economic instability are the work of greedy and irrational black people (through industrial strikes), that white people are inherently hard working, and that the legacy of apartheid does not matter much.

Conclusion

By the end of the first decade of the new millennium, the SABC reinterpreted its mandate as nation-building rather than as transforming or democratizing the airwaves, and its managers became increasingly conflicted between market-driven business models presented to it and the demands of the ruling party. As *Isidingo* and *Generations* experienced ratings dips, pressure increased on producers to pull back on references to the real and instead conform to the conventions of the genre.

Regardless, the impact of soap operas like *Generations* and *Isidingo* on South Africans' relationships to the transition remain. *Isidingo* and *Generations* make real Nancy Signoreilli and Michael Morgan's insight about television: that it both mirrors and leads society.[95] Television serves "as our storyteller; it has become the wholesale distributor of images that form the mainstream of our popular culture."[96] For them, "the world of television tells us about life, people, places, striving, power, fate and family life. It presents the good and the bad, the happy and sad, the powerful and the weak, and lets us know who or what is a success or a failure."[97]

At the heart of soap operas like *Isidingo* and *Generation* are images of a unified, multiracial democracy under conditions of free-market capitalism. There is no state and no need for black empowerment or economic redistribution. Predictably, the shows deal with questions of representation, but political economy barely features. It is almost as if South Africa is imagined as a consolidated democracy on the lines of some Western European and North American states, with little regard for history. Yes, these programs accurately portray middle-class "reality" that has been meaningfully transformed in that it has been deracialized (the size of the black middle class now exceeds that of the white population), but with their focus on aspiration, these shows reflect the drive toward a national ethos that has undermined public institutions. Ironically, the SABC's own strategies for public broadcasting subscribed to such an ethos. In the end, by adding glam and a happy gloss to programming, the producers and the SABC merely continued endorsing the neoliberal transition.

Notes

1. Muff Anderson, "Reconciled Pasts, Fragile Futures, Parallel Presents: Chronotopes and Memory Making in *Isidingo*," *African Identities* 1, no. 2 (2003): 151.
2. Neil McCarthy, interview by the author, June 20, 2007, Johannesburg.
3. "*Sunday Times* Generation Next 8–23 Youth Brand Survey May 2015," http://blackstaradroom.co.za/wp-content/uploads/2016/08/GenerationNextSupplement2015.pdf.
4. Ibid.
5. Dorothy Hobson, *Soap Opera* (Cambridge, UK: Polity, 2003), xiv.
6. Ibid.
7. Matthew Krouse, "TV's New Voices," *Mail and Guardian*, May 31, 2004, https://mg.co.za/article/2004-05-31-tvs-new-voices. Krouse made the same comment in an interview with the author (Johannesburg, June 20, 2007). At the time, Krouse was arts editor of the *Mail and Guardian*.

8. "'All My Children,' 'One Life to Live' Canceled by ABC," *HuffPost*, April 14, 2011, https://www.huffingtonpost.com/2011/04/14/all-my-children-one-life-_n_849304.html.

9. Thinus Ferreira, "SABC Failing in Language, News—Study," Channel24, September 4, 2012, http://www.channel24.co.za/TV/News/SABC-failing-in-language-news-study-20120905.

10. Rebecca Traister, "The Soap Opera Is Dead! Long Live the Soap Opera!" *New York Times*, September 23, 2011, https://www.nytimes.com/2011/09/25/magazine/the-soap-opera-is-dead-long-live-the-soap-opera.html.

11. See Karen Donders, *Public Service Media and Policy in Europe* (Basingstoke: Palgrave MacMillan, 2011); Jeanette Steemers, *Selling Television: British Television in the Global Marketplace* (London: British Film Institute, 2004); Victor Pickard, "Can Government Support the Press? Historicizing and Internationalizing a Policy Approach to the Journalism Crisis," *Communication Review* 14, no. 2 (2011): 73–95; Gregory F. Lowe and Jeanette Steemers, *Regaining the Initiative for Public Service Media* (University of Gothenburg, Sweden: Nordicom, 2011); Gregory F. Lowe and Christian Nissen, eds., *Small among Giants: Television Broadcasting in Smaller Countries* (University of Gothenburg, Sweden: Nordicom, 2011); and Richard Rudin, *Broadcasting in the 21st Century* (Basingstoke: Palgrave Macmillan, 2011).

12. Dimakatso Collins Mashilo, "Redefining and Reshuffling the SABC for 2010 and Beyond" (paper presented at RIPE@2010 Conference, London, September 8–10, 2010), 4.

13. SABC, internal memorandum, undated [ca. early 2000s].

14. Ibid.

15. See Mashilo, "Redefining and Reshuffling the SABC," 6; Aislinn Laing, "South Africa Soap Stars on Strike over Contract Dispute," *Telegraph* (UK), October 18, 2013, https://www.telegraph.co.uk/news/worldnews/africaandindianocean/southafrica/10386332/South-Africa-soap-stars-on-strike-over-contract-dispute.html.

16. Quoted in Mbulelo Mzamane, "Celebrating Thirty Years of Television in South Africa" (speech delivered at the inaugural Golden Plumes Awards, Johannesburg, December 14, 2006), 2.

17. Paul Van Slambrouck, "South African Whites Clamor to Tune in Black TV," *Christian Science Monitor*, February 3, 1984, https://www.csmonitor.com/1984/0203/020318.html.

18. Ruth Teer-Tomaselli, "The Public Broadcaster and Democracy in Transformation: The 1996 Spry Memorial Lecture," *Canadian Journal of Communication* 23, no. 2 (1998), https://www.cjc-online.ca/index.php/journal/article/view/1030/936.

19. Mzamane, "Celebrating Thirty Years," 5.

20. Teer-Tomaselli, "The Public Broadcaster."

21. Although the majority of Afrikaans speakers are colored people, that does not translate into greater representation in Afrikaans media for them. Afrikaans is still very much synonymous with whiteness in media. Most Afrikaans-centered media—satellite TV channel KykNet, public radio station Radio Sonder Grense, *Rapport* newspaper, and so on—are targeted at white speakers of the language and reflect their politics. I explore a number of reasons for this in chapter 6.

22. Mzamane, "Celebrating Thirty Years," 5.

23. Ferreira, "SABC Failing."

24. "The Longer Walk to Equality," *The Economist*, December 6, 2013, https://www.economist.com/graphic-detail/2013/12/06/the-longer-walk-to-equality. See also the yearly updates of economic data in the *South Africa Yearbook* published annually by the Government Information and Communications Systems, Pretoria; and the *State of the Nation* series of books published annually by the Human Sciences Research Council of Pretoria.

25. By "black" here I'm referring to all nonwhite South Africans.

26. Mashilo, "Redefining and Reshuffling the SABC," 6.

27. "*Sunday Times* Generation Next," 12.

28. John Carlin, "Local Soaps Broadcast a New Idea of Normal Life," *Sunday Independent*, December 7, 2003, 10.

29. Muff Anderson, "Intertextuality and Memory in *Yizo Yizo*" (PhD thesis, University of Witswatersrand, Johannesburg, 2004); René Smith, "Yizo Yizo and Essentialism: Representations of Women and Gender-Based Violence in a Drama Series Based on Reality," in *Shifting Selves: Post-Apartheid Essays on Mass Media, Culture and Identity*, edited by Herman Wasserman and Sean Jacobs (Cape Town: Kwela Books, 2003): 249–265; Clive Barnett, "Yizo Yizo: Citizenship, Commodification and Popular Culture in South Africa," *Media, Culture and Identity* 26, no. 2 (2004): 251–271; Jeanne Prinsloo, "Media, Youth, and Sex in the time of HIV," *Journal of Children and the Media* 1, no. 1 (2007): 25–34.

30. René Smith, "Yizo Yizo: This Is It? Representations and Receptions of Violence and Gender Relations" (MA diss., University of Natal, 2001); Litheko Modisane, "Yizo Yizo: Sowing Debate, Reaping Controversy," *Social Dynamics* 36, no. 1 (2010): 122–134.

31. "Yizo Yizo under Fire Again," News24, March 29, 2001, https://www.news24.com/South-Africa/Yizo-Yizo-under-fire-again-20010328; "Controversy over Yizo Yizo," News24, March 16, 2001, https://www.news24.com/xArchive/Archive/Controversy-over-Yizo-Yizo-20010316. Some critics pointed out that there was no moral panic when *Yizo Yizo* depicted rapes of at least two of its female characters, both schoolgirls, by adult men. See Lynette Johns, "Rape OK, but Not Men Having Sex?—Yizo Yizo," IOL News, March 28, 2001, https://www.iol.co.za/news/south-africa/rape-ok-but-not-men-having-sex-yizo-yizo-63097.

32. Krouse, "TV's New Voices."

33. This section is based on an interview with a group of five SABC commissioning editors at the corporation's Johannesburg offices, June 20, 2007, and via email interactions with the group long afterward. Where I want to single out a particular editor, I note them separately.

34. SABC commissioning editors, interview by the author, June 20, 2007, Johannesburg.

35. Ibid.

36. Ibid.

37. Ibid.

38. Muff Anderson, "*Isidingo*: Between Memory Box and Healing Couch" (MA thesis, University of Witswatersrand, Johannesburg, 2001); Catherine Ruth Elliot, "One Nation Viewing: Watching the Local Soap Opera 'Isidingo: The Need' in Context" (MA thesis, University of Witswatersrand, Johannesburg, 2001).

39. Andrew Worsdale, "The Need to Succeed," *Mail and Guardian*, July 5, 1998, https://mg.co.za/article/1998-07-03-the-need-to-succeed.

40. Keyan Tomaselli, Ruth Tomaselli, and Johan Muller, eds., *Broadcasting in South Africa* (Chicago: Lake View Press, 1990).

41. Neil McCarthy, interview by the author, Johannesburg, June 20, 2007.

42. "The Villagers," VintageMedia.co.za, accessed December 15, 2016, http://www.vintagemedia.co.za/television/the-villagers.

43. Incidentally, *Agter Elke Man* also launched the acting career of Afrikaans singer Steve Hofmeyr, a key character in chapter 6.

44. A number of Afrikaans series dealt with terrorism (in which threats from leftist white people and Russians were stand-ins for opposition to apartheid): *Meisie van Suidwes* [Girl from South West] (1984), *Die Rooi Komplot* [The Red Plot] (1983), *Klagstaat* [Charge Sheet] (1982), *Opdrag* [Assignment] (1978), and *Taakmag* [Task Force] (1980–1981).

45. Great Britain's Equity Actors' Union boycott meant South Africans did not see popular UK soaps like *Emmerdale Farm*, *Coronation Street*, or *EastEnders* until after apartheid ended. See Tapio Varis, "The International Flow of Television Programs," *Journal of Communication* 34, no. 1 (1984): 143–152.

46. Flockemann's essay appeared in a volume dedicated to deemphasizing the power of institutions and of "totalizing discourses" of race, class, and gender. The idea was to foreground subjective, individual experience. See Micki Flockemann, "Watching Soap Opera," in *Senses of Culture: South African Culture Studies*, edited by Sarah Nuttall and Cheryl-Ann Michael (Oxford: Oxford University Press, 2000: 145–154). See also Muff Anderson, "Soapies Mirror SA's Soul," *Mail and Guardian*, March 24, 2004. https://allafrica.com/stories/200403250597.html. This chapter and this book take a different approach, of course. For a critique of Flockemann and Nuttall and Michael's overarching thesis, see Rustum Kozain's review of the book in "The Old and the New," *Pretexts: Literary and Cultural Studies* 11, no. 2 (2002): 197–203; and Desiree Lewis, *Feminist Knowledge: African Feminist Studies: 1980–2002* (Cape Town: African Gender Institute, 2000).

47. Larry Strelitz, quoted in Kwame Anthony Appiah, "The Case for Contamination," *New York Times Magazine*, January 1, 2006, https://www.nytimes.com/2006/01/01/magazine/the-case-for-contamination.html.

48. Appiah, "The Case for Contamination."

49. Nguni languages include Zulu, Xhosa, Ndebele, and Swazi.

50. Kevin Bloom, "Egoli Finale: 'Totsiens, My Skat [Goodbye, My Dear]. Until I Return from the Dead,'" *Daily Maverick*, March 2, 2010, http://www.dailymaverick.co.za/article/2010-03-02-egoli-finale-totsiens-my-skat-until-i-return-from-the-dead/.

51. Bloom, "Egoli Finale."

52. Phumza Macanda, "How One Man Turned Storytelling into a Local Gold Mine," *Daily Dispatch*, March 4, 2006, 14.

53. *Generations* publicity material, circa 2007.

54. SABC, "About Generations," accessed June 20, 2007, http://www.sabc1.co.za/sabc/home/sabc1/shows/details?id=c4b9d096-1f71-4c32-8bf7-cbb9850608d9.

55. Ibid.

56. *Prime Time South Africa 1995–1996* (video) promotional material, San Francisco: California Newsreel. http://newsreel.org/video/PRIME-TIME-SOUTH-AFRICA.

57. Ibid.

58. Micki Flockemann, "Watching Soap Opera" quoted in Sarah Ives, "Mediating the Neoliberal Nation: Television in Post-Apartheid South Africa," *ACME: An International Journal for Critical Geographies* 6, no. 1 (2007): 166.

59. Unless otherwise indicated, Vundla's comments are from an interview I conducted with him in June 2007 in Johannesburg.

60. Akin Omotoso, interview with the author, Johannesburg, June 25, 2007; Erica Anyadike, interview with the author, June 23, 2007. Omotoso is an actor and director who had starring roles on both *Generations* and *Isidingo* and directed some episodes of *Generations*. Anyadike was a screenwriter and assistant director on *Isidingo*.

61. Fred Khumalo, "Local Soap Opera Is Tuned-in Escapism," *This Day*, April 26, 2004, 11. See also Pule waSekano, "*Generations* an Insult to Black Culture," *City Press*, May 25, 2003; and Console Tleane, "Is *Generations* Really a True African Soapie?" *City Press*, July 27, 2003.

62. *Generations* publicity material, quoted in Ives, "Mediating the Neoliberal Nation," 165–166.

63. Ibid.

64. Ibid.

65. Vundla, interview by the author.

66. Ibid.

67. Ibid.

68. Ibid.

69. Michele Tager, "The Black and the Beautiful: Perceptions of (a) New *Generation*(s)," *Critical Arts* 24, no. 1 (2010): 115.

70. Lesley Mofokeng, "Popular Soapie Gets Too Smutty for SABC," *Sunday Times*, July 25, 2004, 5; Pule waSekano, "*Generations* Needs a Revamp," *City Press*, August 17, 2003, 3.

71. Tager, "The Black and the Beautiful," 105.

72. Muff Anderson, "Reconciled Pasts, Fragile Futures, Parallel Presents: Chronotopes and Memory Making in *Isidingo*," *African Identities* 1, no. 2 (2003): 151.

73. A stope refers to the production area of a mine where ore is extracted for processing.

74. Also in 1998, the SABC commissioned and aired *Muvhango* [Conflict], a soap opera in which most of the dialogue is in Tshivenda, one of the eleven official South African languages. In 2000 the SABC premiered *7de Laan*, a soap opera mainly in Afrikaans with a mostly white and coloured cast. It is also the most lucrative soap because its target audience—Afrikaans-speaking whites—is the most attractive to advertisers. While both *Muvhango* and *7de Laan* enjoy solid ratings, neither have had the cultural impacts of either *Generations* or *Isidingo*.

75. David Blair, "South African Soap Breaks the Taboo on AIDS," *Telegraph* (UK), July 8, 2006, http://www.telegraph.co.uk/news/worldnews/africaandindianocean/southafrica/1523399/South-African-soap-opera-breaks-the-taboo-on-Aids.html.

76. Ibid. Andile Ndlovu, "ARVs Might Have Saved Angel's Life," TimesLIVE, January 21, 2014. Lesego Motsepe, the actress who played Nandipha from 1998 to 2008, later tested HIV-positive and refused to take ARVs. She committed suicide in 2014. Chapter 5 in this book deals with widespread AIDS denialism in South Africa.

77. Blair, Ibid.

78. "2000 Not Out for *Isidingo*," *Cape Times*, July 7, 1998. https://www.iol.co.za/entertainment/celebrity-news/2-000-not-out-for-isidingo-945670.

79. McCarthy, interview by the author.

80. See Gabriela Soto Laveaga, "'Let's Become Fewer': Soap Operas, Contraception, and Nationalizing the Mexican Family in an Overpopulated World," *Sexuality Research and Social Policy* 4, no. 3 (2007): 19–33.

81. McCarthy, interview by the author.

82. [Name withheld], interview by the author, June 20, 2007, Johannesburg.

83. Ibid.

84. [Name withheld], interview by the author, June 20, 2007, Johannesburg.

85. Ives, "Mediating the Neoliberal Nation," 164.

86. Ibid.

87. Hilary Blecher, quoted in Worsdale, "The Need to Succeed."

88. Endemol.co.za., n.d. (site discontinued). Accessed on June 19, 2007.

89. Ibid.

90. Blignaut, "The Need for Soaps."

91. Elliot, "One Nation Viewing," 12, 17.

92. Anderson, "*Isidingo*," 7.

93. Ibid., 154

94. Ibid.

95. Nancy Signoreilli and Michael Morgan, "Cultivation Analysis: Research and Practice," in *An Integrated Approach to Communication Theory and Research*, edited by Don W. Stacks and Michael Salwen (New York: Routledge, 2008), 108.

96. Ibid.

97. Ibid., 108.

CHAPTER 4

Big Brother MultiChoice

IN JUNE 2012, Koos Bekker, then CEO of South African media company Naspers, was interviewed on the business news television channel CNBC Africa. The subject was the company's bottom line. At the time, Naspers had built its media business from its origins in publishing a pro-Afrikaner newspaper in South Africa nearly a century earlier to a multinational media firm that now dominated cable and satellite television services—through its pay television platform MultiChoice—on the African continent, along with investments in social media in China and Russia and e-commerce in Brazil, India, and Eastern Europe.[1] This made Bekker and his corporation's shareholders very rich. The interview ended with this question: "What are your plans for pay TV [in the rest of Sub-Saharan Africa]?" Bekker responded by summarizing MultiChoice's plans to offer viewers outside South Africa a more affordable option, including digital terrestrial television, then he added, "I expect a lot of growth. . . . The same is not true for South Africa. I see quite little growth for South Africa. . . . If I look ahead, I feel the rest of Africa might be a lot more buoyant than South Africa."[2]

Bekker had reason to be cheery: four years after that interview, by December 2016, MultiChoice had nearly 10.2 million subscribers in forty-eight of the fifty-four countries on the continent, putting it in a place where it dominated the market for television entertainment.[3] To ensure this dominance, Naspers had taken advantage of the weakness of public broadcasting in most African countries. With the exception of South Africa—where the publicly owned SABC still ruled the local airwaves, despite ongoing internal crises—along with public broadcasting systems in North Africa, elsewhere on the continent public broadcasters were underfunded, unimaginative, subject to political interference and weak management, or simply nonexistent.[4] In a few countries where public terrestrial broadcasting had been introduced more recently, MultiChoice was already well-entrenched. MultiChoice also appeared to keep internet streaming services at bay. Most Africans do not have the luxury of access to online television services yet, and low bandwidth means internet-based, on-demand streaming services like Hulu, Roku, or Netflix are limited to only a few countries.[5]

MultiChoice's dominance of the broadcast television market meant that it profoundly shaped mass culture on the continent. For example, the majority of African football fans get the bulk of their football coverage—European club and national team competitions as well as the World Cup—via MultiChoice's SuperSport channels, so much so that SuperSport can largely take credit for the burgeoning fan bases of English Premier League clubs on the continent. In a sense, SuperSport localizes the European leagues: for most African football fans, there are no English Premier League or UEFA Champions League without SuperSport.[6] Even national football leagues and continental football competitions (such as the African Champions League), long subject to dodgy broadcasts, disinterest, and neglect by local television systems, are being rebranded to viewers by SuperSport.[7] But it is perhaps at the level of pop culture that MultiChoice has had more lasting political and cultural effects on the continent and within its diaspora. It is through pop culture offerings—especially reality television—that MultiChoice exports new South African cultures. At the same time, MultiChoice co-opts fledging local cultural forms like Nollywood, the southern Nigerian film industry, for its (MultiChoice's) own ends.[8]

MultiChoice reimagined ordinary South Africans' relationship with other Africans (at least on-screen) and reshaped popular culture elsewhere on the continent. The chapter explores these developments on two fronts: first, MultiChoice's reality television offerings and, second, MultiChoice's attempts to grab some of the huge profits generated by Nollywood. The bulk of the chapter focuses on the reality show *Big Brother Africa*. A South African production company owns the African franchise rights to the original Dutch show, *Big Brother*. *Big Brother Africa* was broadcast live from a house in South Africa's commercial and media capital, Johannesburg. It featured twelve contestants drawn from twelve countries across the continent, including Kenya, Angola, and Nigeria.[9] The composition of the cast set *Big Brother Africa* apart from most other editions of the show elsewhere in the world as well as previous iterations broadcast on M-Net, a local affiliate of MultiChoice in South Africa. The continental format exposed millions of Africans to South Africa's political and social discourses. Not everyone was open to this new development. Some African governments and political and cultural elites objected to *Big Brother Africa*. Ordinary Africans, however, sought out the program. In some cases, *Big Brother Africa* became the space where Africans could openly and matter-of-factly debate identity, class, and gender politics in their own countries—debates from which they were shielded, whether by censorship or "tradition."

While MultiChoice provides most of the continent with satellite television, this does not necessarily translate to cultural dominance. Nigerian music and film, especially Nollywood, compete with MultiChoice for cultural influence among Africans. As this chapter documents, MultiChoice wanted in on profits generated by Nollywood, and its strategy was to commodify and standardize Nollywood rather than put it out of business. By 2012, MultiChoice was screening Nollywood films around the clock on its Africa Magic channels, including Hausa- and Yoruba-specific channels.

MultiChoice's commercial agenda neatly dovetails with the foreign policy and investment agendas of the South African state and South African policy elites, respectively, for the rest of the continent. While MultiChoice and Naspers were not officially part of the South African state's foreign policy goals (nor did they claim to be), the company's policy goals appeared to overlap closely with those of the state. As I show in this chapter, MultiChoice as a company and as a brand as well through its programming inadvertently served as ambassadors for what South Africa (as a nation and an idea) represents. At the same time, MultiChoice's success benefited from South Africa's newfound hegemony on the continent.[10] Significantly, MultiChoice employed pan-Africanist rhetoric or frameworks in gaining a foothold or extending its dominance in key African markets. It also tapped into the aspirations (around class mobility and consumption) of television viewers and the preference of African consumers for South African products, just as major South African retailers such as Shoprite and Woolworths were setting up storefronts in South African–built malls around the continent. Thus, MultiChoice is as much a representative of the power of South Africa as civil authorities—symbolized by the Nando's burger someone lunches on in Dakar, the Vodacom mobile phone contract a consumer purchases in Lagos, or the more than six hundred Shoprite stores around the continent that patrons visit to buy weekly or monthly groceries. According to journalism scholar George Ogola, "Fundamentally, MultiChoice looked at Africa not necessarily as an ideological and political construct but as a market. Its products were targeted at consumers—not Africans."[11]

Part of the story I tell here is that entertainment media, including reality television, have not just given South Africa's business and entertainment industry the opportunity to export the country's cultural products to the rest of the continent, but they have also become the conduit for exporting discourses of aspiration, continental union, and, unintentionally, progressive identity politics. In doing so, the regional globalization strategies of South African media capital do not merely create new identities or aspirations but also co-opt existing cultural products and circuits.

As Koos Bekker knew well, the meteoric rise of MultiChoice into Africa's premier satellite television service coincided with this turn "to Africa" by South African political and economic elites. In interviews with journalists—when he was not being bullish about "Africa"—Bekker promoted the virtues of the African Renaissance, a set of political ideas and a program primarily associated with former South African president Thabo Mbeki. The African Renaissance dates back to May 1996 when, while he was still Mandela's deputy, Mbeki gave his now famous "I Am an African" speech in which he asserted South Africa's identity as an African country and as part of an updated, grand vision of pan-Africanism: "I am born of the peoples of the continent of Africa. The pain of the violent conflict that the peoples of Liberia, and of Somalia, of the Sudan, of Burundi and Algeria is a pain I also bear. The dismal shame of poverty, suffering and human degradation of my continent is a blight that we share." Mbeki also shared Bekker's optimism: "However improbable it may sound to the skeptics, Africa will prosper!"[12]

In subsequent speeches and writings, Mbeki repeated and developed these ideas, eventually arriving at an intellectual agenda organized under the term "African Renaissance." Though some elements of the African Renaissance were vague, its main intention was to pivot South Africa—whose white political elites had historically turned to Europe—to look inward toward the continent culturally, politically, and economically. It also presented South Africa as a continental leader.[13] Naspers and MultiChoice would ride this wave.

That said, economic and political relations with countries north of its border was not necessarily new for the South African state or elements among its business class. During colonialism and apartheid, South African mining corporations and white farmers relied on the state to regulate and facilitate markets for cheap, black labor from bordering states and colonial territories such as Lesotho, South West Africa (now independent Namibia), Mozambique, and Rhodesia (now Zimbabwe).[14] As for foreign policy, South Africa's government was generally hostile to states to the north, and it funded and aided a number of proxy movements outside South Africa to frustrate governments sympathetic to the black resistance at home. The South African army also launched open as well as clandestine attacks against South African political refugees in Mozambique, Swaziland, Botswana, Zimbabwe, Angola, and Lesotho. The relationship "with Africa" (how the rest of the continent was and is often referred to by South Africans) was thus one that derived from the twin policies of extraction and security. When Mbeki succeeded Mandela as president, he actively set about to recalibrate that relationship.

Despite the goodwill that Mandela's stature brought South Africa in the rest of the continent, his administration did not necessarily capitalize on it.[15] In fact, Mandela's Africa policy often backfired (even when it meant well), and South Africa was accused of being both naïve and arrogant at the same time.[16] Mbeki, however, was more successful, leaving a large footprint in the rest of the continent on two fronts: first, through his promotion of the African Renaissance (outlined earlier), and second, through the New Partnership for African Development, or NEPAD. While the African Renaissance provided a cultural and intellectual framework for South Africa's Africa policy, NEPAD was principally an economic development program that aimed to establish a "new framework of interaction with the rest of the world, including the industrialized countries and multilateral organizations," to foster greater economic integration and trade in and among African nations, and to lift African gross domestic product (GDP) growth to an average 7 percent per year.[17] Mbeki managed to co-opt the powerful presidents of Nigeria, Algeria, and Senegal (who had separately also proposed his own economic plan) as well as the UN to endorse his economic framework. In April 2001, the African Union adopted NEPAD as official policy. Mbeki also convinced the leaders of major industrial nations, the Group of Eight, to endorse the program.

The African Renaissance and NEPAD were good for South African business. The South African government vigorously promoted the expansion of business in Africa. It was therefore no coincidence that South African businesses began to dominate regional markets in Southern Africa and elsewhere on the continent and became competitive against better-organized and endowed business rivals from the United States, Europe, and China. Thus, the foreign policy ambitions and soft-power goals of the postapartheid South African state began to neatly coincide with the ambitions of South African capital.[18]

Everything Has a History

Given its origins, it is ironic that MultiChoice became so central to the spread of South African culture in the rest of the continent. Few people pause to remember parent company Naspers's beginnings as the media mouthpiece of apartheid and Afrikaner nationalism for at least eighty years.[19]

Nasionale Pers (National Press)—its original company name reflected its historical ties to the National Party—was founded in May 1915 by a group of Afrikaner nationalists who understood the need for a media outlet for their political aspirations. Two months after its founding, Naspers launched the newspaper *Die Burger* (The citizen) and one year later, the magazine *Huisgenoot* (House companion). Both publications became key cogs in Afrikaner nationalism's media campaigns and would serve as public spaces where the merits of apartheid policy would be debated or various reforms (but never abolition) would be called for.[20] One of Naspers's founders, J. B. M. Hertzog, became prime minister of South Africa between 1924 and 1939, during which time he promoted Afrikaner political aims. When the National Party introduced apartheid in 1948, the founding editor of *Die Burger*, D. F. Malan, became the country's prime minister. Malan's government introduced the key series of apartheid laws that defined South

African political, economic, and social life for the next four decades. Hendrik Verwoerd, a later prime minister described as the "architect of Apartheid" for his role in implementing the homeland (Bantustan) system, previously served as editor of *Die Transvaler*, a rival publication.[21]

Yet despite Naspers's commitments to Afrikaner nationalism and racism, ideology did not get in the way of the bottom line: at various times during apartheid, Naspers adjusted very quickly to changing political conditions, often going against its political principles when it made business sense to do so. For example, Naspers invested in or took over struggling majority black-owned media businesses such as the Sunday newspaper *City Press* and *Drum* magazine in the early 1980s without changing the focuses of those media. Similarly, Naspers's coloured editions of its Afrikaans titles *Rapport* and *Die Burger* became indispensable for coverage of antiapartheid black sports.[22] It also, crucially, made the decision in the mid-1980s to enter the pay television market.

The origins of MultiChoice can be traced back to the introduction of television commercials on the SABC.[23] In 1978, two years after its launch, the SABC begun to flight commercials. This proved lucrative as SABC remained the sole licensed broadcast television service in South Africa well into the mid-1980s.[24] The monopoly cut directly into the revenues of the six biggest print media companies in the country—the white-owned English and Afrikaans companies.[25] In response, these media companies lobbied the government to allow them to introduce a pay television service to rival the SABC to recoup some of their losses. Initially, the new subscription service, M-Net, operated as a consortium, but Nasionale Pers soon emerged as its strongest shareholder.[26] Naspers, as it became known, would eventually become the sole owner. Bekker, who had just returned to South Africa from business school in the United States where he had gained experience working on cable television services, was put in charge of launching M-Net.

In October 1986, M-Net made its first broadcast. The new service required subscribers to buy set-top boxes or decoders. The aim was to attract about nine thousand new subscribers per month, but at the launch M-Net only had about five hundred subscribers. Amid fears that the new company could go bankrupt, M-Net turned itself around and delivered a healthy profit to its shareholders within two years. Over the next decade, M-Net built a successful business through offering various consumer packages.

Researchers have pointed to three key reasons why M-Net turned out to be such lucrative business for Naspers. For one, M-Net offered a mix of cultural and sports programming that reconnected South Africans with a world they felt cut off from. Secondly, and more significantly, M-Net benefited from a government-mandated one-hour, unencrypted time slot, Open Time, to promote the channel to potential subscribers. Regular analogue viewers did not require a set-top box or a cable subscription to watch Open Time programs; it was available free of charge via terrestrial television. Open Time was meant to be temporary (once M-Net had reached a hundred and fifty thousand subscribers), but in 1990 it was increased to two hours. Open Time was finally scrapped in March 2007, but by then it had served as valuable free advertising for M-Net's subscription service.[27] Through Open Time, the SABC in effect generated revenue for a private, commercial media concern that did not have to pay for that privilege and in the process gave "one of the commercial players in the media an unfair edge over its competitors."[28] The third important factor in M-Net's success was that it enjoyed what amounted to a licensed monopoly or state-sanctioned protectionism because no other cable provider existed in South Africa well into the time of the new South Africa.[29] This monopoly would serve it well as it experimented with satellite television.

Perhaps fortuitously, M-Net's foray into the rest of the continent coincided with South Africa's emergence from political isolation. In 1995, one year after the country's first democratic elections and riding on a wave of goodwill for South Africa, M-Net launched MultiChoice, a multichannel digital satellite broadcasting service targeted at South Africans and, crucially, the rest of Africa. The satellite television business soon overtook the cable business. Today, MultiChoice has expanded its service to much of the rest of the continent, with services in multiple languages, niche movie channels catering to regional tastes, live sports events, and African versions of Euro-American pop culture channels (e.g., MTV Africa and Channel O) and continental versions of reality shows like *Idols* and *Project Fame* (in which contestants compete for recording contracts) and *Face of Africa* (in which competitors vie for a modeling contract) as well as the *Big Brother* franchise.

Here Comes South Africa

South Africa has consistently remained the highest-ranking country in Africa in terms of its "global competitiveness" as measured by the World Economic Forum.[30] South Africa has also long dominated its neighbors politically and economically, and the advent of the postapartheid epoch "has certainly not brought about the withering away of the power of South African firms or the South African state."[31] In fact, since 1994 South African firms have expanded across the Southern African region and further afield in the continent; consumers elsewhere have long represented a significant market for South African companies. This expansion by South African capital coincided with large-scale liberalization and the privatization of state enterprises by governments to the north of South Africa, thus easing the entry of South African firms into these newly deregulated markets.[32]

That said, South Africans are not always welcome outside their borders. In a number of countries, South African corporations have been derided as "new imperialists," "subimperial," or "semi-peripheral," basically mimicking the behavior of Western firms[33]—so much so that in March 2004, a senior South African government minister, Jeff Radebe, admitted that "there are strong perceptions that many South African companies working elsewhere in Africa come across as arrogant, disrespectful, aloof and careless in their attitude towards local business communities, work seekers and even governments."[34] In 2013 Zambia's then vice president Guy Scott told a journalist bluntly, "The South Africans are very backward in terms of historical development. I hate South Africans. That's not a fair thing to say because I like a lot of South Africans but they really think they're the bees' knees and actually they've been the cause of so much trouble in this part of the world. I have a suspicion the blacks model themselves on the whites now that they're in power. 'Don't you know who we are, man?' ... I dislike South Africa for the same reason that Latin Americans dislike the United States, I think. It's just too big and too unsubtle."[35]

There are, of course, many different explanations for the hostile reception. Chief among these are accusations of racism, disregard for local production, and ill treatment of workers as well as allegations of corruption. South African retailers like Shoprite are often criticized for contributing to deindustrialization and to undercutting the value of local products by sourcing cheaper goods from South Africa.[36]

More controversial still, South African mining interests have become embroiled in allegations of looting mineral assets abroad, notably in the Democratic Republic of the Congo.[37] Between 1994 and 2008, more than a hundred and fifty South African firms had entered Tanzania, "with virtually every major South African firm active in the region now operating in Tanzania."[38] Also in Tanzania, South African firms are resented for their roles in the rapid privatization of nearly four hundred state-run institutions (e.g., the largest banking chain, national airline, and national brewery), their control of new industries (cell phone service providers, private television stations), and the dumping of cheap South African goods on local markets by retailers. Finally, South African firms dominate the extractive industries (gold, gemstones) on very favorable concessionary terms. A rural Tanzanian activist mocked the South African presence in the following manner: "We now live in the United States of Africa."[39]

White South African representatives of these firms are accused of importing racism from South Africa, and not just in their attitudes. They also establish exclusive schools and social clubs, engage in regular violence against Tanzanians, and push Tanzanians out of lucrative economic sectors. In the gemstone sector, for example,

> hundreds of small-scale miners were forcibly removed from the core of a lucrative tanzanite mining site in the mid-1990s, clearing the way for acquisition by

a South African mining firm. In the ensuing decade, South African security personnel at the mine were implicated in numerous shooting incidents, which resulted in several fatalities and the wounding of dozens of small scale miner "trespassers." The corporate miners later established an exclusive tanzanite brand, which was then used to discredit unbranded gems (like those produced by the small scale sector) as potentially illegal and unreliable.[40]

On the other side of the continent, in 2016, South African mobile telecommunications giant MTN was fined $1.7 billion by Nigeria's communications regulator over unregistered SIM cards.[41] Then in September 2016, on the back of an investigation by a consortium of South African newspapers, MTN was accused of avoiding Nigerian taxes over a ten-year period by diverting $12 billion in profits from its Nigerian subsidiary into bank accounts in Dubai and Mauritius, both well-known tax havens.[42] But is MultiChoice any different?

Big Brother, Africa Is Watching

Cultural exports are at the heart of South African soft and commercial power. For example, MultiChoice exposes large parts of the continent to media discourses in South Africa about gender politics, sexuality, and so on, or the promotion of a new kind of pan-Africanism that has South Africa at its heart. Another way in which culture exports South African power can be gleaned by how MultiChoice's parent company operates as a business. Naspers, argues Martin Nkosi Ndlela, is "a typical example of a horizontally and vertically integrated conglomerate with interests and linkage across Africa."[43] Ndlela suggests that global television production and distribution networks penetrate through state boundaries in highly differentiated ways, "including the export or import of 'canned' television products, joint productions, franchising-licensing agreements as well as other linkages."[44]

The first two seasons of *Big Brother*, broadcast on M-Net, were South Africa–specific, and both seasons stood out for their overwhelmingly white South African casts. In the first season of *Big Brother South Africa*, which aired in the summer of 2003, the majority of the twelve contestants were white, while in the second season, half were white. In each case, the winner of the prize money was a white male. This is not unusual in South Africa: the annual winners of the local *Pop Idols* franchise (*Idols*—another much-watched television show in South Africa) were all white until 2012.[45]

M-Net came under heavy criticism from some commentators in the media and online for *Big Brother South Africa*'s whiteness. The show's producers always insisted this was unfair criticism: only half of the contestants were white in the second season, they retorted. This, they (and some in the media) maintained, represented significant progress, a rather extraordinary statement given that white people make up only about 10 percent of the South African population. M-Net did not want to publicly admit that the rationale behind the skewed demographics of the first two series of *Big Brother* in South Africa was, of course, the fact that white consumers constituted the most desirable sector of the population for marketers and retailers in South Africa and, for this reason, were more attractive to advertisers.

In January 2003, MultiChoice announced that it would host a "continental" series to be titled *Big Brother Africa*. The winner would take home US$100,000. Since that first edition, the title has been altered a few times—for example, season 6 in 2011 was known as *Big Brother Africa Amplified*, season 7 in 2012 as *Big Brother Africa StarGame!*—but most viewers and fans of the show refer to it as *Big Brother Africa*. The numbers of contestants have also increased over time, but the show has largely retained its original format.

Following auditions, twelve contestants—one each from Ghana, Kenya, Uganda, Tanzania, Malawi, Zambia, Angola, Namibia, Botswana, Zimbabwe, Nigeria, and South Africa—were chosen for the inaugural season of *Big Brother Africa*. The group entered a specially equipped house in suburban Johannesburg on May 26, 2003. The house was also wired with twenty-seven cameras and fifty-six microphones (concealed behind mirrors or mounted in walls) running continuously to catch every moment of the housemates' activities.

The footage was broadcast nonstop on one of MultiChoice's satellite channels created specifically for this purpose. In addition, a daily 30-minute highlight program as well as a Sunday night 60-minute "eviction" program were broadcast on a dedicated satellite channel. Agreements with terrestrial broadcasters in a number of African countries also meant the eviction program was broadcast on free-to-air channels. The series attracted huge audiences, averaging thirty million people tuning in nightly throughout its inaugural 2003 run—a feat for the African continent and one that permeated to the African diaspora via the internet as highlights were also streamed on MultiChoice's website.[46] This was all the more remarkable in 2003 because M-Net had only 1.3 million subscribers, 80 percent of whom lived in South Africa.

With the growing success of the show and its visibility on social media—by March 2012 the show's Facebook page had eight hundred thousand "likes"—the producers repeated the formula unchanged in subsequent seasons of *Big Brother Africa* but increased the prize money. *Big Brother Africa* also received millions of text messages. For the 2012 season, at least fourteen million page impressions (number of times a page was viewed or visited) were registered on the show's website and more than four million people viewed video clips online.[47]

For the show's full run—ranging from 106 days in the initial season to 91 days by 2012—producers made sure that housemates were isolated from outside influences. They could not leave their "home" and were banned from access to television, radio, telephone, and other media. To fill the time, each housemate was given special tasks. How well they performed the tasks would reveal how "creative and original" individual housemates were and served to determine their popularity among both their fellow contestants and the public. Each week, viewers voted their least favorite candidate out of the house and off the program. The final contestant walked away with the prize money. The producers' continual emphasis on certain, very particular types of "creativity" and "originality" and on what they termed "a willingness to play the game" determined who stayed in the house and who got evicted. This belied still another of the show's claims: that the winner would be chosen by the audience alone.[48]

Big Brother Africa shared characteristics of the reality program genre that have been well-documented and critiqued in academic literature and popular media alike. As in similar shows elsewhere (*Big Brother* in its US and British iterations and *Loft Story* in France, for example), contestants spent most of their time doing rather ordinary things—eating, arguing, playing in a strategically positioned hot tub, and hamming it up for the camera. By way of carefully chosen camera angles and editing, the producers determined what viewers saw. Activities on the set were driven by daily and weekly story lines, with contestants coming to represent stock characters and stereotypes (in terms of gender or national identity). Audience reactions were actively shaped by these views and plots that were imposed from above.

However, from its first broadcast, *Big Brother Africa* was more than just another reality show and managed to insert itself and its contestants into larger debates about cultural politics and economic globalization on the continent. *Big Brother Africa*'s greatest achievement was to be a representative of continental unity. For one, the relative goodwill among contestants was contrasted with the fragmentation that many in the "North" see as Africa's downfall. "Three decades after the concept of Pan-Africanism fizzled out," reported *Time* magazine, "satellite television is working where liberation philosophy did not: connecting and modernizing the world's poorest continent."[49] And South Africa's *Sunday Times* editorialized, "Big Brother Africa has succeeded where the Organization of African Unity [later the African Union] failed, by unifying the ordinary people of Africa."[50] The Johannesburg correspondent of the *Christian Science Monitor* praised the series and echoed common sentiments, citing *Big Brother Africa* as "an unlikely catalyst for cultural understanding on a continent often divided by ethnic conflict, nationalism, and xenophobia."[51]

Big Brother Africa's producers encouraged such views. Carl Fischer, a veteran producer who oversaw the earlier, all-South African iterations of *Big Brother*, made this claim about the continental version: "For the first time [African viewers] are getting just African images, African people, African heroes, African music."[52] Fischer also insisted that *Big Brother Africa* represented a significant rebuke to generally dour views of the continent: "We are educated, can engage one another and don't always have wars."[53] Marie Rosholt, the series' executive producer, said *Big Brother Africa* was properly groundbreaking: "It's serving to break down misconceptions. There's a perception in the rest of Africa that Nigerians are less than honest, that South Africans are arrogant. I think our show challenges those views."[54] Contestants expressed similar views. Sammi Bampoe, a Ghanaian who appeared in *Big Brother Africa*'s first season, told his country's media that participating on the reality show had no negative impact on his opinion of other African countries or their nationals even after he had been eliminated. In contrast, he had found that the housemates had a lot in common. The only difference, according to Bampoe, "was in terms of food and music. Apart from that we were all the same."[55]

A second feature of *Big Brother Africa* was that it challenged long-held gender stereotypes, sexual identities, and sexual anxieties. Unmarried and single young men and women lived in the same house. Nudity was on full display (during the "shower hour"—the segment that recorded the highest average daily viewership) and sexual relationships between contestants were common. In later seasons, a bisexual contestant was outed (*Big Brother Africa 3*) and the male contestants were openly challenged for their treatment of women (*Big Brother Africa 2* and *Big Brother Africa 3*).[56]

Female contestants were more often than not scorned for their supposed loose morals by media. In turn, these women publicly defended their actions. During the third season, Tawana Lebale, a 31-year-old contestant from Botswana, was criticized variously in media reports and chat rooms as well as via text messaging services for engaging in multiple, often concurrent sexual relationships inside the house. In response, Tawana spoke frankly about her sexuality in a way that was unusual for women in Southern Africa at least: "Nothing happens by coincidence! I felt comfortable sleeping with both Ricco and Munya [the two male contestants] and if they feel they'd played me, I had the most fun. I was spoilt for choice. When I wanted it rough[,] I went with Munya and when I wanted it gentle I did Ricco. I can't speak for them and what they did behind my back. All I know is that there are times when a woman wants to be treated like a slut. And if you think I chased Munya you are wrong. I never went to his bed. He always came to mine. I slept with Ricco because he was open to suggestions. I know morally upright people saw me in bad light but I'm comfortable with what I did. I have no regrets."[57]

Conservative critics of *Big Brother Africa*—mostly government ministers, members of churches, and defenders of "high culture"—regularly invoked tradition to damn the show as "un-African" and "immoral."[58] Essentialized conceptions of African kinship and patriarchal values fast on the wane found common cause with the moralism of missionary Christianity. The series' voyeurism was condemned and notions of privacy—commonly (if erroneously) associated with Western individualism—to "protect the honor of women" were put to work alongside ideals of African cultural heritage. Nobel Prize–winning author Wole Soyinka was particularly brutal in his dismissal of the series' effect on Nigerians: "All we need is to just get some prostitutes on the streets and lunatics. They will go naked for nothing."[59]

Hysterical responses like that of Soyinka to disparage or censor *Big Brother Africa* emboldened its young fans. Campaigns against or attempts to block transmission of the series in Nigeria and Malawi were met with widespread opposition[60] as were criticisms of women on the show. As one young television blogger wrote about *Big Brother Africa 3*, "The truth of the matter is I don't have any problems with Tawana's sex ploits—I fully believe women should be allowed to enjoy and say they like sex in the same way men do and go as wild as they please. To top it all off, I'm annoyed by society in general and feeling trapped by global sexism."[61] Similarly, a columnist in *The Namibian* opined about the same contestant: "[Tawana Lebale has] never been one of my favorite housemates. But I hate the hypocrisy teeming across the BBA3 [*Big Brother Africa 3*] TV text strip [that runs across the bottom of the screen] like maggots swarming over a dead corpse. Munya and Ricco are men and have needs, but Tawana, who quite obviously also has needs, is every unthinkable name under the sun. Some of the messages are downright cruel. Guys do 'it'—as often and as much as they want—and it's all about bragging rights; a woman does 'it' and boy, oh boy, they're all but burnt at the stake. Look it's not my scene, but let's be fair. Tawana should not be made a scapegoat."[62] The promise of new identities—both national and sexual—presented by *Big Brother Africa* was certainly attractive.

Official responses were not exclusively dismissive or negative toward *Big Brother Africa*. In some instances, political elites marshaled the show's discourses for their own political ends. The government of Botswana, for example, actively promoted its nationals who were contestants. Nelson Mandela referred to the winner of the first season, Cherise Makubale (of Zambia), as "an example to African youth."[63] When Makubale returned to Lusaka, Zambia's then president Levy Mwanawasa announced that Makubale would become an "ambassador of goodwill." She would represent Zambia and be granted diplomatic privileges when traveling. Mwanawasa also praised Makubale for exhibiting a supposed set of national traits: "A Zambian woman must sweep and cook and you did exactly that. I am not surprised that you have received so many marriage proposals."[64] Later, Mwanawasa's spokesperson praised Makubale for exhibiting "high moral standards in the house."[65]

Yet as pointed out earlier, that attitude toward the women contestants changed over time among viewers of *Big Brother Africa*. In fact, though a Malawian contestant who resembled Makubale (she cooked and cleaned for the rest of the group) made it to the final round of *Big Brother Africa 3*, she lost out to a male Angolan contestant as viewers and media critics disparaged her for attempting to unite women viewers; she was accused of trying to secure the "kitchen vote."[66]

However, there was more to *Big Brother Africa* than just pan-Africanism and a reworking of gender roles. A close look at the social backgrounds and economic status of the contestants throughout the first three seasons gives a clear sense of the class politics at work: most, if not all, the housemates had finished college, were fluent in English (or Portuguese in the case of Angolan contestants), lived in the major African cities (not their slums or high-density suburbs), had some exposure to the entertainment industry or had worked in it (in television and modeling among others), and had either traveled or lived outside the continent at some time.[67] A leading Ugandan journalist—who was also an emphatic supporter of *Big Brother Africa*—summed up the inaugural series' class politics: "There's been criticism that the bulk of the contestants didn't really grow up [on the continent]—like Gaetano [Kagwa, the Ugandan contestant]—he didn't do most of his schooling here. Some of... the contestants have been criticized for not having been through or probably lived through Africa enough. But you must look at some of the requirements that the show organizers wanted. They wanted people who were fluent in English. They really wanted people who had had some form of exposure—not people who were *really raw*" (emphasis added).[68] As Ndlela posits, "The success of Big Brother Africa derives on the 'transculturality' and cultural hybridity of its audiences, found in the different African countries, and localization of the format in this case is not national but rather the tailoring to an English-speaking transnational audience found in Southern Africa, East Africa and West Africa. In other words, the localization of the Big Brother format is done to suit the requirements of a transnational market rather than a national one."[69]

The choice of contestants made perfect sense to MultiChoice: *Big Brother Africa* and the various continental reality television shows that followed in its path were part of a strategy to secure a greater share of the television market in Africa beyond South Africa. Not surprisingly, the *Big Brother Africa* franchise spawned a number of other shows with a continental flavor such as *Project Fame, Face of Africa*, and *The Apprentice Africa* as well as regional or national versions like *Idols West Africa, Idols East Africa*, and *Big Brother Nigeria*.[70] MultiChoice aggressively pushed a continental version of *Big Brother Africa* in an attempt to encourage middle-class people outside South Africa to subscribe to its satellite television service: "The decision to expand Big Brother across Africa was taken for purely business reasons. M-Net is growing faster in other African countries than in South Africa."[71]

Such considerations were also behind the national choices of contestants for the inaugural *Big Brother Africa* show. Of the twelve contestants in the first series, eleven came from countries where English was the lingua franca among elites, while one contestant was from a Portuguese-speaking country (Angola).

The overwhelming presence of contestants from Southern Africa reflected the region's status as MultiChoice's number one decoder and satellite television services market. Market considerations also dictated the inclusion of Nigeria (because of its size) and Angola—jointly MultiChoice's fastest-growing client bases outside South Africa. That business logic held in subsequent editions of the show.[72]

The maturation of the local pay television market in South Africa meant M-Net had to expand beyond that country's borders. As a result, MultiChoice developed specialized channel "bouquets" specifically targeted at niche markets within the continent. These included a series of channels aimed at Francophone and Anglophone Africans, at Portuguese-speaking countries, and at a large South Asian audience in East and Southern Africa.[73] *Big Brother Africa* helped to increase this market considerably. One report pointed to this effect: "From a business perspective, *Big Brother [Africa]* has been a runaway success for M-Net and MultiChoice. . . . Satellite dishes and cable subscriptions are up since the show began . . . and cellphone usage is booming as well with text messages voting out contestants every week."[74]

The Nollywood Connection

At the start of this millennium, MultiChoice employed a second, equally significant strategy that involved combining American television content, European sports, and South African–produced reality television with an embrace of local—meaning African—media production and entertainment. Rather than seeking to eliminate local successes, MultiChoice incorporated these local media to expand its own markets.[75] A big prize, then, for MultiChoice was flighting "the world's second largest producer of movies by volume"[76]—Nollywood—on its movie channels. MultiChoice proceeded to buy film rights (although Nollywood's informal structure meant directors and producers did not always benefit) and create dedicated channels for Nollywood films on MultiChoice dubbed Africa Magic.

By 2012, MultiChoice was screening Nollywood films twenty-four hours a day on Africa Magic, which also included Hausa- and Yoruba-specific channels. In the process, MultiChoice became the "largest screener of televised Nollywood movies" globally; a number of smaller channels specializing in screening Nollywood films also exist, mainly in the United Kingdom, though they cannot match MultiChoice's output.[77] The effects on Nollywood was quite visible: in May 2015, a Nigerian entertainment website reported that "between 2009 and 2014, Nollywood produced well over 5,000 titles, 80% of which were acquired by the Africa Magic channels, thus giving Nollywood a bigger platform than any other sole broadcaster."[78] As Ogola concludes, "By owning the content delivery and distribution platforms, MultiChoice has been able to create narrowcasted channels which it uses to promote 'products' marketed as 'African.'"[79]

For much of its existence, Nollywood had been relatively independent of global corporations—that is, it was profitable in its own way and existed outside and alongside global media markets.[80] MultiChoice understood that Nollywood was the most financially profitable form of local diversity available in West Africa and wanted a part of it. But could MultiChoice succeed where global media networks had thus far failed? Could it become involved with a local media culture and local production and distribution systems such as Nollywood without necessarily destroying it and remain profitable?[81] MultiChoice's strategy, as already mentioned, was to commodify and standardize Nollywood rather than eliminate it.[82] It made business sense: a monthly subscription fee was low enough "to dissuade interested viewers from going out to buy individual films, and the price paid for broadcast rights [was] high enough to interest the majority of producers and directors."[83]

The relationship with MultiChoice did not guarantee filmmakers or producers wealth or a steady income: because of the informality associated with Nollywood, "there is largely no consistent relationship between these movies being aired and their crews and producers receiving payment for it."[84] Some conclude that this system allowed satellite broadcasters like MultiChoice to intentionally cheat Nollywood producers. Veteran Nollywood scholar Jonathan Haynes noted in 2014 that "M-Net will not publicly discuss how much they pay for the rights to broadcast films." As a result, "filmmakers complain bitterly" about how MultiChoice deals with film rights. Haynes writes of filmmakers getting paid "a mere $700 per film" at one point. Other criticisms include that MultiChoice did not pay royalties to actors and producers and that the offices in Nigeria failed to hire Nigerians in management positions.[85] Other filmmakers blame MultiChoice for a decline in street sales (Nollywood films were often sold by street vendors and in informal stores).[86] But for MultiChoice, it is difficult to figure out who has rights over a film: "In most cases, someone is getting money for supplying the Nollywood movies [to MultiChoice and Africa Magic] and that person is offering to sign over the broadcast rights in return. The problem is that this person is frequently not representing the person who originally produced or made the movie. It can be easy to approach the buying desks at a television channel offering a portfolio of Nollywood movies, as verifying the identities of sales agents will take much more effort than simply buying a piece of documentation from an agent whose word is taken at face value."[87] Predictably, most filmmakers view this process very negatively.[88] MultiChoice's strategy to address this problem has been to commission some films directly, specifying minimum standards in production values and financially supporting the entire production process: "While this [new method of commissioning films] has yet to become a widespread and significant force in Nollywood, the scenario would have the potential to formalize income in Nollywood and cut into the marketers' hold on the industry were it to expand. As it stands now, this relationship serves to formalize the income and productions of the small number of producers who have been able to enter into such an agreement with [MultiChoice]."[89]

Nevertheless, MultiChoice has an impact on Nollywood in other, equally significant ways. One consequence of reality television is that the on-screen talent for Nollywood films—traditionally from television and indigenous theater—emerge more and more from reality shows like *Big Brother Africa*.[90] The Nigerian presenter of *Big Brother Africa* captures MultiChoice's varied influence on Nollywood: "You can't talk about entertainment in Nigeria without talking about MultiChoice. Before the company's involvement, entertainment was considered as a profession for never-do-wells. Today, people can confidently choose to pursue careers in the industry because of MultiChoice's contribution. The company has invested seriously in the entertainment industry and has, in the process, created jobs not just in the front end, but also in the back end. They've created jobs and careers for actors, actresses, screenwriters, producers, directors, presenters and program hosts. People now have real jobs in entertainment because of what MultiChoice has done over the years."[91] The other consequence has been MultiChoice's effect on "New Nollywood" as summarized by Haynes: "[There is] an attempt by independent producers/directors to 'take Nollywood to the next level' by making better films with bigger budgets, films that can survive the aesthetic and technical challenge of being projected in cinemas rather than being released immediately as VCDs . . . or DVDs for home viewing."[92] As for Nigerian audiences, they judge MultiChoice as having had "a positive effect" on Nollywood.[93] Data collected by researchers in the major cities of Lagos, Kanu, and Onitsha report that what matters most to Nigerian audiences of satellite television "is accessibility, which DSTV provides even better than discs [VCDs, DVDs]."[94]

Conclusion

Certainly—and predictably—South African–produced reality television and Nollywood movies tap into and engage with existing discourses about national and, in the case of *Big Brother Africa*, continental identities, gender, and class politics. But as I argue here, it also cements South Africa's place as a globalizing force, separate and independent from those countries, corporations, academics, and researchers usually associated with globalization.

South African–produced reality television exposes millions of Africans to that country's political and social discourses. South Africa is the only nation on the continent that constitutionally protects its citizens' sexual orientation. It also has the most-developed television industry on the continent, both in terms of its reach and resources but also in the diversity of its content. Through reality television, continental audiences—often shielded from such open and robust debate in their countries—are exposed to questions of identity, class, and gender in a very pragmatic way. South African reality television products increasingly take on a continental flavor as they reach more audiences, and South African producers retain either primary or considerable coproduction credits for that content.

Finally, studying reality television in South Africa broadens the manner in which scholars approach cultural phenomena, especially media. Despite increasing attention to reality television and its wider impact, there is still very little scholarly research on the genre in the developing world. The research and commentary that exists deals largely with the North American and Western European contexts and focuses very much on "the implications of questionable production techniques, ethics, and the effects of globalization for television culture and production."[95]

Africa is missing in these analyses, and when developments on the continent are addressed, there is a tendency to transfer insights and conclusions from the rest of the world uncritically to its shores. While some of the characteristics of reality television encountered elsewhere also exist in Africa, it seems clear that generalizations are of little use in analyzing the phenomenon as it presents itself on the continent.[96] An African, and here specifically South African, focus does a lot to alter this scholarly reality.

Notes

1. Jonathan Shieber, "A New $124 Million for Brazil's Movile Proves that Investors Still See Promise in Latin American Tech," Tech Chrunch, July 12, 2018, https://techcrunch.com/2018/07/12/a-new-124-million-for-brazils-movile-proves-that-investors-still-see-promise-in-latin-american-tech/; Ilya Khrennikov, "Naspers $1.2bn Russian Classifieds Bet Pays Off—Fueled by Economic Crisis," BizNews, March 15, 2016, https://www.biznews.com/global-investing/2016/03/15/naspers-1-2bn-russian-classifieds-bet-pays-off-fuelled-by-economic-crisis; Kevin O'Brien, "Naspers of South Africa Moves into East Europe with Acquisition of Tradus," New York Times, December 18, 2007, https://www.nytimes.com/2007/12/18/technology/18iht-naspers.html; T. J. Strydom, "Naspers Investors See Billions Trapped by China Success," Reuters, May 24, 2017, https://www.reuters.com/article/us-naspers-strategy-idUSKBN18KoGN.

2. CNBC Africa, "Naspers Full Year Results with CEO Koos Bekker," YouTube, June 27, 2012, https://www.youtube.com/watch?v=nojMbLOk418.

3. The 10.2 million subscribers were the combined total for 8 million digital terrestrial television (DTT) and 2.2 million direct-to-home (DTH) satellite service subscribers. The 2.2 million DTT subscribers were based in 11 countries and 114 cities across the continent. See Annemarie Meijer, "Digital Television Slowly Coming to African Viewers," Intelsat, November 10, 2016, http://www.intelsat.com/intelsat-news/digital-television-slowly-coming-to-african-viewers/.

4. Amani Milanga, "The Concept of Public Broadcasting in a Changing Africa: A Tanzanian Experience," *Journal of African Media Studies* 6, no. 1 (2014): 7–25; Jesse Geston, "How Has MultiChoice Africa Affected the Way People View Television in Africa?" (MA diss., Grand Valley State University, Michigan, 2006).

5. MultiChoice offers a video-on-demand service, BoxOffice, which in 2015 was available in eleven African countries including South Africa and averaged around six hundred thousand users per month. "MultiChoice Preparing to Compete with Netflix as Profits Fall,"

MyBroadband, June 29, 2015, https://mybroadband.co.za/news/broadcasting/130722-multichoice-preparing-to-compete-with-netflix-as-profits-fall.html.

6. Peter Alegi, *African Soccerscapes: How a Continent Changed the World's Game* (Athens: Ohio University Press, 2010), 107.

7. "DStv Sport Exclusivity Debate Ridiculous: Naspers CEO," MyBroadband, June 29, 2013, http://mybroadband.co.za/news/broadcasting/81081-dstv-sport-exclusivity-debate-ridiculous-naspers-ceo.html.

8. This chapter draws on, expands, and updates arguments made earlier in Sean Jacobs, "Big Brother, Africa Is Watching," *Media, Culture and Society* 29, no. 6 (2007): 851–868; and Sean Jacobs, "Continental Reality Television and the Expansion of South African Capital," in *The Politics of Reality Television*, edited by Marwan Kraidy and Katherine Sender (New York: Routledge, 2011).

9. Even *Big Brother Naija*, a later Nigerian iteration of the show, was filmed in South Africa because of the irregular power supply in Nigeria.

10. CNBC Africa, "Koos Bekker on the Noticeable Absence of China," YouTube, January 26, 2012, https://www.youtube.com/watch?v=rP7SKO20bG4.

11. George Ogola, "Constructing Images of Africa: From Troubled pan-African Media to Sprawling Nollywood," in *Images of Africa: Creation, Negotiation and Subversion*, edited by Julia Gallagher (Manchester University Press, 2015), 14.

12. Thabo Mbeki, "I Am an African" (speech delivered to South African Parliament, Cape Town, May 8, 1996), http://www.mbeki.org/2016/06/06/statement-on-behalf-of-the-anc-on-the-occasion-of-the-adoption-by-the-constitutional-assembly-of-the-republic-of-south-africa-constitution-bill-1996-cape-town-19960508/.

13. Adekeye Adebajo, Adebayo Adedeji, and Chris Landsberg, eds., *South Africa in Africa: The Post-Apartheid Era* (Pietermaritzburg: University of KwaZulu-Natal Press, 2007).

14. David A. McDonald, *On Borders: Perspectives on International Migration in Southern Africa* (Basingstoke: Palgrave MacMillan, 2000).

15. Rob Nixon, "Mandela, Messianism, and the Media," *Transition* 51 (1991): 45.

16. Chris Landsberg, "Promoting Democracy: The Mandela-Mbeki Doctrine," *Journal of Democracy* 11, no. 3 (2000): 107–121.

17. Patrick Bond, "Thabo Mbeki's New Partnership for African Development: Breaking or Shining the Chains of Global Apartheid?," Foreign Policy in Focus, March 1, 2002, https://fpif.org/thabo_mbekis_new_partnership_for_africas_development_breaking_or_shining_the_chains_of_global_apartheid/.

18. See Richard Schroeder, *Africa after Apartheid: South Africa, Race and Nation in Tanzania* (Bloomington: Indiana University Press, 2012); Darlene Miller, "'Spaces of Resistance'—African Workers at Shoprite in Maputo and Lusaka," *Africa Development* 31, no. 1 (2006): 27–49; Darlene Miller, Etienne Nel, and Godfrey Hampwaye, "Malls in Zambia: Racialised Retail Expansion and South African Foreign Investors in Zambia," *African Sociological Review* 12, no. 1 (2008): 35–54; Chris Alden and Mills Soko, "South Africa's Economic Relations with Africa: Hegemony and Its Discontents," *Journal of Modern African Studies* 43, no. 3 (2005): 367–392; and Miller, "South African Multinational Corporations," 2.

19. Tim du Plessis, "Newspaper Management Keeps Quiet about Its Role in Apartheid: In the Afrikaans Press Some Reporters Decide to Testify," *Niemann Reports* 54, no. 4 (1998): 55–56.

20. Ibid.

21. Jacob Dlamini, "Surprising Facts about Verwoerd's Early Career," *Business Day*, October 14, 2010, https://allafrica.com/stories/201010140859.html.

22. After the end of apartheid, *Die Burger* switched to the term "Afrikaanses" as a more inclusive alternative to describe Afrikaans speakers. And the first mass tabloid newspaper aimed at black South Africans, *The Daily Sun*, was published by Naspers. See Herman Wasserman, *Tabloid Journalism in South Africa* (Bloomington: Indiana University Press, 2010).

23. David Williams, "How Pay-TV in South Africa Was Started," *Financial Mail*, August 1, 2008.
24. I argue this point in chapters 1 and 2.
25. Ruth Teer-Tomaselli, "South Africa as a Regional Media Power," in *Media on the Move: Global Flow and Contra Flow*, edited by Daya Thusso, 155–156 (New York: Routledge, 2007).
26. Anton Harber, *Gorilla in the Room: Koos Bekker and the Rise and Rise of Naspers* (Johannesburg: Parktown, 2012).
27. Karin Burger, "Goodbye to MNet Open Time," News24, March 26, 2007, http://www.news24.com/Entertainment/SouthAfrica/Goodbye-to-MNet-open-time-20070325.
28. Ibid.
29. Harber, *Gorilla in the Room*.
30. "How the World Rates South Africa," Brand South Africa, October 2008, https://www.brandsouthafrica.com/investments-immigration/business/economy/globalsurveys.
31. William G. Martin, "South Africa's Subimperial Futures: Washington Consensus, Bandung Consensus or a People's Consensus," *AfricaFiles* 6 (October 2008): 2.
32. Ibid., 7.
33. Patrick Bond, "Towards a Broader Theory of Imperialism," *Review of African Political Economy*, http://roape.net/2018/04/18/towards-a-broader-theory-of-imperialism/; also William G Martin, "South Africa and the 'New Scramble for Africa': Imperialist, Sub-Imperialist or Victim," *Agrarian South* 2 no. 2: 161–188.
34. Patrick Bond, "African Development/Governance, South African Subimperialism and Nepad" (CODESRIA Conference on The Agrarian Constraint and Poverty Reduction, Addis Ababa, Ethiopia, December 17–19, 2004), 38.
35. David Smith, "Zambian Vice-President: 'South Africans Are Backward,'" *The Guardian*, May 1, 2013, https://www.theguardian.com/world/2013/may/01/zambian-vicepresident-south-africans-backward.
36. Miller, "'Spaces of Resistance,'" 28.
37. Craig McKune, Stefaans Brümmer, and James Wood, "Sexwale 'Caught Up' in US Probe of Suspect DRC Mining Deal," *Mail and Guardian*, July 10, 2014, http://mg.co.za/article/2014-07-10-sexwale-caught-up-in-us-probe-of-suspect-drc-mining-deal.
38. Richard A. Schroeder, "South African Capital in the Land of *Ujamaa*: Contested Terrain in Tanzania," *AfricaFiles* 5, no. 12 (2008), http://www.africafiles.org/article.asp?ID=19013.
39. Ibid., 14.
40. Ibid., 19.
41. Yomi Kazeem, "Africa's Largest Phone Company Will Pay $1.7 Billion to Settle Its Nigerian SIM Card Dispute," Quartz Africa, June 10, 2016, http://qz.com/704057/africas-largest-phone-company-will-pay-1-7-billion-to-settle-its-nigerian-sim-card-dispute/.
42. John Bowker and Loni Prinsloo, "MTN Drops as Phone Carrier Faces New Allegations in Nigeria," *Bloomberg*, September 27, 2016, https://www.bloomberg.com/news/articles/2016-09-27/nigerian-mp-mtn-illegally-moved-13-92-billion-from-country.
43. Martin Nkosi Ndlela, "Television across Boundaries: Localization of *Big Brother Africa*," *Critical Studies in Television* 8, no. 2 (2013): 60.
44. Ibid., 59.
45. Lydia Polgreen, "South Africa Has a Black 'Idol.' Surprise Is That It's a First," *New York Times*, October 12, 2012, A1; Munyaradzi Vomo, "IdolsSA Caught between Music Talent, Race," *Sunday Independent*, November 24, 2013, https://www.iol.co.za/sundayindependent/idolssa-caught-between-music-talent-race-1611471.
46. See Ndlela, "Television across Boundaries," 57.
47. MultiChoiceafrica.com, accessed July 20, 2009 (site discontinued).

48. See Emily Wax, "An African 'Big Brother' Unites and Delights," *Washington Post*, July 14, 2003, A1; Michael Dynes, "Africa's Sexy Big Brother Cuts across Great Divide," *The Times* (London), July 16, 2003, 14; Karen MacGregor, "Africa's Satellite Effect: They Are Creating the First Pan-African TV Networks—and Hits," *Newsweek* (international ed.), August 18, 2003, 19; Marc Lacey, "Reality TV Houses Africa Under One Roof," *International Herald Tribune*, September 10, 2003, 20.

49. Simon Robinson, "Reality TV, African Style," *Time*, June 23, 2003, 39.

50. "A Chance to 'Visit' the Birthplace of our BBA Housemates," *Sunday Times* (South Africa), August 24, 2003.

51. Nicole Itano, "Reality TV Hit Unites Africa in 'Brother'-Hood," *Christian Science Monitor*, July 8, 2003: 1. See also "Zambian Churches Demand End to 'Immoral' Big Brother," *Mail and Guardian*, July 4, 2003, https://mg.co.za/article/2003-07-04-zambian-churches-demand-end-to-immoral-big-brother; and Zarina Geloo, "Big Brother Show Irritates the Church," InterPress Service/Global Information Network, July 23, 2003, http://www.ipsnews.net/2003/07/religion-africa-big-brother-show-irritates-the-church/.

52. Robinson, "Reality TV, African Style."

53. "Now KK Joins BBA Winner Cherise Frenzy," *Times of Zambia*, September 12, 2013.

54. Ibid.

55. *Accra Daily Mail*, August 11, 2003.

56. "So, Why Watch *Big Brother*?," *The East African*, September 7, 2008.

57. "'Randy Tawana Says She Just Loves Doin' the Dirty," *SowetanLIVE*, November 18, 2008, http://www.sowetanlive.co.za/sowetan/archive/2008/11/18/randy-tawana-says-she-just-loves-doin_the-dirty.

58. "Big Brother Africa: What Is the Point?," *Accra Daily Mail*, November 25, 2008.

59. Robinson, "Reality TV Houses Africa."

60. "Malawi Bans Big Brother Africa," BBC News, August 6, 2003, http://news.bbc.co.uk/2/hi/entertainment/3128193.stm; Sonnie Ekwowusi, "Nigeria: Punished for Showing Pornography," *This Day*, December 4, 2007, https://allafrica.com/stories/200712050221.html.

61. Tashi Tagg, "Big Brother Africa 3—Is Malawi Going to Clean Up?," *The Namibian*, November 19, 2008, https://www.namibian.com.na/index.php?id=851&page=archive-read.

62. Natasha Uys, "Big Brother Africa 3: Munya, the Bridesmaid," *The Namibian*, November 27, 2008. https://www.namibian.com.na/index.php?id=1112&page=archive-read.

63. Dan Teng'o, "The Lady Who Charmed Africa," *Saturday Nation* (Kenya), September 13, 2003, https://allafrica.com/stories/200309140103.html.

64. "Controversial Big Brother Winner Becomes Zambia's Ambassador," Xinhua News Agency-CEIS, September 10, 2003.

65. *Times of Zambia*, September 12, 2003. It is telling that in September 2004 another Zambian winner of a continental reality television series—Lindiwe Alamu, winner of *Project Fame*, the next big continental reality show after *Big Brother Africa*—was also granted a diplomatic passport by the Zambian government. She was only the third person to have been so rewarded. The other was the former captain of the national football team, Kalusha Bwalya.

66. "Big Brother Africa 3: Coming Oh So Close!," *The Namibian*, November 27, 2008, https://www.namibian.com.na/index.php?id=1113&page=archive-read; Maureen Odubeng, "BB3 Was Quite an Experience—Hazel," *Mmegi*, November 26, 2008, http://www.mmegi.bw/index.php?sid=7&aid=13&dir=2008/November/Wednesday26.

67. See information and descriptions of contestants from various seasons on the official Facebook page, https://www.facebook.com/pg/bigbrotherafrica/about/?ref=page_internal.

68. WNYC Radio, "On the Media," August 8, 2003 (transcript).

69. Ndlela, "Television across Boundaries," 64.

70. "'Project Fame' to Replace 'Big Brother Africa,'" *Accra Daily Mail*, April 13, 2004, https://www.modernghana.com/music/633/project-fame-to-replace-big-brother-africa.html.
71. "Big Brother Africa Sparks Controversy," *Times of Zambia*, July 5, 2003.
72. Jacobs, "Continental Reality Television," 188.
73. "Multichoice Strikes Back," Fin24.com, April 30, 2010, https://www.fin24.com/business/multichoice-strikes-back-20100430?cpid=3.
74. Marc Lacey, "Reality TV Rivets Africa, to the Churches' Dismay," *New York Times*, September 3, 2003, https://www.nytimes.com/2003/09/04/world/reality-tv-rivets-africa-to-the-churches-dismay.html.
75. Ogola, "Constructing Images of Africa," 14.
76. Keyan Tomaselli, "Nollywood Production, Distribution and Reception," *Journal of African Cinemas* 6, no. 1 (2014): 15.
77. Jade Miller, "Global Nollywood: The Nigerian Movie Industry and Alternative Global Networks in Production and Distribution," *Global Media and Communication* 8, no. 2 (2012): 29.
78. Callistus Nwokediuko, "MultiChoice's Effect on Nigeria's Entertainment Industry," Newsbreak.ng, May 20, 2015, https://www.newsbreak.ng/2015/05/multichoices-effect-on-nigerias-entertainment-industry/.
79. Ogola, "Constructing Images of Africa," 15.
80. Moradewun Adejunmobi, "Nigerian Video Film: As Minor Transnational Practice," *Postcolonial Text* 3, no. 2 (2007): 1–16.
81. "Nigeria: John Ugbe—Multichoice Has Invested N55 Billion in Nigeria in 20 Years," August 11, 2013, AllAfrica, http://allafrica.com/stories/201308121646.html.
82. Ibid.
83. Adejunmobi, "Nigerian Video Film," 16.
84. Ibid.
85. Jonathan Haynes, "New Nollywood: Kunle Afolayan," *Black Camera* 5, no. 2 (Spring 2014): 54.
86. Connor Ryan, "Nollywood and the Limits of Informality: A Conversation with Tunde Kelani, Bond Emeruwa, and Emem Isong," *Black Cinema* 5, no. 2 (Spring 2014): 174.
87. Miller, "Global Nollywood," 129.
88. Ryan, "Nollywood and the Limits of Informality," 174.
89. Ibid.
90. Aboubakar Sanogo, "Certain Tendencies in Contemporary Auteurist Film Practice in Africa," *Cinema Journal* 2 (Winter 2015): 141.
91. Nwokediuko, "MultiChoice's Effect."
92. Haynes, "New Nollywood," 53.
93. Matthew Brown and Nyasha Mboti, "Nollywood's 'Unknowns': An Introduction," *Journal of African Cinemas* 6, no. 1 (2014): 5.
94. Ibid., 6.
95. Jacques Vinson, "Review of Shooting People: Adventures in Reality TV by Sam Brenton and Reuben Cohen," *The Velvet Light Trap* 54 (Fall 2004): 80–82. See also Annette Hill and Gareth Palmer, "Editorial: Big Brother," *Television and New Media* 3, no. 3 (2002): 251–254; Paddy Scannell, "Big Brother as a Television Event," *Television and New Media* 3, no. 3 (2002): 271–282; Minna Aslamma, "Flagging Finnishness: Reproducing National Identity in Reality Television," *Television and New Media* 8, no. 1 (2007): 49–67.
96. Some exceptions are Laura Hubbard and Kathryn Mathers, "Surviving American Empire in Africa: The Anthropology of Reality Television," *International Journal of Cultural Studies* 7, no. 4 (2004): 437–455; and Nick Shepherd and Kathryn Matters, "Who's Watching Big Brother? Reality Television and Cultural Power in South Africa," *Africa e Mediterranei* 38 (2002): 67–69.

CHAPTER 5

HIV-Positive Media

THE FIRST DECADE of the twenty-first century witnessed an explosion of social movement activity in South Africa, and the HIV/AIDS activist group TAC was one of the most prominent. Of all the social campaigners of that time period, TAC had the most impact on state policies. TAC built a mass movement—the largest and most visible of that era—to mount a twin assault on capital and the state.[1] TAC demanded that pharmaceutical drug companies lower their HIV medicine prices and that the state roll out a program to supply antiretroviral drugs to HIV-positive pregnant women to reduce their risk of transmitting HIV to their babies either in the womb or when giving birth. For the rest of the decade, TAC turned to campaigning for a full rollout of a combination of drugs known as highly active antiretroviral therapy (commonly referred to as HAART) for all HIV-positive people needing treatment. Media technologies were crucial to TAC's political strategies and its eventual successes. In this chapter, I explore the media politics of TAC.[2]

Thabo Mbeki was at the helm of government; he along with his health minister, Manto Tshabalala-Msimang, emerged as AIDS denialists and thus frustrated the implementation of an AIDS treatment program for at least the next decade. As a result, South Africa, "by any epidemiological standard," was the country with the world's deadliest AIDS epidemic.[3] By the decade's end, however, Mbeki was no longer in office. He had been pushed out in a political coup orchestrated within the ruling party, the ANC. Widespread dissatisfaction over Mbeki's AIDS policies was one reason for his ouster. TAC's legal work, research, civil disobedience, and mass mobilization, including building transnational solidarity networks, combined to play a decisive role in defeating state-supported AIDS denialism in South Africa. Following Mbeki's removal, the government made treatment more accessible to people living with AIDS.

Nathan Geffen was the head of TAC's policy, communications, and research department for much of the first decade of the 2000s and handled the organization's media technology needs. In 2004 Geffen and TAC leadership concluded that having a media strategy would be a substantial resource in achieving its political goals—that is, to end denialism and force the government to implement a treatment strategy—and that shaping public opinion was crucial.[4] TAC recognized that, along with mass protests and civil disobedience, winning the media war meant much of the battle was already won. Thus, TAC became the first postapartheid social movement to seriously assess and engage with media's enormous power. TAC represented a break with how social movements in South Africa had historically related to mainstream media. This included both mainstream media's ability to set political agendas and activist groups' capacity to influence media frames. TAC also set new benchmarks for social movements to exploit new media technologies (especially the internet) to build alternative information infrastructures. This new relationship to media is most evident in the way movements spawned by TAC—the Social Justice Coalition, Equal Education, Reclaim the City, and Unite Behind, among others—have since conceived of media strategy and the internet. It is equally true for movements beyond the TAC umbrella like the Economic Freedom Fighters (EFF) and the hashtag student movements, such as #FeesMustFall and #RhodesMustFall, of 2015–2016.

The chapter begins with a brief review of Mbeki's media politics. Here, in particular, Mbeki's decision to write a weekly online column on the ANC's website and his sourcing of denialist AIDS doctrines via the internet, are examined. For its part, TAC decided early on that the mainstream media would be a critical component of any successful AIDS campaign, as would an online strategy. While a number of publications employed specialist health reporters, the scale of the pandemic and juniorization in newsrooms meant younger reporters with little knowledge of science, AIDS, or medicine were assigned to the health beat. TAC understood the importance of educating these journalists about HIV/AIDS science and denialism. TAC also built an extensive online information infrastructure that, apart from serving as a resource for journalists and the public, countered denialism and provided curriculum for its treatment literacy educators. In addition, TAC was one of the first postapartheid movements to effectively use media spectacle as a form of protest. It particularly employed this approach during its civil disobedience campaigns. In this TAC understood the media's appetite for conflict frames and controversy. Finally, TAC exploited the media's penchant for highlighting individuals and personalities over movements.

The Crisis

From the late 1990s on, South Africa has faced an AIDS crisis of epic proportions made worse by Mbeki's political decisions while in office between 1999 and 2008. For one, Mbeki denied the causal link between HIV and AIDS, which had negative effects on how his government responded to the crisis. Second, without any evidence, Mbeki (who habitually couched his denialism as curiosity; he was just asking questions) claimed that antiretroviral drugs—which prevent HIV from multiplying in the body and therefore allow people with HIV to live longer and healthier lives—were toxic. This he blamed on perceived racism of the medical profession and science. Mbeki's denialism also encouraged all kinds of bogus scientific and health remedies[5] that extended to his government and the ruling party. Tshabalala-Msimang, for example, publicly endorsed discredited AIDS treatments, including promoting garlic, vitamins, and micronutrients as remedies for HIV.[6] Mbeki sowed confusion in a racially divided and unequal society by combining his paranoid views about the alleged toxicity of AIDS drugs with a valid critique of the pharmaceutical industry's price gouging. The toxic brilliance of Mbeki's politics was that he took reprehensible content from AIDS denialism and rearticulated it using radical language and concepts. The confusion spread to journalism, where Mbeki and his supporters exploited reporters' lack of knowledge of HIV and AIDS and preyed on racial tensions among journalists. When Mbeki first began to voice denialism publicly, "most local journalists had never heard of AIDS skeptics."[7] They had not often heard of HIV either: "For many in the media, the science of AIDS was completely unknown and unfathomable territory. There was therefore a real danger of them giving South Africans incorrect information, which could expose the public to the risk of contracting a virus that the government had told them was harmless."[8] Two prominent white journalists, Martin Welz and Rian Malan, defended Mbeki. A noted black journalist once described TAC as "just a harmless but very loud pressure group whose salaries are paid by Americans" and as "a conglomeration of drug-dealers who serve as marketing agents of toxic drugs, which are not even used where they come from, America."[9]

The material effect of Mbeki's actions, not surprisingly, was to frustrate the implementation of any government AIDS policy and to condemn millions of South Africans to painful and unnecessary suffering and death. For a sense of the devastation in South Africa, understand that "more than 330,000 people died prematurely from HIV/AIDS between 2000 and 2005 due to the Mbeki government's obstruction of life-saving treatment, and at least 35,000 babies were born with HIV infections that could have been prevented."[10]

Mbeki's claims about AIDS drugs and his theories about AIDS's causality were unfounded and dismissed as bunk by medical doctors and scientists.[11] Nevertheless, Mbeki sought out and enjoyed the support of a global coalition of AIDS denialists (who referred to themselves as "dissidents") and managed to sway public opinion, including the views of some in his own party.[12] None of this would have mattered if Mbeki was a fringe politician, but as the leader of the largest and most influential, organized political force in the country, his views and actions were decisive; the ANC did not just win large majorities in elections, but due to its leading role in the country's liberation struggle, it was influential in how millions of South Africans reacted on a range of issues, including, crucially, the use of AIDS drugs.[13]

It is worth noting that while South Africa's mainstream media exposed the foolhardiness of Mbeki and his health minister's positions on AIDS, they also provided ample column space where denialists and the ideas they represented were disseminated. When questioned about this, guilty print media (along with the Broadcasting Complaints Commission, a private body covering radio and television coverage) argued that they were merely facilitating free debate and accused their critics of fanaticism.[14] Overall, the effect of AIDS denialism on public knowledge about the pandemic was devastating.

However, TAC would prove to be a formidable opposition force to Mbeki's AIDS stance and would eventually triumph over him. TAC became adept at using its connections to and understandings of mainstream media's logics to organize a successful campaign against denialism and for treatment. Above all, it exploited the potential of the internet—also a key source of Mbeki's denialism—to build an integrative media infrastructure that served to engage policy and media elites as well as complement and amplify its mass campaigns. The chapter argues that, most notably, TAC's media strategies (1) countered denialism through building a web infrastructure to educate and arm its supporters and members with facts and information about treatment and AIDS, (2) employed media spectacle successfully, and (3) capitalized on the media's fascination with political personalities. In the case of the latter, for example, TAC understood the symbolic power of foregrounding the struggle and courage of its charismatic and camera-friendly leader Zackie Achmat or, in rare instances, some of its mostly female, working-class leaders like Sipho Mthathi and Vuyiseka Dubula, who would each later serve terms as TAC general secretary.

When Mbeki was finally pushed out of office in 2008, his interim successor, Kgalema Motlanthe (who served until the next general election), moved swiftly to replace Tshabalala-Msimang with Barbara Hogan, an ANC MP who had close ties to TAC. When Jacob Zuma was elected president of South Africa in 2009, he appointed a respected medical doctor, Aaron Motsoaledi, as health minister. Not much was expected from Zuma. During Zuma's rape trial in 2005—in which he was acquitted—he testified that he took a shower after having unprotected sex with the HIV-positive daughter of his former Robben Island prison cellmate. The shower, he told the judge, protected him from AIDS.[15] While the shower comment was idiotic and ignorant, Zuma was clearly not an AIDS denialist. He was active in the South African National AIDS Council, an advisory body on which TAC served with government officials and the medical profession. His main political constituency was in KwaZulu-Natal, a province devastated by the pandemic and a TAC stronghold. Motsoaledi immediately set out to affirm the government's commitment to science and publicly rebuked Mbeki's denialist stance.[16] Separately, Zuma also affirmed his government's clear commitment to mainstream science on HIV and AIDS's causes and precipitously implemented a government-funded AIDS treatment plan.

As for TAC, after Mbeki's ouster, it had a brief existential crisis (the government had acceded to most of its key demands by 2009) but then recovered to spawn a next generation of social movements that drew on TAC's strategies, including its emphasis on media. The new groups included Equal Education (which fights for good public schools), Social Justice Coalition (which monitors policing and sanitation in informal settlements), and Reclaim the City (which agitates for affordable housing within Cape Town's segregated and heavily gentrified downtown and inner-city suburbs). More pointedly, GroundUp, probably postapartheid South Africa's first news outlet started by a social movement and publishing online only, is a direct descendant of TAC's media politics.[17] It may also be no coincidence, then, that Geffen, TAC's one-time head of policy, communications, and research, became the founding editor and publisher of GroundUp.

The Media Politics of Thabo Mbeki

From the time Mbeki was elected president in 1999—after serving as Nelson Mandela's deputy between 1994 and 1999—until he stepped down in 2008, he developed twin media reputations: that he was preoccupied with South African mainstream media's political power and that he held negative views of that media. His love-hate relationship started one year after assuming the presidency, when Mbeki convinced the editors of *ANC Today*, the ruling party's weekly online newsletter, to allow him to publish a regular column entitled "Letter from the President." It soon grew into a must-read for political observers, party loyalists, and journalists.[18] "Letter from the President" set the daily news agenda in the early 2000s. Most often, local and international media took their lead from Mbeki's column to get a sense of government policy.[19] Readers received unfiltered takes of the president's thought processes and ideas about a wide range of topics, including race and racism, imperialism, foreign affairs, African cultural renewal, and whether South Africa consisted of "two nations" (one rich and white and one poor and black). But a considerable part of Mbeki's intellectual energies in "Letter from the President" were spent unpacking two topics: the role of news media and the HIV/AIDS pandemic. For Mbeki, these two were linked. On the first topic, Mbeki set the tone in his very first column. He wrote that it was clear that the racial and class information deficits of apartheid persisted after 1994. The result was that the dominant tendency in South African politics—represented by the ANC—had little representation whatsoever in mainstream media. This was an unusual state of affairs in any modern democracy. "What masquerades as 'public opinion,'" argued Mbeki, is no more than "minority opinion informed by the historic social and political position occupied by this minority."[20] The average black South African, Mbeki noted, had little or no access to his or her own media, resulting in the black majority having "to depend on other means to equip itself with information and views to enable it to reach its own conclusions about important national and international matters."[21] Mbeki thus used his column to counter the media's one-sidedness and ahistorical reporting and analyses. He presented the internet as the solution to the media problems of the ANC and the government: the internet would empower these entities to counter and bypass the misinformation coming from mainstream media. It became clear very early on, however, that the same internet that Mbeki praised as an information source and as a means to transform public opinion in South Africa was also the source of his denialist views about HIV and AIDS.[22]

One of Mbeki's interventions on AIDS was to question the authority of science, what he termed "dogma." For Mbeki, there was no scientific truth: "schools of thought" about AIDS's causality competed within the public sphere. When asked what he thought about the reaction of the country's leading virologists and intellectuals to his denialism, Mbeki told a television reporter that South Africans were "educated" or "exposed" to only "one school of thought." As a result, he said, "this other point of view [meaning AIDS denialism], which is [deemed] quite frightening, this alternative view, in a sense, has been blacked out. It must not be heard, it must not be seen—that's the demand now."[23]

Most observers wondered where these views came from. Mbeki repeatedly wrote or spoke of studying medical books and medical literature as well as accessing an extensive library of scientific texts that could back up his assertions about HIV and AIDS. This vast literature, Mbeki claimed, proved that "there is a lack of consensus among scientists" and that "both sides of the divide" were not agreed on the causality of AIDS.[24] Where was this huge library located? Mbeki's interlocutors received the answer soon enough. One of his media spokespeople, Tasneem Cassim, told the *Sunday Independent*, "The President has a thick set of documents. He goes into many websites. . . . The president goes into the Net [meaning the internet] all the time."[25] Mbeki later confirmed that he found most of what he claimed to be "scientific knowledge" about AIDS from the internet.[26] It also emerged that most of what he collected seemed to originate from websites denying the causal link between HIV and AIDS or that made claims about the excessive toxicity of AIDS drugs.[27]

The Media Politics of TAC

A small group of activists—most with backgrounds in the ANC, the gay rights movement, and in struggles over public health care—organized TAC in Cape Town on December 10, 1998, which also happened to be International Human Rights Day.[28] The launch coincided with a ten-day fast to bring attention to the rising number of AIDS deaths. TAC made three specific demands: that the government develop a "comprehensive and affordable treatment plan for all people living with HIV/Aids"; that the ministers of health and finance make azidothymidine (AZT) available to HIV-positive pregnant women to "reduce the risk of a woman passing the virus to her unborn child"; and that pharmaceutical companies be pressured to significantly reduce AIDS drug prices.[29] TAC's membership ranks soon swelled, and for the first few months of its existence, TAC's energies were taken up with the issue of AIDS drug prices.

One year earlier, in 1997 South Africa had changed its law governing patent rules; if implemented, the changes to the Medicines Act would significantly reduce drug prices. Two years later, forty multinational pharmaceutical companies, with the support of Bill Clinton's administration in the United States, took the South African government to court to prevent the new law from coming into effect. TAC acted as an amicus curiae (friend of the court) and submitted an affidavit in support of the South African government's position. Initially, TAC employed predictable strategies—marches or testifying in front of the country's parliament to influence pharmaceutical companies. Then the organization's leadership decided that Achmat and another activist, Jack Lewis, would fly to Thailand to illegally import Biozole, a cheap generic brand of fluconazole approved by the World Health Organization (WHO) that can treat opportunistic infections (oral thrush) in people with HIV. A few days later, Achmat and Lewis brought the drugs—three thousand capsules carried in their luggage—into the country. They were moved by the death of a TAC volunteer, Christopher Moraka, who had died of complications from oral thrush. Achmat and Lewis managed to get the drugs past customs without any problems and were welcomed by a large, jubilant crowd. However, outside of TAC's ranks and its supporters and allies internationally, the response was not so welcoming. Political parties such as the liberal Democratic Alliance (DA; at the time the official parliamentary opposition) condemned TAC, and government health officials raided Achmat's house to confiscate the Biozole. Achmat was threatened by the police but was never charged, and the country's medical control council eventually gave special legal power to a doctor allied with TAC to import Biozole to treat AIDS patients. Subsequently, Pfizer, one of the drug companies targeted by TAC, agreed that the government could distribute fluconazole free to public health facilities in South Africa.[30] For TAC leaders, the police decision to not prosecute Achmat, the granting of legal power to import Biozole, and Pfizer's policy change pointed to the power of public opinion. Geffen later cited sympathetic media coverage of TAC's actions as decisive in swaying authorities to TAC's point of view.[31]

The success of this protest strategy eventually led to TAC using similar tactics to illegally import cheap ARVs from Brazil and to score victories against GlaxoSmithKline and Bristol Myers Squibb over reducing the prices of antiretroviral drugs. As a result, the price of AIDS drugs was considerably lowered. In April 2001, the drug companies finally dropped their patent lawsuit against the South African government. Pressure from within South Africa—TAC teamed up with the country's largest trade union federation—managed to embarrass the drug companies for their perceived greed. TAC also organized global public opinion against the drug companies. As Geffen concludes, "It was a huge victory for the South African government, largely engineered by TAC, and a dreadful embarrassment for the drug industry."[32]

Though TAC and the government combined forces on the patent lawsuit, the Mbeki administration—against expectations—quickly developed into probably TAC's most formidable opponent. There were earlier signs of this clash: in 1997 the government promoted an industrial insolvent mixture known as Virodene with fatal side effects as an AIDS drug. Then Mandela's health minister, Nkosazana Dlamini-Zuma, announced that her department would not make AZT available in public hospitals. The biggest setback came when Mbeki made public his views about AIDS causality (that HIV does not cause AIDS) and about the alleged toxicity of AZT. It all came to a head in July 2000 when South Africa hosted the International AIDS Conference in Durban, South Africa's third largest city. The conference, held every two years, is the world's largest and most important meeting on HIV and AIDS, and scientists, activists, and media descend on the host city. Shortly before the start of the Durban conference, Mbeki announced that he would convene a presidential AIDS advisory panel to meet and look at the cause of AIDS. The panel included a number of AIDS denialist scientists, giving them and their views mainstream exposure. In response, TAC coordinated a march to the International AIDS Conference venue. TAC showed its organizational mettle by making sure thousands turn up for the march, but it also wanted to make a media splash. It mattered to TAC leaders that "the march made it on to BBC and CNN."[33] In emphasizing that the march was covered by the two best-known global news networks, TAC activists were most likely channeling the widespread belief—both among activists and analysts at the time—about the perceived "CNN Effect," the idea that coverage of the crisis on global news networks, especially CNN, could embarrass the South African government among its allies or powerful governments who in turn could put pressure on the ANC to effect policy change.[34]

Despite the clear support for AIDS drugs and the need for treatment, Mbeki and Tshabalala-Msimang hardened their stance on denialism and frustrated AIDS treatment in public hospitals for the next few years. TAC countered by taking the government, specifically the minister of health, to court. In 2001, in the first of many court actions, TAC sought to compel the minister of health to allow public hospitals and clinics to provide ARVs to pregnant women with HIV. TAC won the case, but the government appealed. In July 2002, the country's constitutional court eventually ruled in TAC's favor. Mbeki later withdrew from publicly expressing his denialist views, but far-fetched conspiracy theories about AIDS—much of it sourced online—continued to circulate around ANC branches. As for the government and provincial health departments in provinces controlled by the ANC, they had to be compelled through court decisions to implement ARV treatment.

Historically, social movements in South Africa have generally been skeptical of mainstream media. The media's history as extensions, chronologically, of colonialism, apartheid, white monopoly capital, and the political settlement of the early 1990s did not inspire confidence among social movements, particularly movements with mostly black members and supporters. The exceptions were the organic relationship between the new breed of young, photogenic ANC leaders in the 1950s; Steve Biko and other Black Consciousness activists' close relationship with the white editor of a regional newspaper in the Eastern Cape in the early to mid-1970s;[35] and the emergence of the alternative media movement of the 1980s. It was perhaps the latter—that is, alternative media and the social movements it championed—that can be considered direct ancestors of TAC's approach to media. Alternative media coincided with the rise of the UDF, which provided a new impetus to antiapartheid struggle in the 1980s.

TAC obviously operated in a different media environment than that of apartheid and the UDF: now there was media freedom, the country's mainstream media had developed its own voice as a watchdog press, and the internet was growing in influence. Nonetheless, TAC drew on some of the language of the UDF in its campaigns as well as replicated its media tactics. Crucially, TAC also gained inspiration from and mimicked the media campaigns of the first AIDS movement in the United States in the 1980s—groups like ACT UP (AIDS Coalition to Unleash Power) and Gay Men's Health Crisis. This allowed TAC to bring media tactics unseen in South Africa to local AIDS struggles, including its treatment literacy programs.

One of TAC's major tasks, according to Geffen, was to break "Mbeki's hegemony on AIDS" and to convince ANC supporters that the state was wrong about AIDS. Getting the media on TAC's side was central to any strategy: "Key to this success was a multi-pronged approach. We had a well-run national campaign that made effective use of media and the court. Good research was essential for this part of the campaign to succeed. . . . We also put a lot of effort into our relationship with the media, organizing hundreds of interviews between journalists and TAC members. We gave workshops explaining HIV science to reporters. We would spend hours explaining our court cases and actions, such as our highly controversial civil disobedience campaign. This reaped reward. Most journalists were highly critical of Mbeki and very favorable to the TAC."[36]

In fact, veteran journalist Pat Sidley, who covered TAC for many years, testified to the effects of the organization's largely positive relationship with journalists: "For many journalists of my vintage, the [TAC] activists were manna from heaven; they even invoked some nostalgia for the anti-apartheid struggle of old. They were always available, returned phone calls (most of them) and provided mountains of useful, interesting information. They were dealing with a series of complex medical and legal questions, and were always available to teach and explain. Pharmaceutical companies, evasive and secretive at the best of times, retreated further into their shells."[37]

TAC recognized the media's logic and daily work patterns, and it became quite savvy in constructing media frames: "By creating newsworthy events that cannot be ignored by the commercial media (public marches, confrontations with the Health Minister and the disobedience campaign among them), [TAC] inverts a news agenda that has a focus on what the government does and does not do."[38] One such moment presented itself in December 2002 when former president Mandela visited TAC members, first at Achmat's house and later at a Médecins Sans Frontières (Doctors without Borders) pilot ARV program in Khayelitsha township in Cape Town. This was also during the time Achmat refused to take ARVs until the drugs were generally available in public health facilities. When Mandela came to meet Achmat, he encouraged Achmat to take the drugs, but Achmat refused, a position that Mandela admired. Significantly, Mandela wore an HIV POSITIVE T-shirt that had become a TAC trademark by then. The words were printed on the front of the T-shirt in bold, purple, capital letters. For TAC's leaders, the media optics could not be quantified enough: "The symbolism was profound: the world's and the country's most beloved hero had aligned himself with our struggle."[39]

Right from the start, TAC was clear about producing its own media—both online and offline—to capture its work. To produce film, TAC drew on older networks within community and independent media circles that date back to the UDF and alternative media. For example, Lewis, the activist who accompanied Achmat to Thailand to import Biozole, was in charge of a film production company called Community Health Media Trust (CHMT) that was tasked with documenting TAC's work "from the beginning."[40] CHMT originated during the UDF era. Subsequently, CHMT produced campaign videos, a television series about people living with AIDS, and a full-length documentary about TAC's work. These media were disseminated to potential funders, shown at film festivals, and, crucially, made accessible to large numbers of South Africans watching public television.[41] In Geffen's assessment, "CHMT's footage helped to establish TAC's initial footprint in the media."[42]

One of the reasons for TAC's success in framing AIDS debates and struggles was its decision early on to produce its own media. Key among its productions was the magazine *Equal Treatment*, distributed to its funders and the media as well as ordinary members in the townships. At its height, TAC published five issues per year of *Equal Treatment*, which was also translated from English into three local languages (spoken by black people) and with a print run of seventy thousand copies per issue. *Equal Treatment* made law and science accessible to TAC members and regular people without dumbing down the content. The belief that people can understand all the key scientific and legal concepts, no matter their level of education, was central to the whole ethos of TAC. With that belief came a culture of learning in which TAC branches would sponsor reading groups where *Equal Treatment* would be read and discussed. At its peak, it was an extremely empowering publication.[43]

Around the same time, TAC decided to invest resources into building an online presence. Two years into TAC's existence, it still did not have "a proper website," getting by on a web page hosted by another organization. Geffen, who was recruited for this purpose, recalls that TAC proceeded to set up an "extremely simple website" and launched an email newsletter, the TAC Electronic Newsletter. The setup was primitive: "it was all very homemade, clunky and not always reliable." But TAC was the first social movement to send regular newsletters and calls to action through a large emailing list: "Because we were the only or one of the only organizations doing this at the time, the media learned about us and picked up our stories. The electronic newsletter helped spur intense media coverage on TAC. This made a huge difference to public awareness of our campaigns."[44]

Most observers cite a number of instances in which TAC's internet presence enhanced its capacity to organize. The first example came during the International AIDS Conference in July 2000. TAC billed its protest on the opening day of the conference as "a Global March." (This was the first of a series of oppositional marches in South Africa: the march at the AIDS conference inspired protest actions at the UN World Conference Against Racism in 2001 and the World Summit on Sustainable Development in 2002.) In the months leading up the conference, TAC made sure activists coming to South Africa received its electronic newsletter. TAC provided information so that international activists could become quite familiar with its politics and its tactics and take part in organizing the global march as well as coordinate TAC and its alliance partners' actions at the conference.

The second instance in which TAC's internet presence enhanced its capacity to organize offline came during a March 2001 global day of action against the pharmaceutical industry. TAC's website became "the organizing board" for a coordinated, worldwide protest against the pharmaceutical companies that had taken the South African government to court because of its amendments to the Medicines Act. Events related to the protest were advertised on TAC's website and in the electronic newsletter. In the aftermath of the protests, photographs and reports of the protest were posted on the website and put into the newsletter. "Today that seems obvious," Geffen recalls, "what effective organization would not do that? But a decade ago that was unusual and exciting. The global pressure on the pharmaceutical industry was immense and within weeks it capitulated and withdrew its litigation. This level of global activist organizing would have been impossible without websites, email and news lists."[45]

TAC successfully used its internet presence to ratify its status as the privileged interlocutor not only for the AIDS movement but also concerning the AIDS pandemic. TAC provided much of the information for reports about the AIDS situation, and media coverage of AIDS became fused with TAC, its aims, and TAC spokespeople. In the process, TAC's media became a corrective to Mbeki's denialism.

Building an Online Treatment Literacy Infrastructure

Denialism involves "the use of rhetorical arguments to give the appearance of legitimate and unresolved debate about matters generally considered to be settled," argue medical researchers Martin McKee and Pascal Diethelm.[46] They identify at least six key features of denialism: identification of conspiracies, use of fake experts, selective citations, creation of impossible expectations of research, misrepresentation and logical fallacies, and manufacture of doubt. While the AIDS denialist community is small, its impact is not. The internet, in large part, "has made it possible for every conspiracy theory to flourish."[47] One of TAC's main achievements was to build an infrastructure, including an extensive website resource and archive, that contained information on everything from how to counter denialists as well as information about medical ethics, drug trials, drug regimens, pharmacology, the law, science, political economy, and international relations. Achmat describes the effect: "Thousands of TAC members living in poverty-stricken conditions with limited educational backgrounds are [thus] capable of explaining how nevirapine or other antiretroviral medicines prevents mother-to-child transmission. So can many other South Africans as a result of [TAC's] public information campaigns."[48]

TAC's treatment literacy helped its activists work to effectively counter Mbeki when the latter was exploiting links between poverty and AIDS for his denialism. TAC pointed out that Mbeki presented his argument about the connection between poverty and AIDS as some kind of discovery, yet the relationship between poverty and illness was uncontroversial and indisputable. TAC correctly linked poverty to the lack of access to antiretroviral drugs. As the information on TAC's website showed, there was nothing confusing about the obvious correlation between good health and wealth on the one hand and poor health and poverty on the other. Medical researchers, doctors, and activists have advocated this for a while and their empirical research came to the same conclusions.

If AIDS is redefined as a disease of poverty, then the socioeconomic conditions in which one lives becomes as relevant a factor as sexual practices and behavior in understanding the spread of HIV. One is then compelled to confront the reality that the overwhelming majority of people killed by the epidemic worldwide and in South Africa have been poor, mostly black Africans. Redefining AIDS as a disease of poverty highlights the fact that Africa's underdevelopment, created and maintained by racism in the interest of Western countries and the profit motives of multinational pharmaceutical companies, debilitates the health of its citizens. Achmat and other TAC leaders have been unequivocal about the class and racial nature of HIV infections as tied up with South Africa's political economy—that is, that while AIDS as a condition can affect anyone, only middle-class and rich people—including black middle-class people—could afford to treat it. As Achmat himself noted in 2003, "The only reason we don't have this medication in South Africa is because we are poor, not because it does not exist."[49] As Achmat has explained elsewhere, "The vast majority of people who die avoidable and predictable AIDS-related deaths are black people who use the public health services. People who have access to medicines are predominantly middle-class people who have access to private health care. The continued denial of anti-retroviral and other essential medicines reinforces the suggestion that black lives have no value to those in power. It suggests that the lives of the majority of people living with HIV/AIDS are expendable."[50]

The case for a link between poverty and AIDS, as one social anthropologist puts it, "cannot be made, in a denialist way, to the exclusion of mainstream scientific explanations of the viral cause of AIDS in the body of HIV-infected individuals."[51] And as Malegapuru Makgoba, president of South Africa's Medical Research Council during Mbeki's reign and who publicly rebuked Mbeki's AIDS denialism, has pointed out, "All diseases are made worse by poor social conditions. This is so obvious that you would not find a doctor who would say otherwise. However, to conflate this factor with causation by clever wordplay is very dangerous."[52]

TAC also combined its AIDS literacy programs and its media strategies to counter Mbeki and Tshabalala-Msimang's tendency to couch denialism as "African solutions" and as oppositional to white racists. Mbeki railed that the most fervent support for AZT came from white people and the West. When former US president Jimmy Carter criticized Mbeki's AIDS stance, Mbeki accused Carter of treating "our people as guinea pigs, in the interest of pharmaceutical companies."[53] Mbeki likened AZT to the scientific experiments done on African Americans in the first half of the twentieth century in the United States.[54] That most of Mbeki's critics in South Africa were black people, including the bulk of TAC's leadership as well as its membership, somehow escaped Mbeki. Moreover, the country's largest trade union federation, COSATU, and the country's leading scientists also disagreed with Mbeki.

Denialism did more than create uncertainty and confusion among the general public. It simultaneously obscured and complemented the prevailing ethos around neoliberal economic policy within South Africa's government. The government's economic policy, Growth, Employment and Redistribution, or GEAR, was first adopted in 1996 and promoted the privatization (officially referred to as "restructuring") of essential basic services (such as water and electricity) as well as reduced spending on services such as health. These reforms profoundly shaped the government's response to any crisis. In the case of AIDS, GEAR balked at "the drastic increases in public spending that would be required to roll out combination HIV treatment."[55] Even more than that, GEAR "slowed the pace of transformation in the health sector, thus continuing Apartheid-era institutional and economic legacies and prolonging bureaucratic incapacity to implement AIDS programs effectively."[56] What this meant for health policy—and crucially for HIV policy—was that all social policy had to comply with the restrictions of government expenditure in accordance with GEAR. The result was a cocktail of neoliberalism and denialism that combined to deny people living with HIV access to AIDS treatment drugs.

When TAC was formed, its leading activists "knew very little about the science of HIV."[57] Except for a local doctor who joined TAC, most TAC activists needed to study the science of HIV and AIDS, so the organization sponsored reading groups and ran detailed training workshops for TAC volunteers. TAC was not the first AIDS activist group faced with this dilemma. During the 1980s and early 1990s, AIDS activists in Europe and the United States, facing their own and their friends' deaths, proceeded to educate themselves about their health rights, drug therapy, and the science of AIDS. It would be to them that TAC turned to run training courses on HIV and AIDS for its volunteers. "We soon developed members with a useful working knowledge of ARV's, mother-to-child transmission, opportunistic infections, medicine parents, how drugs are developed and much else relevant to our struggles for treatment," Geffen noted.[58] One TAC member later summed up what he understood by treatment literacy:

> Many treatment activists have learned the science and medical treatment of HIV. Many of us educate our communities on these issues. The time when all we knew about medicines is that you take two of the pink pills every morning is over. We must know our medicines by name, how they were found to be effective and how and where in the body they work. Their side effects and how they can be managed, how to monitor the safety of medicines. What food to take and not to take with them. That way we can feel we have some control over our health. We must also follow new scientific research that sheds light on how best to use the drugs we take. All these things are part of what we call Treatment Literacy.[59]

Poor, black South Africans testing positive for HIV also had to deal with stereotypes and stigma. For example, their abilities to manage their own treatment regimens were often doubted. In one notorious instance, Nontsikelelo Zwedala, a TAC activist living with HIV, responded to criticism from Andrew Natsios, then administrator of the United States Agency for International Development under President George W. Bush, who said that Africans could not be trusted to take ARVs daily as many could not tell the time:

> I want to tell the world that I live in a shack in Philippi in Cape Town. I do not have a degree from a university. But I want to tell the world today that I know the names of my medicines. . . . I know how they work. I know nevirapine can cause liver damage so my doctor must monitor my liver function. I know AZT can give me anemia, I know all their side effects. Two months into my treatment I had liver problems. My doctor picked it up and managed it. I am alive today and didn't die. I know what ARVs have done for me. I could not eat any more with thrush and oral herpes. I was losing too much weight. I do not accept this insult . . . that poor people cannot tell time. That we are too poor to be able to learn to look after our own health.[60]

It is a testimony to the effectiveness of TAC's training methods that the organization's treatment literacy teaching document was adapted for use by other movements outside South Africa. The internet's role in this was decisive, though not in the way we might assume. Rank-and-file TAC members had no access to the web or to cyberspace, and Geffen concedes that point: "Unfortunately in the early 2000s few did [have access to the internet]" and few effectively knew how to use it.[61] Instead, ordinary members learned about ARVs from TAC organizers, not the web or any other media. But the internet did help TAC arm trainers and activists with treatment literacy. The internet also gave TAC's leading activists access to information resources such as the US National Library of Medicine's PubMed database and scientific journals like the *Lancet* and the *New England Journal of Medicine* (*NEJM*).[62] Access to information about advances in treatment via the internet reduced the immense costs that TAC would otherwise have had to pay for such information. As Geffen wrote on GroundUp's website in 2012, "It is true that the Lancet and the NEJM existed long before the Internet was popularized, but the paper editions are expensive. Now it is relatively simple for ordinary people—who are unable to access expensive journals—to exchange scientific papers over the Internet, as we have done since the early 2000s. . . . This empowered a small subset of the organization to be able to stay abreast of developments in HIV science, but then use that knowledge to inform the branch members about major developments and update our treatment literacy curriculum."[63]

The Use of Media Spectacle

Even as TAC replicated ACT UP and Gay Men's Health Crisis's treatment literacy campaigns in South Africa, they would also adopt the US groups' affinity for using media spectacle to shock people into action. TAC's HIV POSITIVE T-shirts, for example, resembled ACT UP's bright pink triangle with its attendant slogan,

SILENCE = DEATH. For ACT UP, "SILENCE = DEATH" was "a conscious attempt to transform a symbol of humiliation [the triangle was used to single out homosexuals in Nazi Germany] into one of solidarity and resistance" and "a symbol of gay pride and liberation."[64] Similarly for TAC, HIV POSITIVE served to invert the stigma associated with being HIV-positive or living with AIDS and build solidarity.

Media spectacle would become a critical strategy for TAC in a series of civil disobedience campaigns in 2003 that deliberately courted media controversy.[65] As part of its civil disobedience campaign, TAC members regularly confronted government ministers over the lack of movement on a comprehensive AIDS treatment strategy in the public sector, and while doing so some even got themselves arrested.[66] These disruptive events predictably "generated an enormous amount of publicity."[67]

In one instance, when Tshabalala-Msimang gave a keynote speech at a health conference in Cape Town, TAC members turned up and held placards blaming her for the six hundred deaths daily from AIDS in South Africa. Some of them shouted "Murderer!" at Tshabalala-Msimang. Achmat was photographed "sneering" at Tshabalala-Msimang and insulting her about her wig. Some witnesses to the exchange felt that Achmat was justified in his reaction: Achmat was sweating and Tshabalala-Msimang offered him a tissue but mocked his illness.[68] As Tshabalala-Msimang left the conference, a TAC member threw a shoe at her car. Not surprisingly, the protest and the series of confrontations made the front pages of most local newspapers as well as radio and television news. Some of TAC's supporters and sympathizers in the media and among the middle classes were temporarily turned off by the display. Detractors accused TAC of being rude and disrespectful. One consequence was a media chill: "Some journalists who had previously reported TAC's events positively became more circumspect." Interviewers accused TAC of resorting to "undignified actions."[69]

TAC leaders initially defended their actions. The negative fallout was deemed a necessary hazard in TAC's quest to confront and shame ruling party officials and government ministers. Achmat argued that "it mattered more what our members and people with HIV thought than the polite middle class."[70] This implied that for social movements like TAC that extensively incorporate media into its campaigns, any publicity is good publicity. Achmat eventually apologized for the wig insult, however, showing that Achmat and TAC did care what the media and the middle classes thought of them. Those groups were key to TAC's strategy of building a moral consensus against Mbeki's denialism and for free treatment in public hospitals. Calling Tshabalala-Msimang a murderer was not a problem—that was a widely held perception among South Africans. Making fun of the health minister's wig, however, reflected poorly on TAC when it claimed to occupy the moral high ground. In short, TAC understood that not all media coverage is good coverage if it is not favorable. It sought to present itself to the media as the moral movement taking on an immoral government, and the incident with the health minister damaged that brand.

In apologizing Achmat was also reflecting TAC's sensitivity to black public opinion. Part of TAC's appeal to black South Africans was that it was not an opposition movement aiming to destabilize or bring the government down. In fact, it accepted the legitimacy of the ANC as a people's government with large electoral majorities at the time, and many of its members were staunch ANC members. This was the case during the very public skirmishes with Mbeki and Tshabalala-Msimang. Instead, TAC's "civil disobedience campaigns [were] aimed at enforcing the rights enshrined in South Africa's constitution."[71] It merely wanted to enhance democracy and accountability.

The Personal is Political

With few exceptions, mainstream media coverage of AIDS struggles was largely dominated by clashes between TAC leaders and Mbeki. This predictably made for good copy and headlines. It also reflected the media's penchant for conflict frames. Secondarily, when media coverage did include the experiences of people living with HIV and AIDS, it focused on them mostly as victims in need of help. The media appeared uncomfortable when these same people made explicit demands. A senior TAC leader characterized the media as displaying "ambivalence when the poor do away with decorum, display unmediated anger and break with the law."[72] The same leader, Mark Heywood, suggested that the media focuses "on people they are comfortable with" in the AIDS movement: mostly white, middle class, educated, literate, and camera friendly—in other words, people that look like and are from the same class as journalists. He meant himself or Geffen, but Heywood also included Achmat in this group. At first this would not seem to make sense: Achmat is a black man and a Muslim who grew up in the working class and went to prison for his activism under apartheid.[73] He certainly does not have the typical background of a white South African. However, unlike many of his black colleagues in TAC, Achmat does have a graduate education, is sophisticated, and has traveled internationally; he is therefore both comfortable and fully conversant with elite norms.

One of the costs associated with a media spectacle strategy is that movements can use mainstream media as an ally but only if they present themselves in a particular way. Other working-class and poor people's movements emerged at the same time as TAC. These groups, led by black people and making radical demands on the state about housing and land, had less success with the media. This often led to tensions between TAC and social movements such as Abahlali baseMjondolo, a squatters' rights movement; the Anti-Eviction Campaign; and the Anti-Privatization Forum.[74] The latter discouraged working with the government, openly questioned the ANC's legitimacy, participated in illegal marches and occupations, and for the most part avoided the courts. These groups felt less accepted by mainstream media and were not afforded the kinds of accolades that TAC received. Their actions were mainly dismissed as criminal or classed under a general category as social delivery protests.

For Heywood, most media, by focusing on people they are comfortable with, missed the "social significance" of TAC's mobilization: that "more people with HIV . . . were poor and black" [75] and were the ones who had to deal with extreme forms of stigma and denial in their communities, which spurred them to join the movement to fight for access to affordable treatment. This new activist base (including, after a while, a number of them in TAC's leadership) provided the actual social weight and broad support that TAC could leverage when confronting multinational pharmaceuticals and the South African government over AIDS treatment. It would be the poor, working-class members who would increasingly come to define TAC's agenda. However, one would not know that from the media coverage. "One of the strengths of the TAC was our media profile. One of the weaknesses was that most reporting focused on Zackie Achmat and me," Heywood said. "As a result, the real heroes of the TAC struggle are still largely unknown. The stories we were telling second hand should have been sought from and told by women [whom he considers the "real heroes" of the struggle] like Sarah, Vuyiseka Dubula, Busisiwe Maqongo, Hazel Tau, Joanna Ncala, Portia Serote, Linda Mafu, Portia Ncgaba and many, many others."[76]

To actively work against the media's proclivity to focus on TAC's more white, middle-class, and literate elements, TAC responded with an urgency to produce its own media as well as make many of its black leaders and ordinary activists available to media. Doing so also countered Mbeki's claims that TAC was a "white cabal." The television series *Siyayinqoba Beat It!*, a program flighted on SABC, was a key tool in this regard. Produced by TAC for over a decade, its presenters and reporters were mostly ordinary, usually black TAC members. The program aimed to "demystify health matters" and combined the television series with a range of other media, including "community radio programs, public service announcements, newspaper articles, community engagements, social media, pamphlets and condom wrappers."[77] Later, Jack Lewis would direct and CHMT would produce the 2011 full-length documentary *Taking HAART*, a history of TAC's first decade. The narrator is Vuyiseka Dubula, who rose in the ranks to serve as general secretary at TAC. As with *Siyayinqoba Beat It!*, in the film, it is TAC's black and mostly working-class women membership that feature and tell the organization's history, talking about treatment and taking the lead on-screen in most of South Africa's eleven official languages, which are translated with subtitles.

Furthermore, while it may be true that Achmat essentially became the face of TAC and was the primary leader associated with the movement, other, more ordinary members fronted specific campaigns. Two cases illustrate this. In June 2000, Moraka, the TAC volunteer mentioned earlier, died from a fungal infection of the throat. Moraka could have lived if he had had access to an antifungal medicine called fluconazole. After his death, TAC launched the "Christopher Moraka Defiance Campaign." It was under the auspices of that campaign that Achmat and Lewis traveled to Thailand in October 2000 to illegally import a cheaper, generic form of fluconazole into South Africa. (Months later, Pfizer, which produced fluconazole, made the drug available in public clinics.) In 2002, TAC filed a complaint against drug companies GlaxoSmithKline and Boehringer Ingelheim for the monopoly they had over drug prices and patents. The complaint was lodged in the name of an ordinary, working-class TAC member, Hazel Tau, who lived in Soweto. (The first four complainants were all working-class TAC members. The second respondent, Nontsikelelo Zwedala, for example, lived in a squatter camp outside Cape Town.) The complaint became known in the media and in AIDS law as "Hazel Tau and Others vs GlaxoSmithKline and Others." (The case was settled in 2003 when the companies agreed to lower the prices of antiretroviral drugs.) In other instances, ordinary TAC members testified before Parliament.

Where TAC collaborated with commercial or mainstream producers, it appeared to play along with the media's preference for profiling its more media-savvy members, especially Zackie Achmat. Achmat's biography, particularly his background as an ANC activist and his decision not to take ARVs until they were generally available made for a compelling narrative on film. Even then, because of Achmat's own political convictions and his familiarity with the camera, TAC could exploit the focus on him for building sympathy for its larger health and political goals.

The film that best reflected this tendency was *It's My Life*. The use of first person in the title referred to Achmat. Released in 2002, it was produced as part of *Steps for the Future*, a series of films that focused on AIDS and human rights in Southern Africa and was funded by German and American foundations.[78] The first films in the series were finished in 2001, and by the end of the project, nearly fifty films had been made. The films on South Africa reflect a range of styles and topics. They include exploring the lives of a migrant worker and a single mother with AIDS, following a group of AIDS activists in Khayelitsha, and examining how young people talk about sex as well as telling the story of the black gay ANC activist who had served as inspiration for TAC, Simon Nkoli (*Simon and I*). It was at Nkoli's funeral in 1998 that Achmat first called for a "treatment action campaign" in South Africa.

For *It's My Life*, a small film crew followed Achmat around for five months in 2001 and 2002. The film's shooting schedule coincided with the decision by pharmaceutical corporations to take South Africa's government to court. TAC's decision to file an amicus brief in support of the government case was at the heart of the film—so was Achmat's decision not to take ARVs. The filmmakers had access to the mundane details and rituals of Achmat's life, including his daily routines. It also explored his personal history.

What becomes clear from reviewing TAC's tactics and its own media—and *It's My Life* reflects this—is not that a personality cult around Zackie was a deliberate choice; it just happened, and once it did, it became a deliberate media strategy.

Achmat, born in Cape Town, is a "self-proclaimed socialist" who during the antiapartheid struggle had been arrested or detained five times and operated in the ANC underground.[79] In the late 1980s and early 1990s, he became a prominent advocate for gay rights in South Africa. (Gay rights activists like him played a crucial role in ensuring that very progressive clauses on sexual orientation made it into South Africa's new constitution that was passed in 1996.) Sociologist Peter Dwyer has described Achmat's appeal among TAC members and sympathizers as "Mandela-esque."[80] Dwyer witnessed delegates at a TAC conference in Durban singing struggle songs that venerated Achmat. At one point, conference delegates pointed to Achmat and sang about "how they will follow into civil disobedience even if it means getting arrested."[81] Mandela himself, during his July 2002 visit with Achmat, when Zackie was not taking ARVs, said of the TAC leader that he is "a role model and his action is based on a fundamental principle which we all admire."[82] Outside South Africa, Achmat advanced TAC's mainstream appeal. Achmat was included in *Time* magazine's "100 Most Influential People" list in 2001, and in 2004 he was nominated for the Nobel Peace Prize. Two years later, the *New York Times* named TAC "the world's most effective AIDS group." A media campaign about AIDS awareness by fashion designer Kenneth Cole included Achmat among a dozen or so global celebrities. For the campaign, Achmat posed in the now ubiquitous HIV POSITIVE TAC T-shirt. Throughout this period, however, it became clear that Achmat was quite aware of the limits of his own power relative to that of TAC. Later, when Achmat would finally start taking ARVs, he did so not at Mandela's urging or media pleading but because TAC members publicly voted on it and demanded he do so.

Achmat became the movement—he embodied it. He was a crusading activist against a callous government; a martyr risking his life for the movement. But he did not develop into a demigod. He never became too big for the movement. He remained "a man of the people," able to move between power and ordinary political action—for example, handing out pamphlets with other members on city streets.

Viewers of *It's My Life* tag along as Achmat makes regular visits to his doctor, relaxes or works at home, or campaigns on the street. Even closed-door meetings of TAC, where sensitive information and political strategy are discussed, form part of the narrative. Crucially, Achmat is shown interacting with journalists who come to interview him about the case or his refusal to take ARVs. The effect of this fly-on-the-wall approach is that the media interviews with Achmat became a means with which to explain TAC's policies in very simple terms to viewers.

On camera, many of Achmat's colleagues and fellow TAC members try to convince him to take ARVs. Even his doctor implores him: "Activism is a lot more effective if you stay alive." When the pharmaceutical companies finally withdraw their case, Achmat breaks into dance. Such scenes humanize him.

For the filmmakers, it is clear who the bad guys are: government policy and lack of implementation, the pharmaceutical corporations, Tshabalala-Msimang, and Mbeki. Achmat is brutal about Mbeki's role in the pandemic: Mbeki is "the biggest obstacle" and "presiding over a holocaust of poor people," he says in the film. By contrast, Achmat's interlocutors serve to confirm the righteousness of his cause; one journalist interviewing him likens Achmat's standoff with Mbeki as "like David and Goliath." But the government's decision to question the safety of ARV drugs makes the film end on a pessimistic note. It closes with a debate between Achmat and TAC over whether he should cease his boycott and take ARVs. Achmat, instead, decides that he is sticking to his principles.

In *It's My Life*, Achmat emerges as a leader and a spokesperson for a larger political cause—one that is not just about the struggle against AIDS denialism and for affordable treatment but also about the shape of postapartheid democracy. He becomes a stand-in for the energies of ordinary South Africans taking on a negligent government.

One of the key legacies of *It's My Life* was TAC's success in taking advantage of its connections to and appeal among artists and media workers in South Africa and elsewhere. As a result, its leaders, especially Achmat, appeared as the main interlocutors in films about AIDS.

One of the most controversial aspects of TAC's strategies was its decision to mostly organize within the bounds of the law and not to antagonize the ruling ANC and its alliance partners among trade unions and communists. On the former, TAC decided early on that while it engaged in civil disobedience, it would largely operate within the law and would follow the route of petitions, marches, and court cases. On the latter, TAC recognized the ANC's political leadership and exploited tensions in that alliance. For example, TAC's decision to ally with COSATU, the trade union federation, could be interpreted as within the bounds of this alliance.

We see this side of TAC's media and organizing strategy in the film *State of Denial*, released in 2003 and geared mostly toward an international audience.

(It was edited to match the format of American public television documentaries.) The producer/director, Elaine Epstein, is a South African filmmaker who lives and works in the United States. Epstein picked eight individuals, six of whom were living with HIV and AIDS, including a white couple. A nurse who manages a home-based care service for AIDS patients and a young research scientist and physician round out the cast of main characters. Achmat also appeared for large parts of the film. On camera, he explains what it is like to be sick, rejects government arguments about the financial costs of treatment, and, in a connection to the larger movement, is shown addressing crowds at marches and rallies. The film effectively contrasts TAC's actions with the negligence of the government. TAC is shown as working within the law, practical, and winning its struggle against Mbeki and the state.

Conclusion

From the media-savvy viewpoint of 2018, TAC's media strategies may appear self-evident for any social movement in South Africa; by today's standards, its use of the internet seems tentative and quaint. As Geffen recalled in 2012, its media strategies at the time were uncommon and groundbreaking.[83] The pressure on pharmaceutical corporations and that industry's decision to withdraw its lawsuit against the South African government over patent legislation convinced Geffen that such global activism would not have been possible without the internet and social media.

In this chapter, I propose that TAC represented a break with how social movements in South Africa up to that point had related to mainstream media. I also suggest that TAC constructed a media template for social movements that came after it, such as the Social Justice Coalition, Equal Education, and Reclaim the City. Other, more recent movements, I further posit, can learn from TAC's use of media. The EFF, founded in 2013 in the wake of a massacre of thirty-four mine workers by South African police while the government and politically connected capitalists just looked on, is one such group. The EFF presents itself as a radical parliamentary party whose members wear red berets and overalls and quote the Burkinabe revolutionary Thomas Sankara and the anticolonial theorist and militant Frantz Fanon. Their disruption of Parliament to delegitimize former president Jacob Zuma probably played a decisive role in his eventual ouster. The #RhodesMustFall and #FeesMustFall student movements of 2015 and 2016 on South African campuses, which came to dominate local media coverage of politics, also point to the future of how social movements will exploit media and media technologies, especially social media.[84] I return to these student movements a bit later.

There is obviously a vast difference between how TAC used the internet and how today's movements use social media. In the early 2000s, social media was not the horizontal, user-content-generated sharing machine that it has become. At that time, few South Africans effectively used the internet, but by 2018, millions of working-class South Africans do capably use the internet.

TAC made powerful use of the internet—but as it was then employed—as a publishing mechanism. TACs heyday was in the era of one-directional information—from movements, governments, and the media (i.e., professional communicators) to the public. However, TAC pushed the boundaries of the internet and combined that tactic with a clear strategy for how to utilize mainstream media in its favor. In the early 2000s, TAC emailed its newsletters, but by the second half of the decade, it was using bulk SMS messaging to reach its supporters—most of whom at that stage did not have access to computers or smartphones. By the time Twitter and Facebook took off—and the government by then was implementing a treatment program—many of TAC's core activists had moved on to policing, education, and housing, among other issues. These movements made ample use of the new social media.

One of TAC's strengths and innovations was to use a wide range of media according to the type of audience it aimed to reach: the internet to inform journalists and connect with international activists (elite audiences), movement building on the ground with in-person literacy education supported by pamphlets and booklets, and T-shirts and posters for campaigning and building mass support.

The newer social movements and political organizations that came after TAC learned from TAC but also improved on its model and invented something new. In closing it is worth briefly revisiting what the students pulled off in 2015–2016.

On October 21, 2015, groups of students organized under social media hashtags, especially on Twitter—#FeesMustFall and #NationalShutdown—shut down classes on at least fourteen campuses countrywide in South Africa. (It could be argued that prominent TAC slogans like Treat the People, March for Our Lives, and Fire Manto were basically hashtags before hashtags.) The student movement's hashtags articulated actual events: #RhodesMustFall amplified on an already existing movement, mostly by black students, at the University of Cape Town against a colonial-era statue of Cecil John Rhodes, a notorious white mining magnate from the late nineteenth century in Southern Africa. The movement soon became about more than a statue as students began demanding more black faculty (a small minority of professors at South Africa's top universities are black), that curriculums be updated, and that universities cease their practice of outsourcing services like cleaning, catering, and campus security to private companies and instead empower permanent service staff.

Some of the students in Cape Town marched to Parliament and demanded that the minister of higher education, who is politically responsible for funding public universities, meet with them. The minister refused. The minister of finance, however, was scheduled to give his annual budget speech. Imitating the

American social movement #BlackLivesMatter, the students marched inside the parliamentary grounds with their hands up. Police fired tear gas and stun grenades at them. A number of students were arrested. It soon became clear that the students and those following the protests, mostly on social media, wanted to make older media like television news and print journalism irrelevant to the outcome of their protests. In fact, local television news stations had no choice but to turn their cameras on the protesters and largely cover the protests with little commentary. As media scholar Herman Wasserman and I have argued elsewhere, "television coverage [of the student protests] was of lesser importance, because the revolution wasn't being televised, it was being live-tweeted. Television news only mattered if it placed a camera where the protests were and left it at that."[85] The same could be said for print media. Newspapers and even mainstream online news organizations struggled to keep up with what was happening. Some online news reports consisted exclusively of cut-and-pasted Twitter updates. Most people following the protests, including journalists, were doing so by getting their updates and visuals from Facebook and Twitter.

Social media provided by-the-minute updates on situations as they developed, gave access to students' views and experiences, helped students mobilize (even providing tips on how to deal with tear gas or to ensure their phones were charged), and, crucially, became a platform for alternative narratives to those of the mainstream media: in perhaps the most telling moments, students at the University of Western Cape Town tweeted, "We at #UWCFeesMustFall are in desperate [need] of airtime [for their cell phones], medical and food supplies."[86] In October 2015, #RhodesMustFall activists tweeted: "Tomorrow is another day. Keep your phones on the charger comrade. We need to lead this narrative. It is a revolutionary mandate."[87]

Notes

1. Steven Friedman and Shauna Mottiar, "A Moral to the Tale: The Treatment Action Campaign and the Politics of HIV/AIDS" (School of Development Studies, University of KwaZulu-Natal, 2004), 1–32.

2. A number of people provided comments and suggestions to improve this chapter: Brad Brockman, Kerry Cullinan, Brett Davidson, Ashwin Desai, Steven Friedman, Nathan Geffen, Doron Isaacs, Zachary Levenson, Mia Malan, Mandisa Mbali, Achal Prabhala, Gavin Silber, and Anso Thom.

3. Michael Specter, "The Denialists," *The New Yorker*, March 12, 2007, http://www.newyorker.com/magazine/2007/03/12/the-denialists.

4. Nathan Geffen, *Debunking Delusions: Inside the Story of the Treatment Action Campaign* (Johannesburg: Jacana, 2010), 48.

5. Mark Schoofs, "Learning from HIV: Summing Up the Lessons from Five Years of HIV Reporting," *Village Voice*, August 16, 2000, http://www.thebody.com/content/art2778.html.

6. Edwin Cameron, *Witness to AIDS* (Cape Town: Tafelberg, 2005); Geffen, *Debunking Delusions*.

7. Mia Malan, "Exposing AIDS: Media's Impact in South Africa," *Georgetown Journal of International Affairs* 7, no. 1 (Winter 2006): 44.

8. Ibid.

9. Mark Heywood, "The Price of Denial," *Development Update* 5, no. 3 (2004): 17, https://sarpn.org/documents/d0001195/4-The_Price_of_Denial-Mark_Heywood.pdf.

10. Amy Roeder, "The Cost of South Africa's Misguided AIDS Policies," *Harvard School of Public Health* (Spring 2009), accessed July 9, 2018, https://www.hsph.harvard.edu/news/magazine/spr09aids/; Celia W. Dugger, "Study Cites Toll of AIDS Policy in South Africa," *New York Times*, November 25, 2008, https://www.nytimes.com/2008/11/26/world/africa/26aids.html. Also see, for example, the overview in Malan, "Exposing AIDS."

11. Specter, "The Denialists."

12. Nicoli Nattrass, "AIDS and the Scientific Governance of Medicine in Postapartheid South Africa," *African Affairs* 107, no. 427 (2008): 159.

13. See Martin McKee and Pascal Diethelm, "How the Growth of Denialism Undermines Public Health," *British Medical Journal* 341 (December 2010): 1309–1311; and Cass Sunstein, "Is the Internet Bad for Democracy," *Boston Review*, June 1, 2001, http://bostonreview.net/forum/cass-sunstein-internet-bad-democracy.

14. There were, of course, exceptions like Health-e, a foreign-funded news agency that covered health news with nuance, including syndicating its stories in mainstream South African media. A small number of newspapers employed health reporters, most notably Tamar Kahn at *Business Day* and Judith Soal at *The Cape Times*. See Kerry Cullinan, "The Media and HIV/AIDS: A Blessing and a Curse," *AIDS Bulletin* 10 (July 2001): 35–39; Gideon De Wet, "Agenda Setting and HIV/AIDS News Sources, Implications for Journalism Education: An Exploratory Study," *Ecquid Novi* 25, no. 1 (2004): 94–114; Institute of Media Analysis, "SA Media's Blind Spot on AIDS," *Media Tenor Quarterly Journal*, no. 2 (2004), https://www.files.ethz.ch/isn/141296/2004-02-23_SA.pdf; and Susan Levine, "Documentary Film and HIV/AIDS: New Directions for Applied Visual Anthropology in Southern Africa," *Visual Anthropology Review* 19 (2003): 1–2.

15. For a discussion of the case, see Raymond Suttner, "The Jacob Zuma Rape Trial: Power and African National Congress (ANC) Masculinities," *Nordic Journal of Feminist and Gender Research* 17, no. 3 (2009): 222–236; Shireen Hassim, "Democracy's Shadows: Sexual Rights and Gender Politics in the Rape Trial of Jacob Zuma," *African Studies* 68, no. 1 (2009): 57–77; and Liz Gunner, "Jacob Zuma, The Social Body and the Unruly Power of Song," *African Affairs* 108, no. 430 (January 2009): 27–48.

16. David Smith, "South African Health Minister Sacked as Jacob Zuma Names First Cabinet," *The Guardian*, May 10, 2009, https://www.theguardian.com/world/2009/may/10/jacob-zuma-barbara-hogan; "In Motsoaledi We Trust: Civil Society," eNCA.com, May 24, 2014, https://www.enca.com/motsoaledi-we-trust-civil-society.

17. GroundUp is online at https://www.groundup.org.za. Some COSATU-affiliated trade unions produced media, including online media, but not with the same regularity or the same commitment of resources as GroundUp.

18. Craig Timberg, "South Africa's Mbeki at Once President and Pundit," *Washington Post*, December 24, 2004, A8; David Beresford, "We Are Thabo Mbeki," *The Guardian*, March 21, 2007, https://www.theguardian.com/commentisfree/2007/mar/21/wearethabombeki; Michael Hamlyn, "Zuma Gives Up Mbeki's Weekly Online Column," *Mail and Guardian*, January 18, 2008, https://mg.co.za/article/2008-01-18-zuma-gives-up-mbekis-weekly-online-column.

19. Hamlyn, "Zuma Gives Up."
20. Thabo Mbeki, "Welcome to *ANC Today*," *ANC Today* 1, no. 1 January 26–February 1, 2001), http://www.anc.org.za/docs/anctoday/2001/at01.htm.
21. Ibid.
22. As South African economist Nicoli Nattrass (2008) has pointed out, "AIDS denialists prefer to call themselves 'dissidents.' However, as they simply deny the existing scientific evidence, they are more appropriately termed 'denialists.'"
23. Interview with Thabo Mbeki, *Carte Blanche*, M-Net, April 16, 2000.
24. Marjolein Harvey, "How Can a Virus Cause a Syndrome? Asks Mbeki," iClinic, September 21, 2000, https://archive.li/o9qDo.
25. Schoofs, "Learning from HIV."
26. Martin Wienel, "Expertise and Inauthentic Scientific Controversies: What You Need to Know to Judge the Authenticity of Policy-Relevant Scientific Controversies," in *Between Scientists and Citizens: Proceedings of a Conference at Iowa State University, June 1–2, 2012*, edited by Jean Goodwin (Ames, Iowa: Great Plains Society for the Study of Argumentation, 2012), 432.
27. Allister Sparks, *Beyond the Miracle: Inside the New South Africa* (Illinois: University of Chicago Press, 2009), 287, 289.
28. The history of TAC's founding draws heavily on Geffen's book-length account of his involvement with TAC, *Debunking Delusions*, especially chap. 3.
29. Geffen, *Debunking Delusions*, 49.
30. Pfizer also made similar agreements with other sub-Saharan African national governments.
31. Geffen, *Debunking Delusions*, 48.
32. Ibid., 56.
33. Ibid., 55.
34. On the CNN effect, see, for example, Piers Robinson, "The CNN Effect: Can the News Media Drive Foreign Policy?" *Review of International Studies* 25, no. 2 (April 1999): 301–309; and Monroe Price, "The End of Television and Foreign Policy," *Annals of the American Academy of Political and Social Science* 625, no. 1 (2009): 196–204.
35. Biko wrote a column for the *Daily Dispatch*, among others. Those columns became the basis for his later book of essays, *I Write What I Like: Selected Writings* (Illinois: Chicago University Press, 2002).
36. Geffen, *Debunking Delusions*, 189.
37. Treatment Action Campaign, *Fighting for Our Lives: The History of the Treatment Action Campaign 1998–2010* (Cape Town: Treatment Action Campaign, 2010), 109.
38. Alan Findlay, "Shaping the Conflict: Factors Influencing the Representation of Conflict Around HIV/AIDS Policy in the South African Press," *Communicare* 23, no. 2 (2004): 76.
39. Geffen, *Debunking Delusions*, 62. Mandela's support wasn't unequivocal, however. Geffen relates an incident from February 2003 when TAC planned a march to coincide with the opening of Parliament. The group produced a massive poster with "the salient graphic feature" a photo of Mandela in his HIV POSITIVE T-shirt. Though TAC had verbal permission from Mandela's foundation to use the image, the latter seemingly came under pressure from the ANC, and it discouraged TAC from using the poster. TAC complied.
40. Geffen, *Debunking Delusions*, 52.
41. Rebecca Hodes, "'It's a Beautiful Struggle': *Siyayinqoba / Beat It!* and the HIV/AIDS Treatment Struggle on South African Television," in *Popular Politics and Resistance Movements in South Africa*, edited by William Beinart and Marcelle Dawson (Johannesburg: Wits University Press, 2010): 161–188. See also Rebecca Hodes, *Broadcasting the Pandemic: A History of HIV/AIDS on South African Television* (Cape Town: HSRC Press, 2014).
42. Ibid.

43. Thanks to Anso Thom for this insight.
44. Nathan Geffen, "Information Technology and the Treatment Action Campaign: Successes and Pitfalls," GroundUp, July 18, 2012, https://www.groundup.org.za/article/information-technology-and-treatment-action-campaign-successes-and-pitfalls/.
45. Ibid.
46. McKee and Diethelm, "How the Growth of Denialism Undermines Public Health," 1.
47. Geffen, *Debunking Delusions*, 77.
48. Zackie Achmat, "HIV/AIDS and Human Rights: A New South African Struggle" (John Foster Lecture, Barcelona, October 11, 2004).
49. Samantha Power, "The AIDS Rebel," *The New Yorker*, May 19, 2003, 54–67.
50. Zackie Achmat, Verbatim transcript of address by Zackie Achmat, Chairperson of TAC to the AIDS in Context International Conference on HIV/AIDS, University of the Witswatersrand, Johannesburg, April 7, 2001.
51. Mandisa Mbali, "AIDS Discourses and the South African State: Government Denialism and Post-Apartheid AIDS Policy Making," *Transformation* 54 (2004): 104–122.
52. Malegapuru Makgoba, "Science, the Media and Politics: HIV/AIDS in South Africa" (keynote address, 119th Nobel Symposium, Stockholm, June 7–9, 2001).
53. Mike Cohen, "S. Africa's A.N.C. Criticizes Carter," Associated Press, March 10, 2002, https://www.ourmidland.com/news/article/S-Africa-s-A-N-C-Criticizes-Carter-7094008.php.
54. Thabo Mbeki, "Address at the Inaugural ZK Matthews Inaugural Lecture" (University of Fort Hare, Alice, South Africa, October 12, 2001).
55. Mbali, "AIDS Discourses," 110.
56. Krista Johnson, "The Politics of AIDS Policy Development and Implementation in Post-Apartheid South Africa," *Africa Today* 51, no. 2 (2004): 112.
57. Geffen, *Debunking Delusions*, 52.
58. Ibid., 53
59. "Adapting i-Base Materials," i-base.info.com, March 24, 2016, http://i-base.info/adapting-materials/.
60. Ibid.
61. Geffen, "Information Technology."
62. Ibid.
63. Ibid.
64. Raymond A. Smith and Kevin E. Gruenfeld, "Symbols," TheBody, 1998, http://www.thebody.com/content/art14040.html.
65. See Steven Robins, "Slow Activism in Fast Times: Reflections on the Politics of Media Spectacles after Apartheid," *Journal of Southern African Studies* 40, no. 1 (2014): 91–110.
66. See Alex de Waal, *AIDS and Power: Why There Is No Political Crisis—Yet* (New York: Zed Books, 2006), 34–39.
67. Geffen, *Debunking Denialism*, 66.
68. Power, "The AIDS Rebel," 66.
69. Ibid.
70. Geffen, *Debunking Denialism*, 68.
71. De Waal, *AIDS and Power*, 36.
72. Sean Jacobs and Krista Johnson, "Media, Social Movements and the State: Competing Images of HIV/AIDS in South Africa," *African Studies Quarterly* 9, no. 4 (Fall 2007): 143.
73. Steven Robins, "'Long Live Zackie, Long Live': AIDS Activism, Science and Citizenship after Apartheid," *Journal of Southern African Studies* 30, no. 3 (2004): 651–672.
74. Herman Wasserman, "Is a New Worldwide Web Possible? An Explorative Comparison of the Use of ICTs by Two South African Social Movements," *African Studies* 50, no. 1

(2007): 109–131. ICTs refer to information and communication technologies such as email and the internet.

75. Heywood, "The Price of Denial," 98.

76. Mark Heywood, "Memoirs of an Activist: 'The Real Heroes of the HIV Struggle Are Still Unknown,'" Bhekisisa, June 8, 2017, https://bhekisisa.org/article/2017-06-08-00-memoirs-of-an-activist-the-real-heroes-of-the-hiv-struggle-are-still-unknown. See also Mark Heywood, *Get Up! Stand Up! Personal Journeys towards Social Justice* (Cape Town: Tafelberg, 2017).

77. *Siyayinqoba / Beat It!* home page, accessed July 10, 2018, http://siyayinqoba.co.za.

78. The films in the *Steps for the Future* collection are available at http://stepsforthefuture.co.za/.

79. Peter Dwyer, "South Africa: Dying to Fight," *Review of African Political Economy* 30, no. 98 (2003): 661.

80. Ibid., 661.

81. Ibid., 662.

82. Barnaby Philips, "Mandela Backs SA AIDS Protest," *BBC News*, July 28, 2002, http://news.bbc.co.uk/2/hi/africa/2156588.stm.

83. Geffen, "Information Technology."

84. Tanja Bosch, Herman Wasserman, and Wallace Chuma, "South African Activists' Use of Nanomedia and Digital Media in Democratization Conflicts," *International Journal of Communication* 12 (2018): 2153–2170.

85. Sean Jacobs and Herman Wasserman, "The Day Mainstream Media Became Old in South Africa," *Washington Post*, November 25, 2015, https://www.washingtonpost.com/.../the-day-mainstream-media-became-old-in-south-africa.

86. Ibid.

87. @RhodesMustFall, Twitter, 7:34 p.m., October 21, 2015.

CHAPTER 6

The Second Afrikaner State in Cyberspace

IN 2007 "DE la Rey," a song about an early twentieth-century Afrikaner general, Koos de la Rey, became a surprise "Afrikaner anthem."[1] The song recalled the Anglo-Boer War (1899–1902) when the British, who ruled the Cape and Natal colonies, fought against Afrikaners, the descendants of Dutch settlers to Southern Africa who by the late nineteenth century were organized into two Boer republics. The dispute revolved around a struggle for control over land, mineral resources, and cheap black labor. The Boers (as the Afrikaners were also known) eventually suffered defeat (at least twenty-eight thousand Afrikaners, mainly women and children, died in British concentration camps), but only after General De la Rey had inflicted heavy casualties on the British.[2] The war ended when the two sides signed a peace agreement that amounted to them jointly governing South Africa for their mutual benefit at the expense of the country's black population. The result was the formation of the Union of South Africa in 1910. In the aftermath of hostilities, Afrikaners remembered and commemorated the Anglo-Boer War as a period of suffering and oppression at the hands of the British. A legend developed around the persona of General de la Rey, though after a while he fell out of public consciousness as Afrikaners developed a muscular nationalism. When the National Party won parliamentary elections in 1948 (only white people could vote), Afrikaners took control of the state. Over the next four decades or so, Afrikaner group identity thus shifted from victimhood to an assertive nationalism.

The song "De la Rey," cowritten and performed by Bok van Blerk (born Louis Andreas Pepler)—until then a relatively unknown singer from Pretoria—vividly tells the history of Boer suffering during the Anglo-Boer War. Van Blerk's songs is about "a handful of us against a whole big force" and vaguely predicts that "a nation will rise again." The song includes the catchy refrain: "De la Rey, de la Rey, will you come and lead the Boers?" A music video that accompanied the song's release, with van Blerk in period costume as a bloodied Boer soldier, includes scenes of violence against women and children as well as the wanton destruction of Boer property.

"De la Rey" quickly developed a fan following, forcing Afrikaans radio stations (including the public broadcaster's Radio Sonder Grense) to add it to their playlists. At concerts or festivals where van Blerk appeared, large crowds would rise up as one, wave the flag of apartheid South Africa, and sing along loudly to "De la Rey." Reports of sing-alongs at barbeques, weddings, rugby matches, and other social gatherings abounded. Van Blerk became a star among Afrikaners inside South Africa and also among those in the diaspora in Great Britain, Australia, Canada, the United States, and the Arabian Gulf. Fans of the song posted their own videos on YouTube singing or lip-synching to "De la Rey" or uploaded multiple versions of the music video on video-sharing sites. While the song's lyrics reference the Anglo-Boer War, for some, including its fans, the song is a metaphor for what Afrikaners perceive as their reduced position in postapartheid society: that they are been discriminated against and subject to reverse racism. Others in the community interpret it as an antigovernment uprising. It has also been the subject of some backlash from liberal Afrikaners. For example, journalist and former editor of *Die Vrye Weekblad* (The free weekly paper) Max du Preez (he gained prominence for starting the first openly antigovernment Afrikaans newspaper in the late 1980s) points out: "There's not a word about black people in it. And while the song is in no way racist, it manifests itself—when young people stand there—when they sing about how nasty the British were to the Boer women in the concentration camps, and how general come and lead us, we will fall around you, they're not thinking about the British, they're thinking about black, the enemy is now black."[3] Crucially, the song's popularity coincided with the rise of a new generation of Afrikaner political organizations and activists who presented themselves as civil rights groups and cultural activists. They began to dominate what passed for an Afrikaans public sphere. These included the so-called civil rights movements Solidariteit and AfriForum and media-savvy figures such as Dan Roodt of the Pro-Afrikaanse Aksie Groep (PRAAG; Pro-Afrikaans Action Group) as well as the popular singer/actor Steve Hofmeyr. These groups and individuals openly expressed support for the song and encouraged their followers to play or sing it at every occasion. As if on cue, Afrikaans newspapers, television shows, and blogs began debating the song's lyrics and its implied meanings. The Afrikaans literary website LitNet, for example, encouraged its contributors and readers to send in submissions on the song's political and cultural impact. One submission that stands out is from Beert Jacob Mouw, a regular contributor to LitNet, who wrote about his admiration for van

Blerk and then thanked Roodt and Hofmeyr for their efforts to establish "die tweede Afrikanerstaat in die kuberruim"—literally, the second Afrikaner state in cyberspace.[4] I discuss the Anglo-Boer War's impact on postapartheid Afrikaner identities later, but it is important to note that for a long time after 1902, the war had provided an allegory for Afrikaner marginalization. In the first instance, it underpinned the rise of Afrikaner nationalism. Then a century later, from 1999 to 2002, public remembrance of the war spawned some of the important strands of twenty-first-century Afrikaner identity politics, with "De la Rey" acting as a rallying call.

The idea that Afrikaner identity politics was mostly constructed online is, of course, not an entirely novel insight by itself. Thomas Hylland Eriksen, the anthropologist and scholar of globalization and identity politics, in a survey of nationalism and the internet, made explicit reference to Afrikaner identity movements. Eriksen notes: "Nations thrive in cyberspace, and the internet has in the space of only a few years become a key technology for keeping nations (and other abstract communities) together." Specific to South Africa, Eriksen observes that some Afrikaners have "created a virtual nation, or perhaps a nation-in-waiting, on the Internet."[5] In 2003 expatriate South African novelist Christopher Hope, in a reported piece for *The Guardian* on "new Afrikaner politics," concluded that instead of separate development, new Afrikaner social movements and activists promoted "modernity, minority rights [and] self-reliance." To achieve such goals, pointed out Hope, these groups preferred online politics and were "beating their swords into software."[6] This chapter thus attempts to sketch the contours of this second Afrikaner state in cyberspace and to identify its main players as well what it means for mediated politics.

I argue that for much of its history in the twentieth century, white Afrikaner political identity (as a singular political identity) remained largely uniform and stable, its boundaries effectively policed by a small elite in the state, security forces, schools, universities, clergy, and, crucially, the media, which all contributed to the successful suppression of other Afrikaner identities. The end of apartheid disrupted this status quo; the dominant version of Afrikaner identity lost its political power, the whole identity project became more fluid, and ever since, Afrikaner identities have been up for grabs. Who would come to define Afrikaner identities after apartheid and how would they go about it? What implications, if any, would the changing political environment and a revolution in media technology have for Afrikaner identity politics? This chapter suggests that Afrikaner identities, like most other postapartheid identities, are increasingly formed at the intersection of global identity politics and symbiotic relationships between political activists and online media. Emboldened by the internet, Afrikaner civil society groups or media figures tap into and/or exploit global discourses of identity politics, including right-wing victim discourses about white genocide or more acceptable ones around minority rights. Separately, a symbiotic relationship has developed between three sets of factors: the market imperatives and cultural politics of Afrikaans media, the rise of new media outlets—self-published blogs, online magazines, and social media like Twitter and Facebook—and, finally, the agendas of the new brand of Afrikaans political activists.

It may be useful at the outset to clarify terms and definitions. First, I recognize that contemporary Afrikaner identity "is open and dynamic, loosened both from nationalistic dogma and state control,"[7] and, second, that while the racial whiteness of Afrikaners is disputed, "Afrikaner" means someone who is white and Afrikaans speaking.[8] There have been public—mostly media-infused—debates and social movements in South Africa dating back to late-nineteenth-century colonialism about whether colored Afrikaans speakers "should be drawn formally into Afrikaner civic, if not community, life."[9] Some readers may question the wisdom of focusing exclusively on the political actions of white Afrikaans speakers. Nevertheless, as historian Thembisa Waetjen points out, there is a political reality in which "Afrikaner" means someone who is white in South Africa. Most white speakers of Afrikaans as well as both mainstream and social media mean "white" when they talk or write about Afrikaners.[10] And even more decisive, the new South Africa has not done away with national, ethnic, or racial categories inherited from apartheid; instead they've revalorized them. Thus, Afrikaner as an exclusively white identity continues to have a lot of symbolic and political power.

This does not negate the fact that there have been attempts to redefine what is meant by "Afrikaner" beyond narrow racial or ethnic boundaries. For a while in the early 2000s, *Die Burger* (the ideological arm of Afrikaner nationalism under segregation and apartheid; see chapter 4) in Cape Town used the inclusive term "Afrikaanses" to indicate the diversity of Afrikaans speakers, recognizing that the majority of first-language speakers of the language are not white. Similarly, moves to draw closer to colored Afrikaans speakers (e.g., in literature movements), indicated a preference for a language identity rather than a racial identity. However, such ideas gained little traction among the leading Afrikaner identity movements discussed in this chapter or among ordinary Afrikaners; they preferred a race-based identity. Liberal and left-wing critics of *Die Burger* also viewed rhetorical moves like "Afrikaanses" as rank political opportunism aimed at "boosting Afrikaner demographics and political clout" or expanding market share.[11]

Others may question why I have decided to write about particular groups and individuals (Solidariteit, Dan Roodt, and Steve Hofmeyr) as representative of Afrikaner identity politics. Such critics mainly put forward two arguments: first, that popular support of these movements and celebrities has never been tested in an election and, second, that for every group or individual claiming to speak on behalf of Afrikaners there are political currents or campaigns of equal size countering such claims. For example, when Steve Hofmeyr announced in March 2015 that he would consider a career in politics if he received a million votes on a Facebook page created for that purpose ("Miljoen Stemme vir Steve" [One million votes for Steve]), a parody group, "Miljoen Stemme Teen Steve" (One million votes against Steve), managed to drum up as much, if not more, attention. Similarly, Hofmeyr was barred by the very people he claimed to represent from performing at Afrikaans cultural and music festivals over offensive and racist public statements he had made. So this chapter does not argue that Hofmeyr, AfriForum, or the journal *Vrye Afrikaan* (Free Afrikaner) are fully representative of postapartheid Afrikaner politics. I am mindful of Thomas Blaser and Christi van der Westhuizen's caution that in South Africa, "the processes of identitary reinvention and sense-making amongst former ruling social categories are especially analytically challenging as various fractured forms of adaptation emerge."[12] The only claim made here is that these civil society groups, popular figures, and select media are publicly invested in Afrikaner identity politics and have come to dominate what passes for an Afrikaner public sphere. They have also shaped to a large extent what we understand by Afrikaner political action and define what we mean by the Afrikaans public sphere. It does not matter how large their actual protests are—they manage average crowds of three to four hundred people—rather, I am concerned about the impacts they have on the public sphere.

Afrikaner Identity, Colonialism, and Apartheid

Before 1994, securing white privilege was the preserve of the state. In that sense, white privilege was a public function; it was the task of the state and its auxiliary institutions—the courts, the police, armed forces, churches, education, and the media. In all this, the state remained the power center of white supremacy. This was also the case for Afrikaner media politics. Afrikaans media, whether public or private, were central planks in Afrikaner nationalism's political strategy. The origin tale of Afrikaans media parallels that of Afrikaner nationalism, dating back to the early part of the twentieth century. While the National Party held hegemony over political life, the Afrikaans private press, alongside heavily racialized public broadcast media (monopolized by the state), dominated the public sphere. Media company Nasionale Pers, founded in 1915, was at the heart of this strategy with its stable of newspapers: *Die Burger* (1915), *Beeld* (Picture; 1965), and *Rapport* (Report; 1970). Nasionale Pers also dominated the market for magazines with *Die Brandwag* (The sentry; 1910), *Huisgenoot* (House companion; 1916), and *Landbouweekblad* (Agriculture weekly; 1919) as well as book publishing.[13] Nasionale Pers—as its name suggests—was closely allied to the state and the ruling party and editorialized cheerfully about the supposed morality and beneficent logic of segregation and later apartheid.[14] Complementing this arrangement was state radio, especially the SABC's Afrikaans radio service established in 1937 (changed to Radio Sonder Grense—Radio without Borders—after apartheid), and television, since the latter's introduction in 1976. (One small but significant fact is that satellite television broadcaster MultiChoice, as discussed in chapter 4, has its origins in Afrikaans private media under Nasionale Pers.) For linguist Mariana Kriel (channeling Benedict Anderson's ideas on nationalism), these media "provided the technical means for 'representing' the kind of imagined community that is the [Afrikaner] nation."[15] Historian Isabel Hofmeyr captures the logic of this media universe well: "The pages of *Die Brandwag* and *Die Huisgenoot*, for example, carried articles, advertisements, pictures and stories which took every imaginable phenomenon of people's worlds, and then repackaged all these phenomena as 'Afrikaans.' A brief list would include food, architecture, interior decoration, dress, etiquette, health, humor, landscape, monuments, the plastic arts, music, handicrafts, transport, agriculture, nature study and so on. For the readers of these articles, what had previously been furniture became 'Afrikaans' furniture and what had been a house became an 'Afrikaans' house built in an Afrikaanse bouwstijl (an Afrikaans style of architecture)."[16]

In this public sphere, dissidents were decisively and publicly dealt with; they were isolated and presented as a threat to the consensus even if and when they presented mild criticism of the system. Some of those critics, such as writers André Brink and Breyten Breytenbach or musician Johannes Kerkorrel, were treated mostly like useful idiots and their criticisms used as public relations to shoot down other critics. Colored or black Afrikaans cultural figures, among them writers and academics who offered a more radical vision for Afrikaans identity, had even less success in destabilizing Afrikanerness.[17] Their combined best efforts could not disrupt the identity project of the state and its allies in the SABC, the Afrikaans media, the church (principally the Dutch Reformed Church), cultural organizations (such as the Federation of Afrikaner Cultural Associations, or FAK), public schools, the army, or Afrikaans universities, such as Stellenbosch, Pretoria, Potchefstroom, and Rands Afrikaanse University (now University of Johannesburg). Consider this assessment by historian Albert Grundlingh of the late 1980s Voëlvry (outlaw) Afrikaans music movement, of which the aforementioned Kerkorrel was a key leader: "The embryonic but palpable sense of imminent change and the appeal to new Afrikaner cultural and political sensibilities as well as the enthusiastic following it attracted, certainly gave 'Voëlvry' the appearance of a social movement. But the case should not be overstated. It failed to evolve beyond protest music, lacked wider connections and did not inspire their followers to express themselves in unambiguous and meaningful political terms. At best it can be described as a moderate to weak social movement."[18] Though Afrikaner nationalism would face pressures (mostly from the Right and an emergent middle class) in the 1980s, Afrikanerdom's unity was more or less maintained by the time, in early 1990, President F. W. de Klerk announced the release of Nelson Mandela, the return of political exiles, and the unbanning of liberation movements.

One of the decisive consequences of the political transition was that white privilege and Afrikaner identity politics was privatized: it would no longer be the property of the state. Since it had to find other sources of power, that left cultural and educational institutions: "If state and military power is unattainable, a certain degree of economic and cultural power can still be secured through control of schools, universities, academies, publishing houses and cultural associations. To put it differently: politics is about power, but power can be gained and maintained through institutions other than the state."[19] Crucially, the Afrikaans language retained its status as the organizing principle of Afrikaner identity. At first glance, Afrikaners seemed publicly resigned to the new South Africa. The most visible affirmation of this sentiment was at the 1995 Rugby World Cup final (its political and media significances are discussed in the introduction of this book), where a sell-out crowd of overwhelmingly white Afrikaner fans applauded Mandela at a match that has since taken on a mythical life of its own. The main talk then was of reconciliation and reinvention. As most foreign (and black South African) journalists would later note, it was very difficult to find any white people who would own up to having supported, worked for, or voted for apartheid at any time between 1948 and 1994.[20]

Most public opinion polls and media reporting from the latter half of the 1990s confirmed that although some white people "got on with it" (work, family, consumption, etc.), many others were less enthusiastic about the terms of the new South Africa and were reluctant to publicly confront their complicity in the country's violent history by their support in elections for apartheid or as beneficiaries of what amounted to affirmative action for white citizens.[21] Political expression also took an openly violent and racist turn, whether through right-wing armed attacks on government installations, physical abuse of black workers by employers, or random attacks or murders of black people.

The TRC is cited ex post facto by white South Africans as crucial to their embrace of the new South Africa. Yet while the commission was holding public hearings around the country and dominating media coverage on the nightly news or on the front pages of newspapers, it was met with hysterical, reactionary responses or nonchalance by many white people (see chapter 1). Most analysts of South Africa's political transition were so enamored by the success of the TRC's media campaigns that they missed its mostly negative reception among the white population, especially Afrikaners: "Most say that they did nothing wrong, they just lived their lives as good law-abiding citizens. They never tortured or killed anybody. That they were beneficiaries of a system—kept in place with the help of those who committed the human-rights violations, at the expense of nonwhites is rarely acknowledged."[22] Afrikaans media, in particular *Die Burger*, referred derisively to the TRC as the "lieg-en-bieg-kommissie" (lying and crying commission). In 1997, when a group of Naspers journalists submitted a statement to the TRC's media hearing publicly acknowledging their complicity and regret about the company's support for apartheid, the company, which officially refused to appear before the TRC, severely criticized its own reporters for airing out the company's apartheid history.[23]

One of the biggest media occasions of the late 1990s in South Africa was the publication of *Country of My Skull* (1998) by celebrated Afrikaans poet Antjie Krog. The book recounts Krog's work as a radio journalist reporting on the TRC for the SABC. It contains long passages of reporting from the commission, including transcripts of victim testimonies and amnesty applications. What stands out the most is Krog's attempt to make sense of and peace with the complicity of Afrikaners in apartheid. The book is dedicated to "every victim who had an Afrikaans surname on her lips." Krog is moved to ask, "Was Apartheid the product of some horrific shortcoming in Afrikaner culture? Could one find the key to this in Afrikaner songs and literature, in beer and braaivleis [barbeque]? How do I live with the fact that all the words used to humiliate, all the orders given to kill, belonged to the language of my heart?"[24] *Country of My Skull* became a standard text for what was identified as the "Afrikaner voice" in mainstream media. Outside South Africa, the book was praised as "one of the most remarkable books to come out of South Africa" and "a major, lasting work of non-fiction."[25] In contrast, the book was pilloried in the Afrikaans media and by Afrikaner reviewers. In what became a common retort, journalist Rian Malan referred to *Country of My Skull* as "a guilt-stricken orgy of self-flagellation."[26] Critics objected to Krog's politics (she has self-identified as an ANC supporter, as a liberal, and as a dissident Afrikaans poet during apartheid, all at once), or they thought it suspicious that the book was so well received outside South Africa. The latter reaction was a common refrain of apartheid's supporters and apologists. Dating back to apartheid, most Afrikaner nationalists were wary of foreign opinion, which they felt did not understand fully the "special conditions" of governing South Africa that apparently necessitated black oppression. The truth was that many Afrikaners rejected the TRC.

No apartheid government ministers or senior state security officials appeared before the TRC. In 1996 former president P. W. Botha (the country's leader from 1978 to 1989), referred to the TRC as a "fierce and unforgiving assault" on Afrikaners[27] and refused to testify at one of its hearings, while De Klerk, near the end of the TRC process, only made a general apology for apartheid to the TRC and denied any culpability on the part of the National Party for any human rights abuses committed between 1948 and 1994. De Klerk also threatened a court order to block the final report of the commission unless it removed a reference that he knew about the bombing of the offices of opposition movements in Johannesburg in the 1980s.[28]

A few high-profile cases of the apartheid government's death squads brought before the TRC gave the impression of a wider reckoning, but very few white operatives of the apartheid state came to the TRC. When they did appear, security police claimed they were merely following orders. Most applicants for amnesty to the TRC were black combatants or deserters from the liberation movements or government informers and policemen: "Of the 256 members of the apartheid era security forces that applied for amnesty . . . only 31 had served in the SADF [the apartheid South African Defense Force]. In contrast, there were close to 1,000 applications for amnesty from members of the various armed structures aligned to the ANC."[29]

In general, many white people literally withdrew from the rest of South Africa, hiding behind the high walls of gated complexes and within their own schools and social clubs. This created a kind of internal exile. Others left South Africa. By 2004, an estimated 44,500 white South Africans had left the country, more than double those who left in 1996.[30] By 2009, Afrikaner rights groups claimed that "one million whites" had left South Africa since 1995.[31] Large communities of expatriate whites who identified as "ex-South Africans" sprang up outside major European cities and in other parts of the world.[32]

Though the National Party continued to dominate what passed for white politics in the first two democratic elections, Afrikaner political representation was fragmenting. Small numbers of National Party voters defected to the Freedom Front, then led by Constand Viljoen, an apartheid army general who in 1993 had briefly threatened to derail constitutional negotiations when his separatist demands for a whites-only *volkstaat* (nation-state) was rejected by the ANC. (Viljoen eventually participated in the 1994 elections.) But it was the National Party's decision to leave Mandela's Government of National Unity in 1996 that precipitated the party's final demise.

First, the National Party was swallowed up by the ANC and then, more significantly, by the DA, the latter tracing its origins to white, English-speaking liberalism. In 1999, running on a campaign of "Fight Back" (popularly derided as "fight black"), the DA won 9.6 percent of the national vote, mostly among white citizens. Though the votes of a plurality of colored people added to the DA's improved showing (from a base of 1.7 percent as the Democratic Party in 1994), it was the DA's capture of white, especially Afrikaner, votes that largely contributed to the party's surge and, over time, established the DA as the custodian of white political interests. For some, this shift of Afrikaner voters to the DA appeared out of place given the supposed hostility between white English and Afrikaans speakers dating back to the Anglo-Boer War. Nevertheless, most adult Afrikaners, when they voted, effectively entrusted their political representation to a largely white English leadership. Over time, the DA would increase its share of the national vote to become the second largest electoral party in South Africa.[33]

If the end of the 1990s heralded the death of the National Party, it also ushered in three distinct but related processes that had far-reaching effects for the future direction of Afrikaner politics: (1) the era of President Thabo Mbeki's rule (1999–2007), which marked a refocus on racialized inequalities in South Africa away from Mandela's emphasis on rainbow and reconciliatory politics; (2) transformations to the Afrikaans media sphere, a crucial development explored in this chapter; and finally, (3) the return of identity politics among white people, which borrowed liberally from social movement politics and, more importantly, Western political currents and movements, especially discourse about the cultural effects of globalization, minority rights, and victimhood. It would be into this breach that new kinds of Afrikaner political operatives and social movements would step.

Mbeki's tenure as South Africa's second democratic president has been defined by his stances on the crisis in Zimbabwe and his disastrous AIDS policy (on the latter, see chapter 5), but equally controversial were his policies to tackle entrenched racial inequalities. In 2004, at the start of his second term, Mbeki suggested that South Africa consisted of "two nations"—the one rich and white, the other poor and black.[34] Most public and private agencies that measured racial inequality in South Africa backed Mbeki's assertion. To fight this inequality, Mbeki proposed BEE as official government policy. The aim was to deliver a black middle class. BEE promoted the transfer of some of the equity in white-owned businesses to a new class of black shareholders, the hiring and promotion of black workers (to make workforces more "representative"), and favoring of black-owned firms for government loans or as suppliers to government departments. The policy succeeded: by 2013 the black middle class had "more than doubled in size over the past eight years, exceeding the number of white people in the same bracket and the amount of money they spend."[35] BEE, however, failed to deal with racial inequality and instead became a slur for corruption and cronyism. Ironically, given criticism of BEE from within the white community, the apartheid regime was infamous for its own affirmative action programs for Afrikaners in state-run corporations and for forms of exclusively white economic empowerment.

Importantly, Mbeki's BEE and affirmative action policies set him on a collision course with the white elite, who compared Mbeki negatively to Mandela, a leader they always associated with reconciliation. This white enmity toward Mbeki actually came as a surprise to many observers, given that Mbeki impressed white elites in the late 1980s and early 1990s and that his public statements promoted an inclusive South African identity. Mbeki was also viewed, because of his neoliberal economic views, as a safe option to replace Mandela when the latter retired.[36] In the Afrikaans press, Mbeki became the focus of opposition to what was perceived as a state-led campaign to marginalize Afrikaners economically and politically.

The second area of impact on Afrikaner politics involved the transformation of the Afrikaans media sphere. Like the rest of South African mainstream media aimed primarily at white people, after 1994 Afrikaans media faced legitimacy crises for their open support for apartheid and the National Party. Afrikaans media thus set about self-consciously to rethink their missions. Among others, *Die Burger* and *Rapport*, which had maintained separate editions for their white and colored readers under apartheid, introduced single editions or regional editions. Some Naspers newspapers appointed prominent black people to their company boards and senior editorial positions or hired more black journalists. For example, leading African and colored political figures associated with the ANC joined the Naspers board. The subscription television service M-Net, a division of Naspers, announced a share scheme for black South Africans. When Naspers sponsored Afrikaans cultural festivals (like the Klein Karoo Nasionale Kunstefees [Little Karoo national arts festival] in the rural Western Cape or Aardklop [Earth beat] Festival in the Northwest Province) to defend and promote the language as well as Afrikaans culture, it deliberately targeted colored Afrikaans-speaking audiences and artists but with mixed success. In most cases, white festival audiences balked at the presence of colored and black Afrikaans speakers and artists at these festivals.[37]

Strikingly, these Afrikaans media, long supporters of a blend of state capitalism, national socialism combined with Afrikaner nationalism, now pledged their allegiance to free-market capitalism.[38] This market emphasis dovetailed neatly with new Afrikaner identity politics, as we will see. Naspers could now combine identity politics with its bottom line: the cultural festivals proved very lucrative for Naspers and predictably became ideal venues where certain versions of Afrikaner identity—that is, those of white Afrikaans speakers—held sway.[39]

Overwhelmingly, the Afrikaans media became a ready forum for airing white grievances and victimhood politics. Barely a decade into democracy, Afrikaner groups were openly registering their opposition to affirmative action, claiming that Afrikaners were being oppressed in public life, their children were discriminated against in government schools, and that white people—especially farmers—were deliberately targeted because of their race by black criminals for robberies or violent attacks. There was very little evidence for any of these grievances, and despite many research organizations and government spokespeople disproving these claims—including that the vast majority of victims of crime were not whites, but black people—the grievances only persisted and served to galvanize political action among Afrikaners.[40]

The beginning of the 2000s also coincided with the proliferation of new media forms in South Africa: satellite television had become more popular, cheaper smartphones had become available, and the internet as a means of political communication was coming into its own. While satellite television services gave viewers access to global news and entertainment channels and thus globalized South African audiences, it also spawned the proliferation of private, homegrown television channels broadcasting exclusively in Afrikaans. It soon became obvious that these channels were primarily geared toward white Afrikaans speakers. Among these was KykNet, which was launched in 1999. KykNet targeted Afrikaner audiences who had migrated from the SABC. It transmitted a mix of talk shows, reality television shows, and dramas that mostly peddled nostalgia for Afrikaner symbols. The channel showcased films from a rich archive of apartheid-era Afrikaans cinema and replayed Springbok rugby test matches—featuring all-white teams—from the period of "isolation" (as some white people referred to the sports and cultural boycott during apartheid).[41]

Over time, KykNet would introduce political news programs of variable quality. These gave additional heft to spokespeople of Afrikaner minority rights and victimhood politics. Hofmeyr and the leaders of PRAAG as well as *Vrye Afrikaan* were regularly featured guests on KykNet. The popularity of van Blerk's "De la Rey" owes much to the channel. As for the internet, by the beginning of the 2000s, self-published blogs, new online newspapers, social movement media, and user-generated video sites grew exponentially in South Africa. Because of their economic position relative to most of black South Africans, this technological transformation favored mostly white people at first.

Finally, the advent of the Mbeki regime coincided with the rise of new social movements in South Africa. The crucial difference between these movements and their first-world counterparts was that they were more concerned with material rights, such as housing, health care, AIDS, and education, than with identity politics. That said, South African social movements borrowed liberally from northern rights discourses and mimicked their protest tactics, including the use of court cases to enforce rights as well as spectacular media events. By the early 2000s, South African politics could effectively be characterized as a showdown between the state and these social movements (see chapter 5). These movements—alienated by the mainstream press—were quite adept at using social media to publicize their political programs and demands. Afrikaner social movements were no different in their tactics.

Afrikaans civil rights movements such as AfriForum, PRAAG, and the Solidariteit trade union rode this wave of social movement politics, combining identity politics with material politics and, in the case of Solidariteit and AfriForum, claiming to represent the interests of poor and lower-middle-class white people "left behind" by the new South Africa. Afrikaner social movements "tended to define their mission, depending on the circumstances, as the defense of multilingualism and minority rights, the defense of Afrikaans, or, unashamedly, the defense of Afrikaner rights and interests."[42]

Two events in the early 2000s deserve closer attention for proving decisive in how Afrikaner identity politics rhetorically reconfigured itself to embrace the position of victims after apartheid. The first, in October 1999, was the centennial commemoration of the Anglo-Boer War and the second, in 2000, was what became popularly known as the Boetman debate. In the first instance, postapartheid Afrikaner civil rights groups argued that the violence of the Anglo-Boer War set in motion a chain reaction among Afrikaners that resulted in apartheid in 1948. In this view, apartheid was entirely the fault of British imperialism by forcing Afrikaners—embarrassed by the defeat in the Anglo-Boer War—to adopt a political strategy that emphasized group survival at the expense of other South Africans. In the second instance, Afrikaner civil rights groups and their acolytes in the media argued that the decision of the National Party's leaders (referred to as "fathers") to negotiate a peace with the ANC in the late 1980s and early 1990s had turned the next generation of Afrikaners ("their children") into victims of democracy. In each instance, the media, especially Afrikaans news media, were critical in ensuring that these claims of victimhood were "naturalized" and became commonplace.

The Centenary of the Anglo-Boer War and the Boetman Debate

At the public launch of the Anglo-Boer War commemorations in October 1999 that set off a three-year period of concerts, talks, conferences, and publications, President Mbeki paid tribute to Boer fighters "who in struggle, . . . asserted the right of all colonized people to independence."[43] Mbeki also highlighted the participation of black people in the war (on both sides). A cousin of the British queen, representing the United Kingdom, acknowledged Great Britain's "shameful" role and "dreadful abuses" during the war.[44] The remarks of these two figures represented breaks in how the war had been publicly commemorated in the past by leaders of black political opposition to apartheid as well as by the British.

For much of the twentieth century, the war was colloquially and in official history known as the "white man's war," so the extent to which official government commemorations sought to highlight the suffering of the black population during the war was quite striking. For one, the October 1999 launch was held at the site of a British concentration camp for black people, and for another, government spokespeople emphasized the war as part of a larger heritage—"a South African heritage." As historian Bill Nasson notes, "For successive decades [under apartheid] . . . white and almost exclusively Afrikaner war commemoration and observance carried not a trace of acknowledgement of the experience and losses of the thousands of black people who were caught up in hostilities in one way or another."⁴⁵ The state, academic historians, and elements in the media were thus clamoring to recast the war as "South African" because it involved large numbers of black fighters. This also fit neatly into the government's rainbow nation discourse in which all South African history is celebrated.

Afrikaner pressure groups—whether far-right Afrikaner political organizations, cultural associations, or within Afrikaans media—disagreed. For them, the war was still chiefly about Afrikaners; it represented a period in their history when they perceived themselves as holding a moral high ground (versus the British who were perpetrators) and when they were admired as heroic for standing up to colonialism. (Even Mbeki, perceived as an enemy by Afrikaners at the time of the commemorations, made that point.) Stripped of political power and ashamed by the revelations of the TRC about apartheid (Afrikaners took the brunt of public blame for apartheid, unlike mining capital and English-speaking whites, who were equally implicated in apartheid), those wishing to recast Afrikaners as victims found something appealing in the Anglo-Boer War. Now they needed to figure out "how to go about transforming the meaning of the war, or how to imagine it anew, in a way which faced the future, not the past."⁴⁶

Editorials in Afrikaans media and political party statements abounded demanding war reparations from Great Britain (for damages to farms or for deaths in concentration camps) as well as a symbolic "war crimes tribunal" for British general Lord Kitchener, who was guilty of "genocide" and "holocaust" for his antiguerrilla tactic of concentration camps. These groups demanded a "full apology" from Great Britain.⁴⁷ At a symbolic level, these demands seemed reasonable but at the same time appeared odd coming from people who had until recently strongly objected to calls that black South Africans be granted reparations for apartheid. That said, the Anglo-Boer War commemorations had a lasting impact on postapartheid Afrikaner politics in that they proved useful to political entrepreneurs desiring to put an interpretative twist on how apartheid was rationalized—that it was all British imperialism's fault: "Those who constructed and enforced apartheid were the sufferers of war; thus, in some fundamental way, it was really Britain and Afrikaner nationalism which was culpable for the excesses of white South Africa after 1948."⁴⁸

For a prominent columnist in *Die Burger*, "the war was used in the 1930s to awaken Afrikaner nationalism, because of the impoverishment of Afrikaners." The inevitable result was "an aggressive and intolerant nationalism that flirted with national socialism, and then tried to guarantee its own existence through a massive social engineering program. This chain of reaction had been set in motion by British imperialism."⁴⁹ Such logic was, of course, very powerful and attractive to people recasting themselves as victims. Not surprisingly, it became a widely held sentiment among Afrikaner intellectuals and social movements. Dutch journalist Fred de Vries, writing a book about Afrikaners, interviewed

Dan Roodt and notes that he made a similar point: "[Roodt] does think apartheid was a mistake. The Afrikaners extended the colonialism that the British instituted and then took responsibility for the whole population, black and white. That was stupid. The dream, according to Roodt, is a nation state. Everything about the old South Africa, except apartheid."[50]

Around the same time, in 2000, Willem de Klerk, the brother of F. W. de Klerk, published a book titled *Afrikaners: Kroes, Kras, Kordaat* (Afrikaners: Abrasive, Crass, Plucky). Willem, a former newspaper editor, had a reputation as a *verligte* (reformist) National Party ideologue under apartheid unlike his brother, who had been more conservative. In the book, Willem called for Afrikaners to publicly accept responsibility for apartheid and proposed a more inclusive Afrikaner identity where people could simultaneously be Afrikaners, Africans, South Africans, and Afrikaans speakers.[51] Willem's thesis was not especially controversial. His arguments were fairly common among liberal Afrikaners and vied for attention with right-wing sentiments on the editorial pages of Afrikaans newspapers. The book was generally reviewed favorably in the mainstream Afrikaans press. However, what happened next had a wider and more lasting impact on Afrikaner identity politics.

Chris Louw, an SABC journalist in his forties who had worked for De Klerk in the 1980s at *Die Transvaler* (a newspaper published by a rival of Naspers but firmly in the National Party camp), wrote an "open letter" to the late De Klerk: "Boetman is die bliksem in" (Little man is blind with anger). *Boetman* is a disparaging Afrikaans term used by older men to address younger (sometimes middle-aged) men. Writing in the tone of an aggrieved junior, Louw accused De Klerk's generation—who, he argued, were too young to fight in the Anglo-Boer War or World War II—of never having to physically fight to defend a system they invented and through which they perfected the art of sending their children to war. De Klerk's generation of Afrikaner leaders had conscripted their "sons," like Louw, to fight a senseless, unwinnable war against black South Africans to maintain apartheid and fight "communism" in neighboring countries. (White conscripts referred to South Africa's occupation of Namibia, its proxy wars in Angola and Mozambique, and the occupation of townships as "the border war" or *grensoorlog*.)

According to Louw, Willem de Klerk's generation had negotiated a peace that assisted people like Willem to make a seamless transition to the new South Africa, while Louw's generation was singled out by the TRC as the most visible guilty party for apartheid. Louw's peers were then expected to implement affirmative action at their own expense—in other words, "work themselves out of a job." Louw ends his letter: "I am very sorry. But I have been cheated enough. Now I fight for what is important to me, inside democracy, sure. But not necessarily with the prescribed and outspoken and the politically correct[,] the idiotic masses."⁵² Louw shared his open letter with friends via email, and it quickly gained traction and was widely debated, including by many journalists. This is probably how the *Beeld* editors identified its viral potential and decided to publish it in their newspaper.

The reaction to the publication of Louw's column in *Beeld* was outsized—beyond what the paper anticipated. A debate continued for months about "Boetman" on the paper's editorial pages. Eventually, other Afrikaans media picked up on the debate, and it was soon transformed from a specific debate about Afrikaner media and intellectuals to a wider debate about the future of Afrikaners. Louw later published a book that became a best seller, and a play was written based on the controversy.⁵³

The commemoration of the Anglo-Boer War and the Boetman debate presented opportunities for ordinary white Afrikaners to talk in public about their own experiences and perceptions of apartheid and the new South Africa. A second and probably more significant feature of both the commemorations and the debate was the extent to which Afrikaans media shaped the two: the Anglo-Boer War commemorations were part of an active campaign by Afrikaans papers and book publishers to invoke nostalgia, and in the Boetman case, *Beeld* orchestrated the deliberation around it.

Cut-and-Paste Global Rights Politics

Having then recast the past as a series of disappointments and wrong turns and subject to the vagaries of history, new Afrikaner identity entrepreneurs scanned global political currents for inspiration. This involved combining a diverse, complementary if sometimes contradictory, set of victim discourses to narrow ends: more obvious right-wing discourses, the appropriation of officially sanctioned (by the UN) discourses about first nations and oppressed minorities, liberal and left-wing arguments about multiculturalism, and finally, cultural critiques of globalization.

Euro-American far-right discourses about white victimhood were quite popular. Some Afrikaner groups approvingly quoted "statistics" compiled by right-wing groups—like the US-based Genocide Watch or Stormfront—making a case for Afrikaner genocide (by which they meant alleged targeted attacks on white farmers). Similarly, they cited "evidence" of "cultural discrimination" (the alleged marginalization of Afrikaans). Both Genocide Watch and Stormfront are thoroughly discredited as racist and are considered hate groups by some governments yet were approvingly cited by groups like PRAAG. In May 2010, Roodt, one of the founders of PRAAG, traveled to Europe where he met with representatives of the right-wing Vlaams Belang (Flemish Interest) and the Svenska Motståndsrörelsen (Swedish Resistance Movement). The idea was to establish, in Roodt's formulation, a "worldwide resistance network that would make the then anti-Apartheid movement look like amateurs." During the visit, Roodt also met with a representative of the human rights division of the Swedish ministry of foreign affairs to discuss crime against white South Africans.[54] This was obviously a diplomatic coup. More recently, in 2014 Roodt established the Front Nasionaal (National Front), which mimics the right-wing National Front in France founded by the Le Pen family. Black people are to Roodt's South Africa what African and Asian, particularly Muslim, immigrants are to the French Right.[55]

Sympathy for Afrikaners as an endangered minority has grown among Dutch (and to some extent Belgian) political and media classes. A number of right-wing Dutch parties pushed for official recognition of Afrikaner claims of marginalization, including passing motions in the Dutch parliament, hosting delegations of Afrikaner civic organizations, and popularizing Afrikaner political claims in Dutch media.[56]

The second strategy of Afrikaner civil society groups was to appropriate liberal and left-wing multicultural arguments and tactics. Throughout the 2000s and beyond, it became not uncommon for Afrikaner leaders and cultural activists to make comparisons with the movement for civil rights in the United States and approvingly quote Martin Luther King, Jr., for example.[57] Locally, despite deep antipathy toward the ANC, the new Afrikaner nationalists claimed to draw inspiration from Mandela and the ANC's political tactics against apartheid. In one instance, "De la Rey" singer van Blerk marshalled Black Consciousness leader Steve Biko's politics to make his point about Afrikaner marginalization: "If we [Afrikaners] are not proud about our history, then people would walk around spineless and that would not be cool. In the past Steve Biko told his fellow countryman that we have to share the country with each other but we still had to hold on (to) our identity. It is part of history."[58] The UN provides political cover for conventions and movements that articulate and promote the causes of indigenous groups and first nations (see the UN's 1992 Minorities Declaration). Sān people from South Africa, for example, have used these discourses to make successful land claims against the postapartheid government in South Africa. Some Afrikaners have also sought to appropriate this language and demand these rights. During the 2001 World Conference Against Racism in Durban, South Africa, the Freedom Front erected an information booth next to groups lobbying for Tibetan political self-determination and native people in North America.[59] AfriForum even features the UN's Minorities Declaration on its website. What is lost on AfriForum and Freedom Front, however, is that the UN, in a report defining "minorities under international law," specifically excluded Afrikaner claims from its declaration: "In most instances, a minority group will be a numerical minority, but in others, a numerical majority may also find itself in a minority-like or non-dominant position, such as blacks under the apartheid regime in South Africa."[60] However, this has not discouraged groups like AfriForum or

Solidariteit. It is perhaps cultural critiques of globalization that have enjoyed more traction among mainstream Afrikaner civil society groups—mostly those that claim to do ideological work. Here I am thinking of movements or organizations such as PRAAG and publications like *Vrye Afrikaan*, which operated between 2004 and 2008.

Shortly after Louw's Boetman open letter first appeared, he was invited to a meeting by Afrikaans academics known as the Groep van 63 (Group of 63). The Groep van 63 traced its history to a journal, *Fragmente*, first published in 1998, which focused on "philosophy and cultural criticism" and a "postmodern critique of modernity."[61] Among the four founding editors were philosopher Johann Rossouw and Danie Goosen, a professor of religion at the University of South Africa (UNISA). In May 2000, *Fragmente* organized a meeting of "Afrikaans-speaking writers, philosophers, economists, political scientists, futurologists, educationists, lawyers, historians and classicists" to promote Afrikaner political and language rights.[62] Sixty-three people attended; all white-skinned and mostly male. Rossouw became the first chairperson of the group.

The Group of 63 never properly took off, though its launch was widely reported in Naspers publications. What may have turned off Afrikaner middle classes to the aims of the Groep van 63 was the latter's ambivalence toward the Far Right.[63] One of the goals of the Far Right was a separate homeland for white Afrikaans speakers, which does not mesh with the reality of most Afrikaners, who are comfortable where they are: "To a casual observer, Afrikaans culture hardly shows signs of dying [in the new South Africa]. Rugby matches, where ruddy Afrikaners eat barbecued boerewors, or farmers' sausages, are wildly popular. Afrikaans-language literature sells well, and TV shows in the language are common. Rock music in Afrikaans is exploding."[64] One of the leading members of the Groep van 63 was Dan Roodt. His own organization, PRAAG, existed mostly online but later also published books (including the book version of Louw's Boetman open letter). It gained some prominence in debates about Afrikaner identity, largely because of Roodt's ability to exploit the media's tendency for sensationalism. Apart from PRAAG and Roodt, the other major proponent of the strategy to employ cultural critiques of globalization was *Die Vrye Afrikaan*.

By 2003, the key people behind the Groep van 63, Rossouw and Goosen, gained control of FAK, which enjoyed status as a mainstream Afrikaner cultural organization. FAK had a large membership and considerable resources. Under apartheid, it had a reputation of being a front for the Broederbond. Goosen was appointed FAK chair and Rossouw was appointed communications and research officer. Rossouw's job was "to communicate the new vision of the FAK to the broader Afrikaans world in a comprehensive and appropriate manner."[65] To that end, Rossouw and Goosen used FAK's resources and networks to launch a new online magazine, *Vrye Afrikaan*.

From the outset, *Die Vrye Afrikaan*'s editors worked to craft a new discourse around Afrikaner identity. They liberally borrowed from French cultural critiques of globalization. In its inaugural edition in 2004, the editors stated the most explicit formulation of this politics. They connected the plight of Afrikaners to that of a worldwide unease with globalization. They decried the universalizing tendencies of globalization, which undermined minority languages and cultures.[66] *Die Vrye Afrikaan* drew explicitly on the ideas of French philosopher Alain de Benoist, considered a hero of European right-wing and fascist groups (though he denies those connections). De Benoist champions "ethnocultures" and is opposed to the idea of the nation-state. *Die Vrye Afrikaan*'s editors favored "communities" and called for "new forms of politics" to counter "party politics and the market economy." While capitalism brought progress to the West, they argued, it also "destroyed [the West's] political and community life and increasingly transformed their societies into the vision of the market." To counter this process, the fifteen largest languages understood or spoken by 85 percent of Africa's people must be considered key to Africa's future and need to be cultivated and promoted. In what included a neat piece of historical revisionism, Afrikaans' experience in South Africa may have lessons for other African languages: "Afrikaners can play a key role here. In the first decade of the twentieth century, the language [Afrikaans] exhibited how much mother tongue education can mean for a community. We also believe that Afrikaners can share knowledge with the rest of Africa about what not to do, since Afrikaans witnessed in the second half of the 20th century what happens to corporatize and tie your community to the state."[67] The editors summed up by imagining a South Africa "where all South Africans are [not] the same, but a nation of communities, where we are also allowed to be different." The "new Afrikaner" (presumably white) would "work together" with the "new African" (implied to be black) in an Africa and on a planet "where people can choose what they believe, what language they want to speak, and what jobs they want to do—because they know who they are." Though this was consistent with *Vrye Afrikaan*'s critique of the "universalizing tendencies of globalization," it also harked back to the language of apartheid with its reference to a "nation of communities" and its claims of religious and language persecution. As for explicitly endorsing a political party, the editors suggested the DA was "already tapping into these emotions and providing a political outlet" for Afrikaner political frustrations. They also supported the Afrikaans trade union Solidariteit, which offered a vehicle for the interests of white workers.[68]

In a public lecture, Goosen identified "three related phenomena" that are "signals of crisis": (1) Afrikaners' experience of alienation stemming from "being left without any meaningful say in their own affairs"; (2) the "centralizing tendencies" of the nation-state as an artifact of colonialism; and (3) the impact of globalization on the Afrikaans "speaking community."[69] For Goosen, Afrikaner alienation resulted in a "collective farewell to public life," including emigration to countries such as Australia: "The real cause behind Afrikaner privatization, and eventual Afrikaner emigration, is the collective feeling of being alienated from social-political realities. Afrikaners are privatizing and emigrating because they can't see a future for themselves as a cultural and historical community in our country."[70] Thus, in Goosen's view, democratic rule was "Afro-nationalism" (which he equated with the ruling ANC). The nation-state was the same as colonialism with its "centralizing tendencies." Goosen went on to equate "Afro-nationalism" to Afrikaner nationalism: "Although [Afrikaner nationalism] was exclusive, certainly, and [Afro-nationalism] inclusive, both strategies share a pathological inability to recognize the diversity of communities. While Afrikaner nationalism excluded diversity from its own ranks, the present nationalism tends to absorb diversity without remainder within an inclusive unity. In short, despite differences, both strategies share a resistance against a meaningful policy or policies of recognition for the diversity of voices, communities etc. I think the real challenge for the future is to do away with both manifestations of enmity against diversity and the colonialist legacy still informing these intolerant practices."[71] He argued further that "globalization does not signal the demise of the nation-state but is in fact a hyper-extension of the nation-state's project of subsuming the local under the universal."[72] The most legitimate response to globalization, according to Goosen, would come "from those Afrikaners who argue in favor of an alternative process of globalization. That is, Afrikaners who accept globalization as inevitable but at the very same time challenge the new liberal power structures directing this process. Alternative globalization is the one that both recognizes the local, original and particular community, and emphasizes their radical interdependence."[73] Finally, in what both reflected and prefigured the direction of postapartheid Afrikaner politics, Goosen suggested that Afrikaners become "radical democrats" by encouraging civil society or social movement politics: "Afrikaners have to recommit themselves to the so-called intermediary spaces between the state and the individual." This meant that in "reinterpreting themselves along post-nationalist lines, Afrikaners may become a radical and democratic community seeking the very rationale for a meaningful existence in its commitment to those places where real political events may still be possible."[74] These spaces would be "communal." In practical terms, Rossouw and Goosen were lobbying for a "politically-negotiated and state-supported representative council."[75] This both reflected the ethnic politics of apartheid and the appeal for a *volkstaat* by right-wing Afrikaner groups.

Die Vrye Afrikaan proved very successful in gaining mainstream legitimacy for its views. The editors were regulars on the opinion pages of South African newspapers, and they even convinced the leftist French monthly magazine *Le Monde Diplomatique* of their bona fides. *Vrye Afrikaan* was appointed as *Le Monde Diplomatique*'s South African partner, which is perhaps how an opinion piece on South African politics by Rossouw, first published in *Le Monde Diplomatique*, later made it onto the opinion pages of the *New York Times* website.[76] In Kriel's estimation, Rossouw and Goosen "recognized the potential of myths and symbols to unite and mobilize a nation (or an ethnic/cultural community as they would call it) and to sustain its identity and cohesion over time. By 2000, these philosophers had come to see their primary task as 'myth-making' or, in Goosen's own words, as the production of 'a viable network of meaning-giving symbols and space-creating myths' that could 'unleash new cultural-political energy and lead Afrikaners out of the cultural-political impasse of the present.'"[77] However, for effective nationalist mobilization to occur, "philosophy [had] be translated into appropriate ideology . . . and . . . ideology [had] to be simplified and concretized."[78] *Die Vrye Afrikaan*, it can be argued, succeeded on the first, but failed the second condition. By 2008, *Die Vrye Afrikaan* had run its course when Rossouw emigrated to Australia (partly to earn a PhD) and Goosen was replaced as the CEO of FAK. The new FAK CEO's rationale for closing down *Die Vrye Afrikaan* was that it was "an elitist political newspaper" and "went over the heads of ordinary people."[79] To reach ordinary Afrikaners required a different, more accessible and legible kind of media politics.

The Celebrity Activist

Three characteristics about the postapartheid public sphere stand out: first, the dominant media position of white people inherited from apartheid—and their social capital—meant that they were well-placed to exploit the opportunities presented by the restructuring and transformation of apartheid media. Second, that same position allowed them to grasp early on the utility of social media forms, especially self-published blogs and user-generated video sites, for rhetorical struggles. In 2010 the (colored) writer and award-winning poet Rustum Kozain summarized this web universe of white right-wing South African blogs and forums thus:

> Some [of these websites] present a dry, professional political image with historical and constitutional analyses, seeking legal precedent and constitutional justification for a white Afrikaans volkstaat. Some factions seek an all-white volkstaat, other factions feel anyone who speaks Afrikaans as mother tongue might be welcome. There are many factions amongst this broad movement of white dissatisfaction with the New South Africa. Some talk about armed resistance, while others caution against such "irresponsible" talk. Some blogs focus on recording violent crime statistics, especially where crime victims are white. However, some blogs have now started to include all violent crime, irrespective of the victim's race, so as to avoid accusations of racism. Some of these blogs are conceptually and mildly racist. But several blogs are filled, post after post, comment after comment, with hysterical, ugly racist vitriol and with a sustained, tangible rage. Much of this can also be found in comment threads on any online newspaper's site.[80]

The largest media company in South Africa has its origins in Afrikaner nationalism. Outside of English, Afrikaans has the only viable book publishing industry in South Africa. The Afrikaans commercial music industry is the country's most lucrative, while Afrikaners, as the second biggest market in South Africa, are a sought-after segment for brands and advertisers.[81]

Finally, there is the symbiotic relationship that develops between entertainment (represented by media) and politics. In what is not unique to South Africa, entertainment figures take on political significance and are frequently turned to for political commentary and seen as political leaders. In time, cultural figures come to enjoy an agenda-setting role within mainstream media. Hollywood actors are the most visible examples of this tendency. American actors George Clooney, Ben Affleck, and Don Cheadle have emerged as leading figures on foreign policy questions in the United States, consulting with presidents and members of Congress. In some instances, entertainment figures have contested and won office. Fascination with these figures' private lives and success as entertainers lend credibility to their claim to political authority.

Afrikaans political culture has historically featured popular entertainment figures in politics. Under apartheid, Eugène Terre'Blanche—a former policeman, amateur poet, and actor—was one such figure. He founded the neo-Nazi AWB, and one of Terre'Blanche and the AWB's first acts was to literally tar and feather an academic who had called for the repeal of a public holiday associated with Afrikaner nationalist mythology.[82] Consistent with celebrity culture, Terre'Blanche's private life was also the subject of much speculation and rumor. The Voëlvry movement (discussed earlier) also produced Afrikaner music celebrities. Unlike Terre'Blanche, however, those involved in Voëlvry never aimed to establish a political movement, and their political program was quite vague. But both Terre'Blanche and Voëlvry operated during a period when Afrikaner identity easily dealt with such political challenges.

Postapartheid, a number of Afrikaner entertainment figures have emerged with claims to be *volksleiers* (national leaders). Though these figures usually act alone, they share some links with social movements or so-called civil rights organizations such as Solidariteit, AfriForum, or PRAAG and often feature at the latter groups' public events. More than that, they share a preference for media-based activism.

Sunette Bridges is a singer-activist whose fame partly derives from being the daughter of Bles Bridges, a popular singer who dominated Afrikaans music charts in the 1980s. Though Bles Bridges performed during the most violent period of apartheid, he never really wrote or performed political music.[83] In fact, the Voëlvry movement was partly a reaction against the kind of musical expression represented by Bles Bridges. In contrast, Sunette Bridges courts political notoriety and is known more for her activism than her singing. At one point on her website, she described herself thus: "I am a 45-year-old Mother of 5, Afrikaner,

Artist, Writer and often described as a Human Rights Activist. I see myself rather as a concerned citizen of the once prosperous country called South Africa."[84] Most of her campaigns focus on the claim that there was a white genocide in South Africa, that white South Africans are deliberately targeted by criminals, and that the South African government and police are aiding and abetting violent crime against white citizens.

Bridges also favors media-spectacle protests. She played one of the three most prominent roles in the Red October campaign in 2013, along with Steve Hofmeyr and Dan Roodt. Red October, which deliberately trolled the South African Communist Party, accused the South African government of failing the white population. On October 10, 2013, supporters of the Red October campaign gathered in a number of cities across South Africa as well as in the diaspora (in front of the South African High Commission in London) to release red balloons. The protest also had a strong online component. Bridges later claimed Red October protests "trended worldwide," though her detractors point out that most of the tweets were opposed to Red October.[85]

Reactions to Bridges are generally negative in mainstream Afrikaans media; her speeches and appearances have found more traction online.[86] Bridges was investigated by the South African Human Rights Commission after a complaint was brought against her for racist postings by her fans and followers on her Facebook page. She was forced by the country's equality court to "regularly monitor her Facebook pages and remove any content that amounts to hate speech, harassment, or the inciting of violence."[87] In April 2015, Bridges chained herself to a monument of former Boer leader Paul Kruger to protest plans to remove it.

Unlike Bridges, van Blerk, who cowrote "De la Rey" with two seasoned record producers and popularized it in his performances, was more ambivalent about his position as a leader (the Sunday paper *Rapport* referred to him as a *volksleier*) and about the song's various appropriations. Van Blerk vacillated between publicly rebuking fans who wanted to make connections between "De la Rey" and nostalgia for apartheid (he removed an old South African flag from his guitar when a fan attempted to attach it while he was on stage, telling his audience about the need to "move on"). At the same time, van Blerk agreed to meet leaders of the Boeremag (Boer militia), a paramilitary group who planned terrorist attacks against the South African government, and said he would be willing to play for the Boeremag as long as they paid him.[88]

More successful than either Sunette Bridges or Bok van Blerk at exploiting the space between celebrity, activism, and the media is the singer Steve Hofmeyr, who has on occasion been described as "the most famous and visible Afrikaner activist."[89] Born in part of Pretoria now called Tswhane in 1964, Hofmeyr is the grandson of the leader of the Ossewa Brandwag (in English: Wagon sentinel). During World War II, the Brandwag were followers of Adolph Hitler's Nazi

Party, and Steve Hofmeyr senior acted as leader of the Brandwag's stormtroopers, which were a copy of the Nazis. Steve Hofmeyr has proudly paraded this family connection and wrote in a 2005 autobiography of his admiration for his grandfather.[90] After doing his national service in the early 1980s (all white men were conscripted from the mid-1970s), Hofmeyr became a popular television actor by the end of the decade. He then parlayed that fame into a career as a popular singer. Throughout the 1990s and 2000s, Hofmeyr remained one of the top-selling artists in South Africa, earning a South African Music Award (the South African Grammys) a number of times. In 2004 Hofmeyr was included at No. 32 in a poll of "Great South Africans."[91]

For much of the first decade of democratic rule, Hofmeyr was apolitical. When he made headlines, it was mostly over his complicated personal life. In the mid-2000s, Hofmeyr started a blog, Steve se Spoeg Blog (Steve's spit blog). Over time, he became increasingly vocal about politics. His politicization coincided with the rise to prominence of PRAAG, AfriForum, and Solidariteit. Increasingly, Hofmeyr attended and spoke at public rallies organized by Roodt as well as Solidariteit. Throughout this time, however, Hofmeyr insisted on his nonpartisan stance and ideological independence; he referred to himself as merely a "concerned South African." However, his views clearly dovetailed with that of far-right Afrikaner groups. The local press, especially Afrikaans media, showed a fondness for contacting Hofmeyr for comment, and unsurprisingly, with that media attention and his blog, he was able to promote his brand of Afrikaner politics through a range of media-friendly stunts.

By the time Hofmeyr shut down Steve se Spoeg Blog in 2008—mostly to reprise its contents for his 2010 memoir—*Mense van My Asem* (People of my breath)—he had emerged as one of the leading *volksleiers* online. This may have been why one of his supporters praised him on LitNet for presiding over the struggle to establish "the second Afrikaner state in cyberspace."

Many of Hofmeyr's campaigns revolved around crime. Like AfriForum and Solidariteit (which joined Hofmeyr in his anticrime crusades), he claimed to have empathy for all victims regardless of race, but like Bridges, Solidariteit, and other Afrikaner activists, Hofmeyr only highlighted criminal attacks on white people and consistently held black South Africans responsible for crime. As he wrote to his followers on Facebook, "Do follow my Twitter time-line to see something of the black attitude towards crime. . . . It's quite revealing. It explains why (a) we won't solve violent crime anytime soon and (b) why the majority of these black South Africans really need to keep this kind of government in power."[92] To protest the perceived targeting of white citizens by criminals, in March 2010 Hofmeyr fronted an AfriForum protest at the ANC's main offices in Johannesburg to hand over a list of sixteen hundred names of victims of crime. Separately, Hofmeyr organized a protest of white South Africans at embassies in South Africa's capital city Tswane to protest violent crime and in April 2013 joined Roodt and Bridges's Red October campaign.

Apart from what he perceived as the racial profiling of white people, Hofmeyr objected to what he termed the marginalization of Afrikaans in public life. In addition to his campaigns around language, he promoted campaigns about heritage and historical memory. Most of these campaigns were linked to struggle symbols, which Hofmeyr deemed as affronts to white people. Like Solidariteit and AfriForum, Hofmeyr publicly objected to songs associated with the liberation struggle. He insisted on openly exhibiting apartheid symbols and singing racist colonial songs as retaliation. For example, in March 2011 he composed a song in honor of Terre'Blanche that included the "Kaffir" slur (equal to the N-word in the United States) as a response to what he claimed was the racism of a song sung by ANC members, "Dubul' ibhunu" (Kill the Boer). Later in 2014, Hofmeyr sang the apartheid anthem, "Die Stem" (The call) at an Afrikaans music festival along with forty thousand concertgoers. After the festival organizers announced that he would not be welcome again, Hofmeyr vowed to include "Die Stem" on his *Toeka* album series (on which he featured songs nostalgic of the apartheid-era) to "annoy his critics." At the time, he also announced that he would record the song "Ken jy die land waar die boerevolk woon?" (Do you know the land where the Boer nation lives?), the anthem of the nineteenth-century Boer Transvaal Republic.[93]

Apart from language activism, Hofmeyr worked to recoup the history of apartheid's army conscripts. In *Mense van My Asem*, he wrote about his own experience as a conscript, and in January 2007, he led protests against Freedom Park, South Africa's version of a war memorial. The site, opened in March 2004 in Tshwane, serves as a memorial for soldiers who fought in the struggle for "humanity and freedom" and includes a wall of names. Freedom Park is not far from Klapperkop, another war memorial for soldiers who fought in apartheid wars. Of the two memorials, Freedom Park has more legitimacy and prestige.

A debate soon developed about whose names should be included and whose names omitted at Freedom Park. Mongane Wally Serote, Freedom Park's CEO, argued that soldiers who served in the SADF—the apartheid army—had fought to preserve apartheid and defeat the struggle for liberation and would thus not be honored there. Soon after, "a pressure group led by Afriforum executive Kallie Kriel and Hofmeyr sought to have the names of SADF members killed while fighting for their country included in the roll of honor. The group also objected to the fact that the memorial wall was to include the names of Cuban soldiers who died in Angola fighting the SADF."[94] The group led by Hofmeyr responded to this perceived snub by erecting its own memorial on the access road to the park, inscribed as follows: "For All Those Who Fell heeding the Call of Their Country including those whose names are not on the Freedom Park wall. So We May never Forget the Dearly Fought Freedom of all Ideologies, Credos, and Cultures and their Respective Contributions to our rich South African Heritage."[95]

Hofmeyr's media profile feeds off the Afrikaans media's obsessions with his private life and his shrewd use of online platforms (first his blog and later via Facebook and Twitter) to shape media coverage of his campaigns. He is well aware of his media power. As he responded to the editors of *Beeld* and *Huisgenoot* at one point, "More South Africans watch DSTV (17%) and own computers (18%) then the 6% who reads *Huisgenoot/You*."[96] Hofmeyr has been accused of using his notoriety as an Afrikaner activist to fuel his career and to promote his concerts and records. By 2014, his *Toeka* albums—which include a number of songs deemed objectionable by black South Africans—had combined sales of 350,000.[97] In a Facebook post in January 2015, Hofmeyr compared himself to the journalists and cartoonists at the French satirical magazine *Charlie Hebdo*, which had been attacked after publishing cartoons of Muhammad (Hofmeyr: "I get Charlie Hebdo'ed everyday"), and announced that he would "retire from politics if people support the [art and music] festivals that boycott him." He wrote, "This year I am testing the political waters. If Afrikaners, Boere and whites support the festivals that boycott me, I will know to step out of the debate and to not stand up for our interests. . . . I can't place the safety of my family, my career and our survival on the cultural altar if my work isn't perceived seriously there. . . . Maybe by 2016 I will again just be a normal Afrikaans singer without an opinion. I take YOUR guidance this year. Where do YOU want me to go? This year I will know."[98]

Nevertheless, Hofmeyr remains a controversial figure. While many mainstream and liberal Afrikaners distance themselves from him, in 2007 Hofmeyr was invited along with leaders of AfriForum, PRAAG, and the filmmaker Leon Schuster to a *braai* (barbeque) with then South African president Jacob Zuma.[99] (The meeting was organized as a publicity stunt by the Afrikaans magazine *De Kat*.)[100] The cookout was as much a reflection of Zuma's own political ideology—that is, that South African politics is inherently tribal—but also confirmed Hofmeyr's status as a populist figure. In April 2009, the *Washington Post* reported that Zuma told a gathering of Afrikaner organizations, "Just as I cherish being a Zulu, so should you cherish being Afrikaners. I've always said we are a unique country. We've got a tribe, a white tribe, that is African in every respect." Afrikaner groups like AfriForum saw an ally in Zuma. In the same article, Kallie Kriel, CEO of AfriForum, told the *Washington Post*, "People actually feel that government is not governing or serving us, they're actually governing against us. . . . Jacob Zuma shows more sensitivity to these issues."[101]

Conclusion

Accounts of Afrikaner identity usually end by referencing attempts to overcome narrow identitarian politics. The tendency is to point to figures that transcend the narrow politics of those cited in this chapter (for example, white Afrikaans rappers or writers and thinkers who act as countervailing forces to right-wing, race-based identities). Some note the increasing numbers of black Afrikaans speakers becoming more prominent in popular cultural spaces. Still others point to changes in voting that indicate a move away from elections as a racial and ethnic census. My conclusion is less hopeful. I suggest that old hierarchies and separations are reinforced in new terms ("multiculturalism," "minority rights") and through new technologies that provide a space for such discourse: culture-talk has replaced race talk.[102]

I end by referring to the tactics of the Afrikaner trade union Solidariteit. The union has been variously described as an "influential identity entrepreneur" and lauded for successfully "reinventing" itself organizationally after apartheid. It has its roots in the whites-only Mynwerkersunie (Mine Workers' Union), rebranded as Solidariteit (for the Polish union) in 2001.[103] Like other Afrikaner identity movements, Solidariteit agitates around language and crime (on this it collaborates with Hofmeyr) but "mixes a politics of recognition with class struggle." Solidariteit's main focuses are improving the position of "poor whites" through charity and workplace issues: on the latter, it emphasizes the impacts of affirmative action on lower-middle-class and working-class Afrikaners. Solidariteit does not oppose affirmative action outright but insists that it be "balanced" and "not create new inequalities."[104] The result, argues Jacob Boersema, is that Solidariteit "represents a peculiar exemplar of the new global vernacular of whiteness" that safeguards privileges inherited from the past within the framework of South Africa's new democratic constitution.[105] What is striking, however, is how integral Solidariteit views media, especially the internet, as part of its political strategy: internet-based activism is equated to community politics and held up as the future of Afrikaner politics.

In March 2010, Dirk Hermann, then deputy secretary general of Solidariteit, wrote a post on the union's blog reviewing Solidariteit's "three social media successes" that year.[106] The first was a campaign to force a local bank, FNB, to allow white employees to apply for in-house scholarships meant to assist black staff; the second involved delivering twenty-three thousand protest letters to President Zuma's Cape Town residence; and the third victory they claimed was having forced Julius Malema, an ANC Youth League leader at the time, to delete his accounts from Facebook. The blog post stands out for Hermann's use of metaphors and terminology from social media and marketing textbooks—for example, he equates Solidariteit to an internet "cult brand" and "positive trade mark" and suggests Solidariteit's responsibility to its membership is to assist them in "self actualization."

More importantly, Hermann concludes that these victories point to a "new kind of politics which the full impact has not been discovered yet. Our people think party politics and to vote is the highest form of democracy. That is simply not the case. It's not party politics that forced FNB's hand, but community politics."[107]

In sum, if Afrikaners, in Eriksen's terms, have created a virtual nation—or perhaps a nation-in-waiting—on the internet, then it seems the internet is also providing a new language for that nation.

Notes

1. Michael Wines, "Song Wakens Injured Pride of Afrikaners," *New York Times*, February 27, 2007, https://www.nytimes.com/2007/02/27/world/africa/27safrica.html. "De la Rey" is written by Bok van Blerk, Sean Else, and Johan Vorster. For an analysis of the reaction to "De la Rey," see Andries Bezuidenhout, "From Voëlvry to De la Rey: Popular Music, Afrikaner Nationalism and Lost Irony" (Department of History seminar, University of Stellenbosch, September 5, 2007).

2. "The Escape of De La Rey: Details of Kitchener's Latest Sweeping Movement—179 Boers Captured out of about 1,500," *New York Times*, March 29, 1902, https://www.nytimes.com/1902/03/29/archives/the-escape-of-de-la-rey-details-of-kitcheners-latest-sweeping.html.

3. Max du Preez, quoted in Bezuidenhout, "From Voëlvry to Del la Rey," 3.

4. Beert Jacob Mouw, "Gesoek: een Afrikanerleier vir 'n rewolusie!" LitNet, April 20, 2009, http://argief.litnet.co.za/article.php?news_id=65045.

5. Thomas Hylland Eriksen, "Nationalism and the Internet," *Nations and Nationalism* 13, no. 1 (2007): 1.

6. Christopher Hope, "Great White Hope," *The Guardian*, May 5, 2003, https://www.theguardian.com/world/2003/may/06/southafrica.features11.

7. Thembisa Waetjen, "Between Explanation and Apology: Giliomee and the Problem of the Afrikaner Ethnic Past," *Transformation* 58 (2005): 87–96.

8. Suren Pillay, "The Demands of Recognition and the Ambivalence of Difference: Race, Culture and Afrikanerness in Postapartheid South Africa," in *Limits to Liberation after Apartheid: Citizenship, Governance and Culture*, edited by Steven Robins, 57–73 (London: James Currey, 2005).

9. Ibid., 58.

10. Waetjen, "Between Explanation and Apology," 94.

11. Christi van der Westhuizen, *White Power and the Rise and Fall of the National Party* (Cape Town: Struik, 2008), 324. See also Herman Wasserman, "Learning a New Language: Culture, Ideology and Economics in Afrikaans Media after Apartheid," *International Journal of Cultural Studies* 12, no. 1 (2009): 61–80.

12. Thomas Blaser and Christi van der Westhuizen, "Introduction: The Paradox of Post-Apartheid 'Afrikaner' Identity: Deployments of Ethnicity and Neo-Liberalism," *African Studies* 71, no. 3 (2012): 382.

13. *Die Brandwag* and *Huisgenoot* were tabloid magazines in the tradition of *People* magazine. *Huisgenoot* still publishes, as does *Landbouweekblad*, which, as its name suggests, is a weekly aimed at farmers—white farmers in particular.

14. Naspers is the overall holding company. Media24, under which newspapers and magazines and news and entertainment websites fall, is its media subsidiary.

15. Mariana Kriel, "A New Generation of Gustav Prellers? The *Fragmente/FAK/Vrye Afrikaan* Movement, 1998–2008," *African Studies* 71, no. 3 (2012): 433. Gustav Preller (1875–1943)

was an Afrikaner journalist and historian who played a key role in constructing myths of Afrikaner nationalism. See also Benedict Anderson, *Imagined Communities: Reflections on the Origin and Spread of Nationalism* (London: Verso, 1983).

16. Isabel Hofmeyr, "Building a Nation from Worlds: Afrikaans Literature, Language and Ethnic Identities 1902–1924," in *The Politics of Race, Class and Nationalism in Twentieth Century South Africa*, eds. Shula Marks and Stanley Trapido (London and New York: Longman, 1987), 111, quoted in Kriel, "A New Generation," 433.

17. These included poets Adam Small, S. V. Peterson, and P. J. Philander; literary scholars Vernon February and Hein Willemse; theologian and political activist Allan Boesak; and university president (and Afrikaans professor) Jakes Gerwel. As late as 2005, Gerwel—who also worked as Mandela's chief of staff and was later recruited to the M-Net board—made a public call for "nonracialism in Afrikaans ideally under black leadership." Kriel, "A New Generation," 429.

18. Albert Grundlingh, "'Rocking the Boat'? The 'Voëlvry' Music Movement in South Africa: Anatomy of Afrikaans Anti-Apartheid Social Protest in the Eighties," *International Journal of African Historical Studies* 37, no. 3 (2004): 498.

19. Mariana Kriel, "Fools, Philologists and Philosophers: Afrikaans and the Politics of Cultural Nationalism," *Politikon* 33, no. 1 (2006): 53.

20. Gunnar Theissen, "Between Acknowledgement and Ignorance: How White South Africans Have Dealt with the Apartheid Past" (Center for the Study of Violence and Reconciliation, Johannesburg, 1996); Fred Khumalo, "Closet Racism Uncovered, Thanks to Social Media," *Rand Daily Mail*, January 23, 2015.

21. Theissen, "Between Acknowledgement and Ignorance."

22. Mads Vestergaard, "Who's Got the Map? The Negotiation of Afrikaner Identities in Post-Apartheid South Africa," *Daedalus* 130, no. 1 (2001): 26.

23. Wasserman, "Learning a New Language." Naspers finally apologized for its behavior in 1997 at the company's centenary celebrations in July 2015.

24. Antjie Krog, *Country of My Skull: Guilt, Sorrow, and the Limits of Forgiveness in the New South Africa* (New York: Broadway Books, 1998), 238.

25. Melanie McFadyean, "More Than Black and White," *The Guardian*, January 15, 2000, https://www.theguardian.com/books/2000/jan/15/politics. Separately, *Country of My Skull* also became the basis for a less successful Hollywood film, *In My Country* (dir. John Boorman, Columbia TriStar, 2004), which featured French actress Juliette Binoche (playing a character resembling Krog) and American actor Samuel L. Jackson (as a fictitious black American journalist with whom the married Krog has an affair).

26. Rian Malan, "A Guilt-Stricken Orgy of Self-Flagellation," *Finance Week* 76, no. 26 (1998): 36.

27. "Apartheid Former Strongman Lambasts S African Witchhunt against Afrikaners," *The Independent*, November 22, 1996, https://www.independent.co.uk/news/world/apartheids-former-strongman-lambasts-s-african-witchhunt-against-afrikaners-1353589.html.

28. "De Klerk Accusations Cut from Report," *BBC News*, October 28, 1998, http://news.bbc.co.uk/2/hi/africa/202367.stm.

29. Gary Baines, "Site of Struggle: The Freedom Park Fracas and the Divisive Legacy of South Africa's Border War/Liberation Struggle," *Social Dynamics* 35, no. 2 (2009): 339.

30. "Why White South Africans Are Coming Home," *BBC News*, May 3, 2014, https://www.bbc.com/news/world-africa-27252307.

31. Karin Brulliard, "White Afrikaners in S. Africa Hear Inclusive Voice from ANC Leader," *Washington Post*, April 14, 2009, http://www.washingtonpost.com/wp-dyn/content/article/2009/04/13/AR2009041302994.html.

32. Martha Evans, "'Uit die Blou' [Out of the blue]: Nostalgia for the 'Old' South Africa on YouTube," *Journal of Global Mass Communication* 3, no. 1–2 (2009): 47–65.

33. The DA won 12.4 percent of the vote in 2004, 16.6 percent in 2009, and, significantly, 20.2 percent in 2014.

34. Thabo Mbeki, "Statement at the Opening of the Debate in the National Assembly, on "Reconciliation and Nation Building," National Assembly, Cape Town, May 29, 1998.

35. Janice Kew, "South Africa's Black Middle Class Doubles, Study Shows," *Bloomberg*, April 29, 2014, https://www.bloomberg.com/news/articles/2013-04-29/south-africa-s-black-middle-class-doubles-stuady-shows.

36. See Mark Gevisser, *A Legacy of Liberation: Thabo Mbeki and the Future of the South African Dream* (New York: Palgrave McMillan, 2009).

37. Compare Temple Hauptfleisch, "The Eventification of Afrikaans Culture—Some Thoughts on the Klein Karoo Nasionale Kunstefees (KKNK)," *South African Theatre Journal* 15, no. 1 (2001): 167–177.

38. See Wasserman, "Learning a New Language."

39. Megan Lewis, "(Un)patriotic Acts of an Imagined Community: The Klein Karoo Nasionale Kunstefees (KKNK) (review)," *Theatre Journal* 60, no. 4 (2008): 654–659; Dror Eyal, "Beer Cans and Boer Wars," *Mail and Guardian*, April 4, 1997, https://mg.co.za/article/1997-04-04-beer-cans-and-boer-wars; Gabriel Bothma, "Sinergie as politiek-ekonomiese strategie by *Die Burger*, 2004–2005," *Ecquid Novi* 27, no. 2 (2006): 137–158.

40. Nechama Brodie, "Are SA Whites Really Being Killed 'Like Flies'? Why Steve Hofmeyr Is Wrong," AfricaCheck, June 24, 2013, https://africacheck.org/reports/are-white-afrikaners-really-being-killed-like-flies/; Julian Rademeyer, "Do 400,000 Whites Live in Squatter Camps in South Africa? The Answer Is No," AfricaCheck, accessed November 22, 2016, https://africacheck.org/reports/do-400-000-whites-live-in-squatter-camps-in-south-africa-the-answer-is-no/; Johan Burger, "Why It Is More Dangerous to Be a Farmer Than a Policeman in SA," AfricaCheck, November 6, 2013, https://africacheck.org/2013/11/06/why-it-is-more-dangerous-to-be-a-farmer-than-a-policeman-in-south-africa/.

41. "Isolation" is how the sports or economic sanctions period was described in apartheid-era publications and in speeches by politicians. Some white commentators still used the term "postapartheid."

42. Kriel, "A New Generation," 427.

43. "South Africa Remembers Boer War," CNN.com, October 9, 1999, http://www.cnn.com/WORLD/africa/9910/09/anglo.boer.war.01/.

44. Ibid.

45. Bill Nasson, "Commemorating the Anglo Boer War in Post-Apartheid South Africa," *Radical History Review* 78 (2000), 150. See also Albert Grundlingh, "Reframing Remembrance: The Politics of the Centenary Commemoration of the South African War of 1899–1902," *Journal of Southern African Studies* 30, no. 2 (2000): 359–375.

46. Nasson, "Commemorating the Anglo Boer War," 155.

47. Ben Wilson, "Queen Offers No Apology over Boer War," *The World Today ABC* (Australia), http://www.abc.net.au/worldtoday/stories/s65787.htm. The charge of genocide against Great Britain is quite common on right-wing Afrikaner websites.

48. *Die Burger*, October 9, 1999, cited in Nasson, "Commemorating the Anglo Boer War," 160.

49. Ibid.

50. Fred de Vries, *Rigtingbedonnerd: Op die Spoor van die Afrikaner Post '94* (Without direction: Following the tracks of the Afrikaner Post '94) (Cape Town: Tafelberg, 2013).

51. See van der Westhuizen, *White Power*. See also Willem de Klerk, *Afrikaners: Kroes, Kras, Kordaat* (Cape Town: Human and Rousseau, 2000).

52. Chris Louw, "Boetman is die bliksem in. 'Baie jammer, ek is genoeg verneuk en boonop gatvol,'" (Little man is blind with anger Very sorry, I have been conned enough and on top of it, I'm fed up), *Beeld*, May 5, 2000, 13.

53. Chris Louw, *Boetman en die swanesang van die verligtes* [Boetman and the swansong of the reformers] (Cape Town: Human and Rossouw, 2001).
54. Dan Roodt, Twitter, May 26, 2010, https://twitter.com/danroodt/status/14778119566.
55. Thorne Godinho, "Front Nasionaal Stokes the Embers of the Afrikaner Right," *Mail and Guardian*, April 25, 2014, http://mg.co.za/article/2014-04-24-front-nasionaal-stokes-the-embers-of-the-afrikaner-right.
56. Tom Devriendt, "The Dutch Disease," *Africa Is a Country* (blog), October 20, 2011, http://africasacountry.com/2011/10/the-dutch-disease/.
57. Christi van der Westhuizen, "The White Angst of Red October," *Thought Leader* (blog), October 14, 2013, http://thoughtleader.co.za/christivanderwesthuizen/2013/10/14/the-white-angst-of-red-october/.
58. "Just a Song?," News24.com, February 7, 2007, http://www.news24.com/SouthAfrica/News/Just-a-song-20070205.
59. Pillay, "Demands of Recognition," 68.
60. Office of United Nations Human Rights, *Minority Rights: International Standards and Guidance for Implementation* (New York and Geneva: United Nations, 2010), 2–3, quoted in Adriaan Basson, "White First. African Second," News24.com, September 26, 2011, http://www.news24.com/Columnists/GuestColumn/White-first-African-second-20110926.
61. Kriel, "A New Generation," 438.
62. Ibid.
63. See van der Westhuizen, *White Power*.
64. Brulliard, "White Afrikaners."
65. Kriel, "A New Generation," 439, quoting from an official FAK history.
66. Johan Rossouw, "'n Ander wereld is moontlik," *Die Vrye Afrikaan*, September 3, 2003, http://blik.co.za/artikel/36.
67. Ibid.
68. Ibid.
69. Danie Goosen, "The Afrikaners: Who Are They? What Is Their Future?" (paper for Harold Wolpe Memorial Seminar, Edge Institute, Johannesburg, April 6, 2005), 3. The venue for Goosen's talk was an odd choice. Harold Wolpe was a Marxist sociologist who was also a prominent ANC activist. He fled South Africa in the early 1960s and spent the rest of his life living in political exile in the United Kingdom. Wolpe was not particularly enamored of identity politics or minority entitlements.
70. Ibid, 2.
71. Ibid, 4
72. Ibid, 4.
73. Ibid, 5.
74. Ibid., 6.
75. Kriel, "A New Generation," 437.
76. Johann Rossouw, "South Africa's Last Chance," *New York Times*, April 13, 2009, http://www.nytimes.com/2009/04/14/opinion/14iht-edrousouw.html. The opinion article is fairly straightforward but includes criticism of the South African government over skilled white emigration to Australia, New Zealand, Canada, and the United States. Rossouw quotes statistics by the South Africa Institute of Race Relations that "more than a million whites have left since 1994, with nearly half of the white men between 20 and 40 years of age now out of the country." Rossouw then makes the claim that "the A.N.C. government has done very little to stem this unaffordable outflow of crucial skills," accusing it of "often signal[ing] that it is not too unhappy about it." His evidence? "The government had to be forced through legal action to allow South Africans outside the country to vote in the coming elections."
77. Kriel, "A New Generation," 436.

78. Ibid., 430–431.
79. Ibid., 441.
80. Rustum Kozain, "Waar die kranse antwoord gee," (Where the cliffs give answer) *Groundwork* (blog), WordPress.com, April 11, 2010, https://groundwork.wordpress.com/2010/04/11/waar-die-kranse-antwoord-gee/.
81. Megan Chronis, "Afrikaans vs English: Comparing SA's Top Markets," The Media Online, July 11, 2012, http://themediaonline.co.za/2012/07/afrikaans-vs-english-comparing-sas-top-markets/; "The Afrikaans Market Is the Second Biggest Market in South Africa," TheMarketingSite.com, September 28, 2016, http://www.themarketingsite.com/news/45026/the-afrikaans-market-is-the-second-biggest-market-in-south-africa.
82. Alan Cowell, "To the Far Right of Apartheid," *New York Times*, November 23, 1986, https://www.nytimes.com/1986/11/23/magazine/to-the-far-right-of-apartheid.html.
83. Despite his so-called nonpolitical stance, Bles Bridges identified with the apartheid government. For example, he titled his 1982 album *Die Onbekende Weermagman* (The unknown army man) in homage to soldiers occupying neighboring Namibia.
84. Sunette Bridges, "Biosketch," Sunettebridges.co.za/bio, accessed April 15, 2015.
85. *Dagbreek* [Daybreak], KykNet, October 23, 2013.
86. Willemien Calitz, "Rhetoric in the Red October Campaign: Exploring the White Victim Identity of Post-Apartheid South Africa" (MA thesis, University of Oregon, 2014).
87. Isaac Mengena, "Equality Courts Orders Sunette Bridges to Ensure She Does Not Promote Hate Speech, Harassment and Violence on her Facebook Page," South African Human Rights Commission, March 31, 2015, http://www.sahrc.org.za/index.php/sahrc-media/news-2/item/317-equality-courts-orders-sunette-bridges-to-ensure-she-does-not-promote-hate-speech-harassment-and-violence-on-her-facebook-page.
88. "De la Rey Rides Again," *Carte Blanche*, M-Net, February 18, 2007.
89. "The Tribe Has Lost Its Rudder," News24.com, July 21, 2012, http://m.news24.com/news24/Archives/City-Press/The-tribe-has-lost-its-rudder-20150429.
90. See Steve Hofmeyr, *Mense van My Asem* [People of my breath] (Pretoria: Zebra Press, 2010); and Phyllis Green, "Steve Hofmeyr gesels oor sy nuwe boek" (Steve Hofmeyr talks about his new book), *Sarie*, March 7, 2014, https://www.netwerk24.com/Sarie/Argief/steve-hofmeyr-gesels-oor-sy-nuwe-boek-20170914.
91. The opinion poll itself was the subject of ridicule and scorn. The SABC, which organized the poll, decided it would not exclude racist personalities. As a result, racist figures such as Hendrik Verwoerd (14) and Eugène Terre'Blanche (24) scored higher than a number of figures associated with the struggle against colonialism and apartheid. Furthermore, the prohibitive cost of telephones (landline and mobile phones) meant white responders dominated among the voters.
92. Steve Hofmeyr, Facebook page, January 15, 2015.
93. "Die Stem on Steve's Album 'By Request,'" Independent Online, August 27, 2014, http://www.iol.co.za/tonight/music/die-stem-on-steves-album-by-request-1741597.
94. Baines, "Site of Struggle," 224.
95. Ibid., 336.
96. *You* is English-language version magazine of *Huisgenoot*.
97. "Die Stem on Steve's Album."
98. "Steve Hofmeyr Will Quit Politics If You Support the Festivals That Boycott Him," Channel24, January 15, 2015, http://www.channel24.co.za/Music/News/Steve-Hofmeyr-will-leave-politics-if-you-support-festivals-that-boycott-him-20150115.
99. "Zuma, Afrikaners Bond at Braai," News24.com, March 27, 2007, https://www.news24.com/SouthAfrica/Politics/Zuma-Afrikaners-bond-at-braai-20070327-2.

100. Less prominently, in July 2015 a marginal group calling for a *volkstaat* named Hofmeyr as a "traditional Boer leader." Though the honor came from a fringe Afrikaner group, it was enough for Hofmeyr's followers to both celebrate and debate the meeting on his Facebook page.

101. Brulliard, "White Afrikaners." See also Pierre de Vos, "A Note on Afrikaners and Tribalism," *Constitutionally Speaking* (blog), May 9, 2012, http://constitutionallyspeaking.co.za/a-note-on-afrikaners-and-tribalism/.

102. On culture talk, see Mahmood Mamdani, *Good Muslim, Bad Muslim: America, The Cold War and the Roots of Terror* (New York: Doubleday). On race talk, see Paul Gilroy, *Small Acts: Thoughts on the Politics of Black Cultures* (London: Serpents Tail, 1994). For example, Solidariteit works closely with the liberal South African Institute of Race Relations (Thomas Blaser, personal communication with the author, July 31, 2015).

103. Jacob Boersema, "Between Recognition and Resentment: An Afrikaner Trade Union's Brand of Post-Nationalism," *African Studies* 71, no. 3 (2012): 410.

104. Ibid, 413.

105. Ibid., 422.

106. Dirk Hermann, "Voetsool veldbrand—lesse vir die volgende veldtog," [Footpath veld fire—lessons for the next campaign] *Solidariteit Blog*, March 30, 2010, https://blog.solidariteit.co.za/voetsool-veldbrand-lesse-vir-die-volgende-veldtog/.

107. Ibid.

Conclusion

SINCE THE END of apartheid, groups of South Africans have periodically enacted xenophobic violence against so-called foreigners—specifically and exclusively black African nationals from elsewhere on the continent who make their homes in South Africa. There have been sporadic attacks on Somali street traders in Cape Town, migrants have been thrown off trains and attacked in the streets of Johannesburg, and immigrants (including South Africans deemed "too dark") have been rounded up and held in cramped, inhumane detention centers to be put on overnight trains out of the country.[1] In general, these migrants are seeking economic opportunities or are refugees in quest of political stability in the Southern African subregion and in the continent's most developed nation. In April 2015, such violence revisited South Africa. The immediate cause of this spate of killings was a speech by Zulu king Goodwill Zwelithini, who demanded that African immigrants and refugees leave South Africa, comparing them to "lice" and "ants."[2] Shortly after his speech, locals attacked migrants in and around Durban in KwaZulu-Natal Province (parts of which Zwelithini claims as his kingdom). The violence became national news once it spread to South Africa's industrial capital, Johannesburg. After a week of violence, at least eight people were dead and five thousand others were left homeless.[3] The media and immigrant rights groups pressured Zwelithini to express regret, occasioning a kind of half apology on his part; Zwelithini blamed a "third force" and demanded that "the media must also be probed for its role in the violence."[4]

For all its claims to pan-Africanism and even as its multinational corporations mine other African countries for profits and markets (see chapter 4), South Africa has an onerous immigration regime and has become notorious for its mass deportations of African migrants.[5] At the height of the violence, the most senior official in the ruling party proposed "tightening immigration laws" and establishing refugee camps as a solution to xenophobic violence. Then the police and army launched Operation Fiela (sweep the dirt), an initiative ostensibly aimed at rooting out prostitution, illegal guns, and drugs. But more than half of those arrested happened to be undocumented migrants.[6]

Like so much else in South Africa, xenophobic violence has been highly mediated. When South Africans were quizzed on the sources of their negative attitudes toward foreigners, most cited public utterances by political leaders and public officials or, more significantly, the images circulating in popular and news media. Zwelithini's xenophobic comments were not that unusual, rather they were consistent with statements by government leaders and political figures with close ties to the ruling party. The head of the country's Congress of Traditional Leaders (CONTRALESA), who doubled as an ANC MP, supported Zwelithini's claim that the Zulu king's hate speech was misunderstood, simply lost in translation. But more damning, as monitoring organization Africa Check reported, were the outbursts of some of then president Jacob Zuma's cabinet ministers. Only weeks before Zwelithini's comments, Nomvula Mokonyane, the minister of water and sanitation, wrote on Facebook that in one Johannesburg township, Somali and Pakistani immigrants were orchestrating "a subtle takeover" of local shops. And in January 2015, one week after South Africans looted Somali-owned shops in Soweto, Lindiwe Zulu, the minister of small business development, said foreign businesses "are here as a courtesy" and should share their "trade secrets" with South Africans. Government policy on migration, when it comes to other Africans, also reflects these attitudes. African visitors complain of harassment, arbitrary arrests, or at regular intervals, mass deportations.[7]

In 2005 a research study by the Southern African Migrancy Program had shown that South African media coverage of foreigners in a wide range of South African media news sources (from television news to broadsheet newspapers to tabloids) was overwhelmingly negative and relied on stereotypes about foreigners as "criminals," "illegals," and "job stealers" despite there being little evidence to substantiate such views.[8] It also turned out that South Africans—regardless of class, race, or education—displayed an extraordinary consistency in their antagonism toward foreigners, particularly those from other countries in Africa and especially those deemed illegal immigrants, despite few South Africans having any or little contact, beyond the incidental, with migrants or refugees.[9]

Xenophobic violence in South Africa is a postcolonial problem that on some levels is not exceptional. Recall Uganda's forced ejection of Asians in the early 1970s, the mass expulsions of emigrants from Nigeria and Ghana in the 1980s, the struggle over *Ivoirité* that broke Côte d'Ivoire apart, or the ways the Kenyan state has mistreated its Somali citizens since independence. The specifics in South Africa may be different, but the ways in which South Africans respond follow a similar pattern. The problems of South Africa since 1994 are rooted in its unsatisfactory political settlement in which the enormity of the troubles it inherited is papered over by feel-good politics, a failure to revisit the political terms on which the "new South Africa" was constructed, and the neoliberal course it has embarked on since. Although it does not justify xenophobic violence, a major contributing cause for it is the desperation of poor black South Africans living in subhuman conditions. Most of these people have consistently voted for the ANC but have witnessed how a small elite enriched themselves, how white citizens have actually benefited from freedom, and how the majority of black citizens still live in poverty with high rates of violence and illness. Instead of revolting, the poor and desperate turn against foreigners.

The country has been more successful in changing the terms of belonging, at least at the level of national discourse. They may not share in its bounty, but there is no more denying that poor, black South Africans are part of the rainbow nation, the most advanced and politically celebrated democracy on the continent. Ironically, after the democratic transition what has bound black and white South Africans together is a kinship based on shared experience of colonialism and apartheid; it does not matter whether you were a perpetrator or a victim, you have a claim to South Africa. Years of political maneuvering and contests over what the nation was and who belonged, through conquest and expansion (wars, the "homelands," use of pass books, and group areas), settled those debates. Now debates over who belongs and can make a claim on rights in the new South Africa, as I argue in this book, are contested in television commercials and on television soap operas. That's where the boundaries of the new South Africa end.[10] At elite levels, migrants may be celebrated for the contributions their countries of origin made to South African freedom, such as hosting exiles, training guerrillas, and incurring attacks by the apartheid army, but these portrayals rarely make their way into popular media. If you come from another African country, you can never become fully South African, even if you become a citizen.

Just as this new sense of belonging is a product of apartheid and the compromises that ended it, so are Zwelithini and the forms of violence he incites. As Daniel Magaziner and I have argued elsewhere, the April 2015 outbreak of xenophobic violence was hardly sui generis.[11] The early 1990s, in which the "miracle transition" took place, were characterized by tremendous violence in KwaZulu-Natal and around Johannesburg. The unrest was fueled in part by the apartheid government's efforts to sustain itself by promoting the idea that South Africa consisted of many nations. Rivalries between the country's traditional or tribal authorities and nationalists affiliated with the ANC were particularly useful in this regard, and as is now well-documented, the apartheid authorities armed ANC opponents, particularly those associated with the Inkatha Freedom Party (IFP), and stood by as violence raged.[12] The TRC reported that "from the start of the negotiations in mid-1990 to the election in April 1994, some 14,000 South Africans died in politically related incidents" and that "between July 1990 and June

1993, an average of 101 people died per month in politically related incidents—a total of 3653 deaths."[13] Zwelithini was the symbolic leader of the Zulu-dominated IFP. The king's brand of ethnic chauvinism appealed especially to poor, young men. Along with KwaZulu's chief minister and IFP leader Mangosuthu Buthelezi and a host of far-right white organizations, Zwelithini repeatedly threatened to sabotage the landmark 1994 election.

One of the ANC's triumphs in the mid-1990s was to co-opt nationalist leaders like Zwelithini and Buthelezi into the new South Africa without requiring them to give up their Zulu chauvinism.[14] Zuma was a key figure in these negotiations.[15] Traditional leaders like Zwelithini were put on the state's payroll as part of CONTRALESA. As a result, in large parts of five of South Africa's nine provinces, traditional authorities like Zwelithini are responsible for local government and control resources such as land. In relying on chiefs, the postapartheid government continued its own version of indirect rule, the system employed to good effect by colonialism (across the continent) and apartheid.[16]

While incorporating elements like Zwelithini, Buthelezi, and the IFP in the new South Africa brought political peace to KwaZulu-Natal and the parts of Johannesburg that had seen the most violence, it also provided legitimacy to a form of ethnonationalist politics that the ANC had officially opposed during the antiapartheid struggle. In the interest of governing, the ANC opened its ranks and offered support to a range of ethnic and regional interest groups, including elements of the former apartheid regime and traditional leaders. But it also incorporated a new kind of nativism that threatened democracy, one that Zuma himself exploited in his own battle for the presidency.[17] Thus the past lives on in the postcolony.

As much as it stemmed from the nature of South Africa's violent past and its incomplete transition, xenophobic violence and the reaction to it were also globalized and mediated in distinctly twenty-first-century ways. The internet has in the space of only a few years become a key technology for facilitating identity politics in South Africa. As we see in this book, the internet has allowed Afrikaners in particular to create a virtual nation, or perhaps a nation-in-waiting, online.

Responses to the April 2015 violence on the part of officials and commentators alike were highly sensitive to questions about the nation's image—that is, its brand. One of the defining (and most horrifying) images of the April 2015 violence was a series of photographs by James Oatway published on the front page of the *Sunday Times* in Johannesburg. The multiple photos depicted the murder of a Mozambican national, Emmanuel Sithole, in Alexandra Township, Johannesburg, on April 18, 2015. Sithole (a businessman in Alexandra who owned a small grocery store) was stabbed, and images show him falling on the side of a road into a pile of garbage. Sithole was taken to a hospital by the photographer and a journalist but survived only for another hour; he was the eighth person to die in the violence.[18]

The day after the photographs were published, the ruling party held an anti-xenophobia forum at its headquarters in Johannesburg. Speaking at the forum, Zuma turned away from the causes and responses to the violence to focus on media portrayals of it. He questioned Oatway's motives for taking the photos and the *Sunday Times* for publishing them on its front page.[19] Zuma told his audience, "People who live in rough townships have never seen such a scene. And I was sitting and I was saying to myself, what are we telling the world about ourselves?"[20] As journalist Ranjeni Munusamy reported for the website *Daily Maverick*, Zuma "likened the situation to a family with an errant member. Zuma asked whether that family would expose the deviant member as representing them." This was about the South African brand: Oatway's images, for Zuma, "conveyed that 'all South Africans are carrying knives, are killing one another.'" Zuma then contrasted the reporting with media in Mexico and the United States. Zuma told his audience that Mexico's media "does not represent their country in a negative light despite the high crime rate." As for the United States, "after the September 11 attacks, the US media did not show pictures of the dead bodies out of respect for those who perished."[21]

Strikingly, the media followed Zuma's lead with respect to this question. That is, they turned to nation-branding specialists for their opinion. They wanted to know how South Africa's image was affected by this violence. Many sought out Thebe Ikalafeng, the founder and managing director of Brand Leadership Group and Brand Africa and a member of the boards of South African Tourism and Brand South Africa (I discuss the latter in chapter 2). Ikalafeng offered that xenophobia was "negatively affecting *the South African brand*" (emphasis added).[22] For Ikalafeng, if South Africa lacked the kind of clear cultural identity that might characterize other African nations, "we have other virtues" like "unity and diversity. . . . We're the only country that has inspired the world by solving our conflicts."[23] The calls to counter these supposedly negative images of South Africa were swift. The government, nongovernmental organizations (NGOs), and popular black figures partnered on a series of marches (thirty thousand people marched in Johannesburg and another five thousand in Durban), a series of hash tags trended on Twitter (#WeAreAfricans, #SayNoToXenophobia, and #PeaceMarch), and graffiti artists painted a series of murals promoting tolerance and continental identity on the sides of buildings.[24] The government announced a "South African Migrants Awards" to present an image of South Africa as connected to the continent by " honor[ing] and celebrat[ing] outstanding migrants who reside in South Africa" as well as "South Africans working beyond the borders of the country."[25]

While on the one hand media were sites for papering over conflict, on the other, they launched a defense of the South African brand. But new media technology also lent a salutary dose of reality to the conversation. When news of his xenophobic remarks first appeared, Zwelithini claimed that he was the subject of a smear campaign, blaming the media for misconstruing his words. These denials were getting strong support from his followers and elements within the Zulu royal family. The denials also gained plausibility from Zuma's unwillingness to unequivocally condemn Zwelithini's words or even the violence itself. However, a YouTube video of his remarks existed, and Independent Online, the collective web portal for Independent Newspapers, one of the legacy media companies in South Africa, posted the video. Zwelithini was soon forced to make his half apology. The original video, while no longer available, was hardly sensational. It opened with an Independent Online logo and consisted of about two minutes of audio from Zwelithini's speech with English subtitles scrolling over a still photo of the king in traditional gear. The words "foreigners must pack up and leave the country" were unmistakable.[26] A Capetonian filed a complaint of hate speech and human rights violations against Zwelithini at the country's Human Rights Commission, and newspaper editorials questioned the government salary paid to Zwelithini.[27]

During the apartheid period and much of the initial period of freedom, local South African mainstream print media competed mostly with mass party politics for influence over identity formation, cultural politics, and political representation. Now, mass-based parties and unions provide much less competition. But as we have seen, a host of new forms of mediated communication has stepped into the breach. The growth and lower cost of satellite television means that South Africans increasingly get their news and entertainment from global news organizations like BBC World News, Al Jazeera English, and Fox Studios' various international television and web affiliates. Already, large sections of minority white Afrikaans audiences watch and read specialized, privatized media. The SABC, which long held a monopoly over local audiences, is challenged by MultiChoice/M-Net's cheaper subscription offers for poorer viewers. Global advertising campaigns and the internet have increased demand among the middle classes for popular US television serials and Hollywood films. The latter used to make their debut in South Africa months, sometimes more than a year, after their US premieres but now are readily available via satellite or, even more significantly, via a lucrative black market for hard drives full of entertainment. Young black people (just below 40 percent of the population) increasingly turn to social media sites and illegal downloads, primarily through internet-enabled mobile phones.[28]

On the tenth anniversary of South African democracy (in 2004), Paul Gilroy declared that "critical consideration of South Africa's democratic transition can inspire new responses to the current geo-political situation."[29] The experience of the April 2015 violence and my own study of the impacts of popular media on postapartheid political life in South Africa suggests a mixed bag. For example, the uses and ownership of mobile phones have grown at significant rates in South Africa.[30] In 2012 South Africa boasted more than four million Facebook users.[31] And a 2012 study of Twitter in Africa found that the most active Twitter users on the continent live in South Africa.[32] Some parliamentary parties—the DA and the EFF, for example—conduct much of their politics on social media, whether Twitter, Facebook, Instagram, or WhatsApp. So do disgruntled members of the ruling ANC. This points to all kinds of new research questions: What does it mean for political organization, for how ideological battles are fought, or for how parties formulate policy? More than political parties, young people present a potent political force online. The impact of social media and video-sharing sites on political debate and political mobilization in places like South Africa cannot be underestimated. Social media open political debate and deliberation beyond national borders where democratic states and governments have more control.

What will be the impact of South Africa's fractured diaspora—its legions of white ex-pat South Africans in Australia, the United Kingdom, and Canada and its new generation of migrant black professionals in the Arabian Gulf or the United States—on political debate back home? With satellite television and the internet providing cheap, accessible outlets for all kinds of identity politics, it remains to be seen what pitfalls and possibilities lie ahead, from articulations and mobilizations of ethnic-based nationalisms to more inclusive understandings of South African identity.

Notes

1. See Michael Neocosmos, *From "Foreign Natives" to "Native Foreigners:" Explaining Xenophobia in Post-Apartheid South Africa* (Dakar: CODESRIA, 2010).

2. Dan Magaziner and Sean Jacobs, "South Africa Turns on Its Immigrants," *New York Times*, April 24, 2015, https://www.nytimes.com/2015/04/25/opinion/south-africa-turns-on-its-immigrants.html.

3. "South Africa's Johannesburg Marches Against Xenophobia," *BBC News*, April 23, 2015, https://www.bbc.com/news/world-africa-32432205.

4. Matuma Letsoala, "Zwelithini Refuses to Take Responsibility and Blames Media for Violence," *Mail and Guardian*, April 21, 2015, https://africasustainableconservation.com/2015/04/21/south-africa-zwelithini-refuses-to-take-responsibility-and-blames-media-for-violence/.

5. "Zimbabwe and South Africa's Cat and Mouse Game of Deportation," *The Daily Vox*, July 2, 2015, http://www.thedailyvox.co.za/zimbabwe-and-south-africas-cat-and-mouse-game-of-deportation/.

6. Daniel Finnan, "Immigration Controls Tightened in Wake of South Africa's Xenophobic Attacks," Radio France International, April 16, 2015, http://en.rfi.fr/africa/20150416-immigration-camps-not-solution-stopping-south-africas-xenophobic-attacks; Andrew Konstant,

"An Unwelcoming Place—The Mistreatment of African Immigrants by the South African State," Oxford Human Rights Hub, June 19, 2015, http://ohrh.law.ox.ac.uk/an-unwelcoming-place-the-mistreatment-of-african-immigrants-by-the-south-african-state/.

7. See Kate Wilkerson, "Analysis: Are Foreigners Stealing Jobs in South Africa?," Africa Check, February 8, 2015, https://africacheck.org/2015/02/08/analysis-are-foreigners-stealing-jobs-in-south-africa-2/.

8. David A. MacDonald and Sean Jacobs, "(Re)writing Xenophobia: Understanding Press Coverage of Cross-Border Migration in Southern Africa," *Journal of Contemporary African Studies* 23, no. 3 (2005): 295–325. See also Neocosmos, *From "Foreign Natives" to "Native Foreigners"*; and Belinda Dodson, "Locating Xenophobia: Debate, Discourse, and Everyday Experience in Cape Town, South Africa," *Africa Today* 56, no. 3 (2010): 2–22.

9. MacDonald and Jacobs, "(Re)writing Xenophobia."

10. Sisonke Msimang, "Belonging—Why South Africans Refuse to Let Africa In," *Africa Is a Country* (blog), April 15, 2014.

11. Magaziner and Jacobs, "South Africa Turns on Its Immigrants."

12. Terry Bell and Dumisa Ntsebeza, *Unfinished Business: South Africa, Apartheid and Truth* (New York: Verso, 2003).

13. Truth and Reconciliation Commission, *Truth and Reconciliation Commission of South Africa Report*, vol. 2, chap. 7, "Political Violence in the Era of Negotiations and Transition, 1990–1994" (Pretoria: Truth and Reconciliation Commission, 1998), 584, 585.

14. Thembisa Waetjen, *Workers and Warriors: Masculinity and the Struggle for Nation in South Africa* (Urbana Champaign: University of Illinois Press, 2004).

15. Chitja Twala, "Jacob Zuma's 'Zuluness' Appeal during the April 2009 Elections in South Africa: An Attempt to Break the IFP's grip on Zulu Social and Political Structures?," *Journal for Contemporary History* 35, no. 2 (2010): 68–83.

16. Mahmood Mamdani, *Citizen and Subject: Contemporary Africa and the Legacy of Late Colonialism* (Princeton, NJ: Princeton University Press, 1996); Lungisile Ntsebeza, *Democracy Compromised: Chiefs and the Politics of Land in South Africa* (Leiden: Brill, 2005).

17. Liz Gunner, "Jacob Zuma, the Social Body and the Unruly Power of Song," *African Affairs* 108, no. 430 (January 2009): 27–48; Thembisa Waetjen and Gerhard Mare, "Tradition's Desire: The Politics of Culture in the Rape Trial of Jacob Zuma," *Theoria* 56, no. 118 (2009): 63–81.

18. Beauregard Tromp, "The Final Moments of Emmanuel Sithole," TimesLIVE, April 26, 2015, https://www.timeslive.co.za/news/south-africa/2015-04-26-the-final-moments-of-emmanuel-sithole/; Beauregard Tromp and James Oatway, "The Brutal Death of Emmanuel Sithole," TimesLIVE, April 19, 2015.

19. Ranjeni Munusamy, "Xenophobia and the Media: Where Truth and Patriotism Intersect," *Daily Maverick*, April 22, 2015, https://www.dailymaverick.co.za/article/2015-04-22-xenophobia-and-the-media-where-truth-and-patriotism-intersect/.

20. Brent Swails, "Xenophobic Killing in South African Township Caught by Photographer," CNN.com, April 21, 2015, https://www.cnn.com/2015/04/20/africa/south-africa-xenophobia-killing-photos/index.html.

21. Munusamy, "Xenophobia and the Media."

22. Thebe Ikalafeng, quoted in "Xenophobic Attacks Shatter South Africa's Brand—Expert," SABC, April 20, 2015.

23. Ibid.

24. Elizabeth Sejake, "Photo Story: Art on Walls," *City Press*, October 29, 2015, https://city-press.news24.com/Trending/Photo-Story-Art-on-walls-20151029.

25. "SA launches Migrants Awards," eNCA, May 10, 2015, https://www.enca.com/south-africa/sa-launches-migrant-awards.

26. The original video was accessed April 20, 2015.

27. Jenni Evans, "Rights Violation Charge Laid Against Zulu King," *Mail and Guardian*, April 16, 2015, https://mg.co.za/article/2015-04-16-rights-violation-charge-laid-against-zulu-king; Fred Khumalo, "King Zwelithini Is Living Up to His Name After All," *Rand Daily Mail Online*, May 15, 2015.

28. Alf James, "Performing a Protecting-Constitutional Balancing Act," *Business Report*, June 7, 2013, 22; Natalie Primo and Libby Lloyd, "South Africa," in *Media Piracy in Emerging Economies*, edited by Joe Karaganis (New York: Social Science Research Council, 2011), 113.

29. Paul Gilroy, *Between Camps: Nations, Cultures and the Allure of Race* (London: Penguin, 2000), 243.

30. Matthew Buckland, "Mobile Surpasses Traditional Web in South Africa," *Matthew Buckland* (blog), November 19, 2008, http://matthewbuckland.com/?p=573; Percy Zvomuya, "Computer Geek Becomes a Laughaholic," *Mail and Guardian*, August 3, 2012, https://mg.co.za/article/2012-08-03-00-geek-becomes-laughaholic.

31. Chris Roper. "South Africa and the Media: Looking Back at 2011, Looking Ahead to 2012," *Regional Report* (Johannesburg: Konrad Adenauer Stiftung, January 17, 2012), http://www.kas.de/wf/doc/kas_29931-1522-2-30.pdf?130205225732.

32. David Smith, "African Twitter Map Reveals How Continent Stays Connected," *The Guardian*, January 26, 2012, https://www.theguardian.com/world/2012/jan/26/african-twitter-map-continent-connected.

Index

Note: Major discussions are indicated by **bold** page numbers.

Achmat, Zackie: about, 125, 128, 129; class and HIV infection, 121; as face of TAC, 112, 127, 128; film about, 127–28; importation of fluconazole, 115; in media spectacle, 124; meeting with Mandela, 118; in *State of Denial*, 130; on treatment literacy, 120
activism in media, 70, 109–10, 129
ACT UP (AIDS Coalition to Unleash Power), 117, 123–24
advertising: dominant firms, 58n2; and identity construction, 35, 36; industry's struggle with *Isidingo*, 79; and moral leadership, 36; and politics, 36–38; print advertising in the new South Africa, 41; SABC's revenue stream, 66. *See also* television commercials and branding South Africa
advertising industry, 36, 58n2, 58n6, 75, 79
affirmative action policies (BEE), 52, 146, 147, 151–52, 163
Africa Check, 172
Africa Magic, 101
African National Congress (ANC): Chris Hani's role in, 24; co-optation of nationalist leaders, 174; handling of AIDS crisis, 7; relationship with TAC, 125, 129; representation in the media, 113–14; strength of, 16–17; use of culture and media, 20, 22–23; and white emigration, 167n76. *See also* Mbeki, Thabo
African Renaissance, 90
AfriForum, 138, 141, 148, 153–54, 160, 162

Afrikaans identity politics, 8, 139, 140–41, 162–63. *See also* Afrikaner state in cyberspace
Afrikaans media sphere, 8, 72, 146, 147, 157–58
Afrikaans speakers, 83n21, 86n74
Afrikaner, definition of, 140
Afrikaner nationalism: emergence of, 137, 142–43, 150; and foreign opinion, 144; Goosen's conception of, 156; media voice of, 91; myths of, 164–65n15; and rugby, 25
Afrikaners (Boers): emigration of., 145, 156, 167n76; enmity toward Mbeki, 146–47; marginalization of, 139, 146–47, 152, 153, 155, 161; as radical democrats, 156; in South African history, 137
Afrikaner state in cyberspace, **137–64**; adoption of global rights politics, 152–57; "Afrikaner anthem," 137–39; Afrikaner identity under colonialism and apartheid, 141–49; Anglo-Boer War commemoration, 149–51, 152; Boetman debate, 151–52; celebrity activists, 7, 157–62; definition of Afrikaner, 140; impact of apartheid's end on Afrikaners, 139–40; individuals and groups as representative of Afrikaans identity, 140–41; Solidariteit tactics, 163
Afrikaner Weerstandsbeweging (AWB; Afrikaner Resistance Movement), 24, 158
Afro-nationalism, 156
Agter Elke Man (Behind every man) (SABC, 1985–86), 72, 84n43

AIDS and HIV: addressed on soap operas, 78; AIDS crisis, 7–8; campaigns in the United States, 117; denialism, knowledge, and information sources, 110–12; as disease of poverty, 120–21; free debate over epidemic, 112, 133n14; government actions to address, 112–13, 115; morbidity and mortality in South Africa, 111; treatment literacy, 120–23, 131. *See also* government actions; Treatment Action Campaign (TAC)
AIDS campaigners, alternative politics of, 7
Alegi, Peter, 56
Al Jazeera, 12, 176
Allsorts candy advertising, 41
American commercials, 37–38
American popular culture, 21–22, 158, 176
American soap operas, 72–73
"America of Africa," 10
amnesty applications, 145
ANC. *See* African National Congress (ANC)
Anglo-Boer War (1899–1902), 137, 139, 149–51, 152
Anti-Privatization Forum, 125–26
antiretroviral drugs: availability to AIDS sufferers, 115, 116–17, 120, 121; highly active antiretroviral therapy (HAART), 109; Mbeki's claims about, 111; TAC's importation of, 115–16, 127
apartheid: Afrikaners' complicity with, 143–44, 150, 151; beginning of, 91–92, 149; control of media, 4, 21; as form of colonialism, 10; indirect rule and, 174; and liberation from, 2; and a nation of communities, 155; nature of, 3, 19; notion of heritage under, 45; public opinion about, 28; purity of language, 30n14; relations on the continent, 90; shared experience of, 173; symbolism of Ford Bantam car, 51; television dramas under, 70–73, 74. *See also* language politics; Naspers
Appiah, Anthony, 73
aspirational politics, 63–64, 75, 79–81
Association of Communication and Advertising, 50
athletes in advertising, 54–55, 56–57
AWB. *See* Afrikaner Weerstandsbeweging

Baker, Beathur, 30n14
Bampoe, Sammi, 98
BBC World News, 116, 176
BEE. *See* affirmative action policies (BEE)

Beeld (Picture), 141
beer as marker of national identity, 43
Bekker, Koos, 87, 90, 92
Benoist, Alain de, 155
Big Brother Africa: about, 6–7, 96–97; challenges to gender and sexual stereotypes, 98; class politics in, 100; critics', viewers', and elites' responses to, 98–99; as representative of continental unity, 97–98; television market for, 100–101
Biko, Steve, 19, 20, 117, 134n35, 153
bilingualism, 68
Biozole (generic fluconazole), 115, 127
black Afrikaans speakers, 142, 147, 163, 165n17
Black Consciousness, 153
black consumer market, 40–41
black economic empowerment, 64, 65. *See also* affirmative action policies (BEE)
black middle class, 41, 146. *See also* aspirational politics
"Black Pimpernel," 23
black South Africans: in Afrikaans media, 147; changing culture and economy of, 21; and history of resistance, 23; soap operas as models for, 6; suffering of in Anglo-Boer War, 149–50; in television commercials, 38–41; wealth of, 75–77
black student protest, 131–32
black television stations, 19
black working class, 90. *See also* aspirational politics; *Isidingo* (SABC, 1998 to present)
Blaser, Thomas, 141
Blecher, Hilary, 80
Blignaut, Charl, 81
blogs, 157, 162, 163
Boehringer Ingelheim, 127
Boeremag (Boer militia), 159
Boers. *See* Afrikaners
Boersema, Jacob, 163
Boetman, definition of, 151
Boetman debate, 149, 151–52
Bolsmann, Chris, 56
Bonita milk advertising, 41
Boraine, Alex, 28
Botha, P. W., 144
BoxOffice, 104n5
boycotts, 2, 19, 20, 84n45, 148, 166n41. *See also* Soweto uprising
BP Corporation advertising, 41
branding in South Africa. *See* television commercials and branding South Africa

Brand South Africa: extension fo Brand Africa, 62n78; "Football Fridays," 56; "Invest in South Africa" commercial, 53–54; rhythm of life commercial, 54; "Today I woke up . . ." commercial, 54–55, 62n76; "We've Done It Again" commercial, 55; World Cup 2010 tournament, 62n83
Brandwag, 159–60
Die Brandwag (The sentry), 141, 142, 164n13
Breytenbach, Breyten, 142
Bridges, Bles, 158, 168n83
Bridges, Sunette, 158–59
Brink, André, 142
Bristol Meyers Squibb, 115
British Equity Actors' Union boycott, 19, 84n45
British imperialism, 149, 150, 166n47
British ITN interview of Mandela, 23
Broederbond (Brotherhood), 67
Die Burger (The citizen), 91, 140, 141, 144, 147
Buthelezi, Mangosuthu, 174

Calvinist Christianity, 19
capitalism: Afrikaner media support for, 147; and aspirational viewers, 6; and community life, 155; conveyed through *Generations*, 77–78; in image of South Africa, 82; influence of popular media, 4, 64
Carlin, John, 27
Carter, Jimmy, 121
Cassim, Tasneem, 114
Castle Lager commercials and branding, 40, 43–45, 46–48, 60n44
Catsam, Derek, 57
celebrity activists, 157–62
Charlie Hebdo, 162
CHMT. *See* Community Health Media Trust
Christopher Moraka Defiance Campaign, 115
Chrysler Corporation, political ad for, 37–38
citizenship, meaning and shapers of, 5, 9, 11, 15
civil disobedience campaigns, 124, 125
civil rights movements, 138, 148–49, 153
civil society organizations, 9, 67, 139–40, 141, 153–54, 156
class mobility. *See* aspirational politics
Clinton, Bill, 115
CNN effect, 116
Coca-Cola advertising campaigns, 55, 56
Coetzee, J. M., 27
Cole, Catherine, 28
Cole, Kenneth, 128

colonialism: Afrikaners' extension of, 151; centralizing tendencies of, 155, 156; history of in South Africa, 2; indirect rule and, 174; media under, 117; place of Afrikaners under, 140; relations on the continent, 90; shared experience of, 173
Comaroff, Jean and John, 10
Community Health Media Trust (CHMT), 118, 126
concentration camps, 149, 150
Congress of South African Trade Unions (COSATU), 20, 121, 129
Congress of Traditional Leaders (CONTRALESA), 172, 174
consensus politics, 2
CONTRALESA. *See* Congress of Traditional Leaders
COSATU. *See* Congress of South African Trade Unions
Cosby Show, The, 21
Country of My Skull (Krog, 1998), 144, 165n25
court actions regarding antiretroviral drugs, 116–17
crime, victims of, 160, 163
cult of personality, 112, 125–30
cultural archive, media as, 11–12
cyberspace and nationhood, 139. *See also* Afrikaner state in cyberspace; internet

Dayan, Daniel, 29n1
De Klerk, F. W.: comments before the TRC, 144–45; conscription of fighters, 151; control of media and Mandela's release, 16–17; response to Chris Hani's murder, 24; SABC board nominations, 67–68
De Klerk, Willem, *Afrikaners: Kroes, Kras, Kordaat* (Afrikaners: Abrasive, Crass, Plucky, 2000), 151
"De la Rey" (Van Blerk), 137–39, 148
Democratic Alliance (DA), 115, 145–46, 155, 166n33
democratic elections: Afrikaner representation in, 145; commercial referring to, 55; first, 2, 25; and new mediated politics, 5, 15
denialism: AIDS denialists, 134n22; effects on neoliberal economic policies, 122; features of, 120; Mbeki's denialism, 78, 109, 110–12, 114, 120, 121
Derby-Lewis, Clive, 24
Diethelm, Pascal, 120
disabled athletes, 54

Dlamini, Jacob, 21
Dlamini-Zuma, Nkosazana, 116
Drogba, Didier, 56
Drum Magazine, 22
Dubula, Vuyiseka, 112, 126
Dwyer, Peter, 128

Eastwood, Clint, 37–38
Economic Freedom Fighters (EFF), 110, 130
economy, South African: dominance on the continent, 89; economic development, 35, 91, 103; growth and success of, 10–11, 93; recession, 80
Egoli (M-Net, 1992–2010), 73–74
electronic newsletters, 119
emigration, 145, 156, 167n76
Endemol, 80–81
entertainment media, 9, 13n12. *See also* MultiChoice; reality television; soap operas
entrepreneurship, 80
Epstein, Elaine, 130
Equal Education, 110, 113, 130
Equal Treatment, 119
Eriksen, Thomas Hylland, 139, 164
ethnicities, differences in, 19
ethnocultures, 155
ethnonationalist politics, 174
exceptionalism of South Africa, 10
expatriate population, 44, 53, 55, 145

Facebook users, 176
Federation of Afrikaner Cultural Associations (FAK), 154, 157
#FeesMustFall, 110, 130, 131
feminism, in television soap operas, 76
filmmakers and film rights, 102
First National Bank (FNB), 56, 62n79, 163, 164
Fischer, Carl, 97–98
Flockemann, Micki, 72–73, 85n46
fluconazole, 115, 127
football (soccer), 48
football (soccer), television coverage of, 88
"Football Fridays," 56
Ford Bantam (bakkie) commercial, 51–52
Ford car commercial, 39
Ford South Africa, 51
foreigners, attitudes toward and media coverage of, 172
foreign investment, 53, 55
Fragmente, 154
Freedom Front, 145, 153

Freedom Park, 161
Front Nasionaal (National Front), 153

gay men, 78
Gay Men's Health Crisis, 117, 123
Gaz'lam [My Friend] (SABC, 2002–2005), 69
Geffen, Nathan: about, 109–10, 113; access to medical information, 123; CHMT films, 118; history of TAC, 134n28; TAC's goals and strategies, 115, 116, 117, 122, 130; on use of Mandela on poster, 134n39; website creation and use, 119, 120
Generations (SABC, 1994–2014), 6, 74–77, 82
genocide, 139, 152, 159, 166n47
Genocide Watch, 152
Gerwel, Jakes, 165n17
Gibson, Angus, 30n14
Gilroy, Paul, 11, 176
Glass, Charles, 46–48
Glaxo-SmithKline, 115, 127
global competitiveness, 93
global identity politics, 139
globalization, critiques of, 154, 155, 156
global news, access to, 176
global rights politics, adoption of, 152–57
Goosen, Danie, 154, 155–56, 157, 167n69
Gorbachev, Mikhail, legacy of, 17
government actions regarding AIDS: access to AIDS drugs, 114–15, 116–17, 122, 127; commitment to treatment, 113, 122, 129; Mbeki's denialism, 78, 109, 110–12, 114, 120, 121
government actions regarding higher education, 131–32
Government of National Unity, 145
Great South Africans opinion poll, 160, 168n91
Groep van 63 (Group of 63), 154
GroundUp, 113, 133n17
Growth, Employment and Redistribution (GEAR), 122
Grundlingh, Albert, 27, 142
guidelines for television programming, 70

HAART. *See under* antiretroviral drugs
"Hamba nathi mkhululu wethu" (hymn), 48
Hani, Chris, murder of, 24–25
Harris, Kevin, 18
Haynes, Jonathan, 101, 103
"Hazel Tau and Others vs GlaxoSmithKline and Others," 127
Henry, Thierry, 56

Hermann, Dirk, 163–64
Hertzog, Albert, 17–18
Hertzog, J. B. M., 91
Heywood, Mark, 125, 126
HIV treatment, 7–8
Hofmeyr, Gray, 72, 74, 80, 81
Hofmeyr, Isabel, 142
Hofmeyr, Steve: about, 84n43, 159–60; media coverage of, 162; *Mense van My Asem* (People of my breath, 2010), 160, 161; political activities of, 138, 141, 159, 160–62; *Toeka* albums, 161, 162; as traditional Boer leader, 169n100
Hogan, Barbara, 112
Hollywood actors, 158
Hollywood films, 176
Holt, Alexander, 36, 40
homosexuality on *Isidingo*, 78
Hope, Christopher, 139
Huisgenoot (House companion), 91, 141, 142, 164n13

Ibrahim, Abdullah, "Today I woke up . . ." commercial, 54
ICASA. *See* Independent Communications Authority of South Africa
identity, class, and gender politics, 7, 8, 88–89, 103–4. *See also Big Brother Africa*
identity entrepreneurs, 8
identity politics: facilitated by the internet, 174; global, 89, 139. *See also* Afrikaans identity politics
IFP. *See* Inkatha Freedom Party
Ikalafeng, Thebe, 174–75
IMC. *See* International Marketing Council of South Africa
immigration regime of South Africa, 171–72
Independent Communications Authority of South Africa (ICASA), 65
Independent Online, 176
indigenous groups, UN promotion of rights for, 153
indirect rule, 174
information infrastructures, alternative, 110
Inkatha Freedom Party (IFP), 173, 174
International AIDS Conference (Durban, South Africa), 116
International Marketing Council of South Africa (IMC), 55; launch of, 53
International Rugby Board (IRB), 25
internet: and facilitation of South African identity politics, 174; internet streaming, 88,

96; multiple uses of, 10; role in treatment literacy, 123; as solution to government media problems, 114; as source of information, 114; TAC's use of, 119–20, 130, 131; use of by Solidariteit, 163. *See also* social media
Invictus (film), 27
IRB. *See* International Rugby Board
ironic pragmatism, 51–52
Isidingo (SABC, 1998 to present): about, 6; compared to *The Villagers*, 77–78, 81; economic politics of, 80–81; ideals of rainbow nation, 77; producer, 72; ratings drop, 82
It's My Life (TAC, 2002), 127, 128, 129
Ives, Sarah, 80

Jameson, Fredric, 9

Kaká, 56
Katz, Elihu, 29n1
Kerkorrel, Johannes, 142
Kitchener, Lord, 150
Kit Kat television commercial, 41–42
Klapperkop, 161
K'Naan, "Wavin' Flag," 56
Kozain, Rustum, 157
Krabill, Ron, 9, 21, 28
Kriel, Kallie, 161, 162
Kriel, Mariana, 142, 157
Krog, Antjie, *Country of My Skull* (1998), 144, 165n25
Kwaito music, 47, 49
KykNet, 148

Lampard, Frank, 57
Landbouweekblad (Agriculture weekly), 141, 164n13
language identity, 140
language policies, 19, 30n14, 68, 71, 73–74
language politics, 22, 30n14, 39, 68, 147, 155, 163. *See also* Afrikaans speakers
language use in commercials, 45
Lebale, Tawana, 98, 99
Le Monde Diplomatique, 156–57
"Letter from the President" (Mbeki), 113
Lewis, Jack, 115, 118, 126
liberation movements: and exceptionalism, 10; isolation of regime, 20; media control of, 2; packaging as commercial resource, 57 (*See also* television commercials); unbanning of, 2, 16, 143; US policy toward, 19

Lindstrom, Martin, 43
LitNet, 138, 160
Loerie Awards, 36
Louw, Chris, 151–52, 154

Madikizela-Mandela, Winnie, 16
Magaziner, Daniel, 173
Mager, Anne Kelk, 45
Makgoba, Malegapuru, 121
Makubale, Cherise, 99
Malan, D. F., 91–92
Malan, Rian, 111, 144
Malema, Julius, 163
Mandela, Nelson: at 1995 Rugby World Cup final, 2–3, 26–27; on Cherise Makubale, 99; image on TAC poster, 134n39; images of during apartheid, 16; as media star, 22–24; meeting with TAC's Achmat, 118, 128; and new political consciousness, 2; release from prison, 5, 15–17, 22–24; stature of South Africa, 90; televised address following Chris Hani's murder, 5, 15, 24–25; "Today I woke up . . ." commercial, 54; and use of 'rainbow nation,' 42
masculinity in television commercials, 43–44
Matlala, Jacob, 54
Mbeki, Thabo: "African Renaissance," 3, 90–91; African solutions to AIDS treatment, 121; and Afrikaner politics, 146; as AIDS denialist, 7–8, 78, 109–12, 114, 120, 121, 129; on AIDS drugs, 116; black economic empowerment, 6, 64; commemoration of Anglo-Boer War, 149; distancing from 'rainbow nation,' 42; economic framework of, 91; media politics of, 113–14; and new political consciousness, 2; policies regarding racial inequalities, 146; "Today I woke up. . ." commercial, 54; white enmity toward, 146–47
Mbembe, Achille, 11
McCarthy, Neil, 71–72, 79
McCluskey, T., 21–22
McKee, Martin, 120
media: as archive of cultural knowledge, 11–12; control of during apartheid, 2; fascination with personalities, 112, 125–30; impact of technology, 147–48; pervasiveness of, 12; socially driven understanding of, 65; South African media development, 11; as window into South Africa's transition to modern state, 4–5. See also Afrikaner state in cyberspace; MultiChoice; soap operas on SABC; South Africa's media history during the transition; television commercials and branding South Africa; Treatment Action Campaign
media event, concept of, 29n1
media spectacle, use of, 110, 112, 123–25, 159
mediated politics, events that prompted, 5, 15, 27–28
Medical Research Council, 121
Medicines Act, 115, 119
Messi, Lionel, 56
Mexico's television firms, 12
Middleton, Mike, 48
miner's strike, 72, 78
mining industry, 80, 94
mining town, representation of, 71–72
Minor, Michael, 35
minorities under international law, definition of, 153
minority rights, 163. See also Afrikaners (Boers)
M-Net (cable TV), 73; Big Brother's whiteness, 95–96; competition with SABC, 67; first postapartheid soap opera, 73; Jakes Gerwel, 165n17; launch of MultiChoice, 93; as lucrative business, 92–93; profitability and ratings, 64, 66; as response to SABC monopoly, 92; subscribers, 96, 176; transformation of, 147
mobile phones, 175–76
Mokonyane, Nomvula, 172
Molson Canadian, branding of, 37
Moraka, Christopher, 115, 127
moral leadership, 36
Morgan, Michael, 82
Motlanthe, Kgalema, 112
Motsoaledi, Aaron, 112–13
Mouw, Beert Jacob, 138–39
Mpufane, Jerry, 49
Mthathi, Sipho, 112
MTN in Nigeria, 95
MultiChoice, **87–104**; Big Brother Africa, 95–101; business strategies of, 6; challenge to South African Broadcasting Corporation (SABC), 176; cross-continent growth of, 87–91, 90, 104n3; history of, 91–93; as 'middle power,' 12; origins in Nasinale Pers, 142; relationship with Nollywood, 6, 7, 89, 101–3; South African dominance in Africa, 93–95. See also M-Net (cable TV)
multiculturalism, 163

multiracial democracy, 82
multiracial interaction in commercials, 40
Munusamy, Ranjeni, 175
Mwanawasa, Levy, 99

Nandos' advertising campaign, 38
Naspers (Nasionale Pers/National Press): apartheid and nationalism, 91; domination strategy of, 87, 141; M-Net as lucrative business, 92–93; policy goals, 89; structure of, 95; subsidiary, 164n14; transformation of, 147; before the TRC, 144, 165n23
Nasson, Bill, 149–50
national allegories, 9
national ethos, 82
national identity. *See* South African identity
National Party, 16, 17, 18, 19, 91, 145
nation building, 81–82
Natsios, Andrew, 122–23
Nattrass, Nicoli, 134n22
Nazis, followers of, 159–60
Ndebele, Njabulo, 68
Ndlela, Martin Nkosi, 95, 100
neoliberal economics, 10, 35, 57, 80, 122
neoliberalism, power of, 11
New Partnership for African Development (NEPAD), 91
New York City, use of in commercials, 43–44
Nigeria: cultural influence of, 89; misconceptions about, 98; MTN, 95; and MultiChoice, 102, 103; production of *Big Brother Naija*, 105n9; transmission of *Big Brother Africa* in, 99, 101. *See also* Nollywood
Nkoli, Simon, 127
Nobel Peace Prize nomination, 128
Nollywood, 6, 7, 88, 89, 101–3
Nomvete, Pamela, 54, 55

Oatway, James, photographs of, 174–75
Obama, Barack, 38
Ogola, George, 89, 101
"one nation viewing," 6, 64, 81
Open Time, 74, 92–93
Operation Fiela (sweep the dirt), 172
oral thrush, 115
Organization of African Unity, 97
Otto, J. C., 18
Oyedele, Adesegun, 35

pan-Africanism, 95, 97, 171
patent lawsuit, 115, 116
patriotism, 56, 62n79
pay TV, 87
Pepsi advertising campaigns, 55, 56–57
Pfizer, 115, 127, 134n30
pharmaceutical industry: court case against South Africa, 115–17, 128, 129; global day of action against, 119–20; price gouging of, 109, 111, 115–16, 127
Pienaar, Francois, 26
Pietersen, Hector, 55
political and business elites, 5, 9, 90, 99
political economy, media engagement with, 55, 64
political identity, media as shapers of, 11
political parties, supplantation of, 9
politics, social media's role in, 9
popular culture, 4, 9–10, 88
postapartheid public sphere, characteristics of, 157
poverty and the poor: AIDS as disease of, 120–21; and health management, 122–23; media ambivalence to, 125–26; social movements representing, 148; and social weight behind TAC, 126; and xenophobic violence, 173
power through nonstate institutions, 143
PRAAG. *See* Pro-Afrikaanse Aksie Groep
Preez, Max du, 28, 138
Preller, Gustav, 164–65n15
privatization: and Afrikaner emigration, 156; of Afrikaner identity politics, 143; and growth of South African economy, 93, 122
Pro-Afrikaanse Aksie Groep (PRAAG; Pro-Afrikaans Action Group), 138, 148, 152, 154
protest marches, 119, 131–32, 134n39
public broadcasting, 64, 65, 87–88. *See also* South African Broadcasting Corporation (SABC)
Puma commercial, 62n83

race and class stratification, 113, 163; and AIDs treatment, 121; in apartheid dramas, 71–72; under Mbeki's government, 146; SABC's reconfiguration to address, 68–69
race relations, 35; 1995 Rugby World Cup's impact on, 27; change through soap operas, 65
racial inequality: depicted in television commercials, 39–40; Mbeki's policies regarding, 146; reversal of in commercial, 49–50, 51–52
racism, persistence of, 52, 157, 159, 161

racism, reverse, 138
Radebe, Jeff, 94
radio media, 21, 67, 142
Radio Sonder Grense (Radio without Borders), 83, 83n21, 138, 142
Radio Zulu, 21
rainbow nation and rainbowism: coining of term, 42–43; limits of, 8; marketing of, 55; public acceptance of, 5; and SABMiller marketing campaigns, 3; and shaping of media discourses, 3; in soap operas, 65; success of vision, 173
Rapport (Report), 141, 147
reality television: analysis of African reality television, 103; and export of South African culture, 88; genre characteristics, 97; as public space, 4; reshaping of culture, 6; talent for films, 103; in Western countries, 65. See also *Big Brother Africa*; MultiChoice
Reclaim the City, 110, 113, 130
reconciliation and forgiveness, 3, 27, 146
Red October campaign, 159, 161
Reith, John, 66
Rey, Koos de la, 137–38
Rhodes, Cecil John, 131
#RhodesMustFall, 110, 130, 131, 132
Rivonia Trial, 16
Rolux lawn mower commercial, 39
Roodt, Dan, 138, 151, 152–53, 159
Rosholt, Marie, 98
Ross, Robert, 43
Rossouw, Johann, 154, 157, 167n76
Rove, Karl, 38
rugby, 2, 25, 27, 48
Rugby World Cup finals (Johannesburg, 1995), 2–3, 5, 15, 25–27, 143

SAB. *See* South African Breweries (SAB)
SABC. *See* South African Broadcasting Corporation
SABMiller: division of Anheuser-Busch In Bev, 12n1; marketing campaigns of, 3; television commercial depicting South African collective effort, 1, 2, 4
satellite television, 147–48, 176. *See also* MultiChoice
scientific truth, Mbeki's views on, 114
Scott, Guy, 94
Serote, Mongane Wally, 161
sexuality and sexual orientation, 78, 98, 99, 103
Sidley, Pat, 118

Signoreilli, Nancy, 82
Silver Apex Award, 50
Simunye, meaning of, 43
simunye commercials, 43, 49
Sithole, Emmanuel, 174–75
Situ, Zanele, 54
Siyayinqoba Beat It! (TAC, TV series), 126
Slabbert, Frederik van Zyl, 17
soap operas, 12, 173
soap operas on SABC, **63–82**; *7de Laan,* 86n74; analysis of advertising on, 5–6; under apartheid, 70–73; aspirational politics of, 63, 79–81; *Generations,* 63–64, 73–77; *Isidingo,* 63, 64, 77–79; *Muvhango* (Conflict), 86n74; restructuring of SABC, 67–70; success of, 63, 64–66
soccer. *See* football (soccer)
Social Justice Coalition, 110, 113, 130
socially conscious television, 69
social media: in actors' communication strategies, 10; change in use of, 130–32, 176; for entertainment, 157; multiple uses of, 10; political debate and deliberation on, 176; as public space, 4; use by *Big Brother Africa*, 7; use by social movements, 148. *See also* blogs; Twitter coverage; YouTube videos
social movements: characteristics of, 142; and material rights, 148; use of media, 110, 117, 125–26, 130–31
Solidariteit, 138, 148, 154, 155, 160, 163, 169n102
songs, racist, 161
Sono, Ephraim "Jomo," 54
Soul City (SABC, 1994–2015), 69
South Africa: AIDS epidemic in, 109; creation of Union of South Africa, 137; exceptionalism of, 10; first democratic elections, 1, 2; foreign policy and investment, 89, 90; as globalizing force, 103; as nation of communities, 155; ranking in global competitiveness, 93; relationship to the African continent, 10, 89, 90; vision of, 4, 5. *See also* Afrikaner state in cyberspace; apartheid; economy, South African; South African identity
South African Breweries (SAB), 1, 43–44, 45–49, 48. *See also* SABMiller
South African Broadcasting Corporation (SABC): under apartheid, 67; challenge from MultiChoice, 176; double mandate of, 66; financial health, 65–66; impact of television commercials, 92; incorporation of national identity as resource in branding, 42–45;

language politics of, 22; launch of additional channels, 19; mass media event coverage, 25; as 'middle power,' 12; "Mzansi fo sho" (South Africa for sure) slogan, 50–51; soap operas on, 5–6; "Ya Mampela" (the real thing) slogan, 49–51
South African citizenship, 5
South African Communist Party, 24
South African companies, derision of, 93–94
South African Defense Force (SADF), 145, 161–62
South African Human Rights Commission, 159
South African identity: in advertising, 35, 42, 48–49; and *Big Brother Africa*, 88–89; in Castle Lager commercials, 47–48; in globalized context, 12; media defense of, 175–76; and 'rainbow nation,' 3, 42; soap operas as key sites for cultivating, 6, 63, 64, 79–80, 103; and success, 53–57, 62n75; and unity, 80
South African languages, 30n14, 68, 85n49, 86n74
South African Migrants Awards, 175
South African Music Award, 160
South African National AIDS Council, 112
South African Rugby Union, 25, 26
South African unity, compelling story of, 3–4
South Africa's media history during the transition, **15–29**; 1995 Rugby World Cup final, 25–27; debate over meaning of citizenship, 15; deracialization and democratization of media, 20–21; introduction of television to South Africa, 17–21; Mandela's release from prison, 15–17, 22–24; Mandela's televised speech following Chris Hani's murder, 24–25; reform of media, 21–29; TRC public hearings, 27–29
Southern African Migrancy Program, 172
Soweto uprising, 19, 47, 48, 55, 61n53
Soyinka, Wole, 97
sports personalities, 54
Springboks. *See* Rugby World Cup finals
Standard Bank commercial, 39–40
Stark, Friedrich, 74
State of Denial (TAC, 2003), 129
Steps for the Future (film series), 127
stereotypes: gender stereotypes, 98, 99; HIV positive Africans, 122–23; soap opera challenges to, 76; in television commercials, 36, 39, 60n44; white farmers and their Bantams, 51
Steve se Spoeg Blog (Steve's spit blog), 160

Stormfront, 152
Stransky, Joel, 54
Strelitz, Larry, 73
Super Bowl commercials, 37–38
SuperSport channels, 88
Svenska Motståndsrörelsen (Swedish Resistance Movement), 152
symbolism and myth-making, 157

TAC. *See* Treatment Action Campaign (TAC)
TAC Electronic Newsletter, 119
"Take Another Look at Msanzi" (SABC commercial), 49–50
Taking HAART (CHMT, 2011), 126
Tanzania, 94–95
Tau, Hazel, 127
Taylor, Ella, 27
telenovelas, 79
Telesur news service, 12
television: under apartheid, 17–19; commercials' impact on print media, 92; as communication space for politics, 9, 25; dramas as public spaces, 4; as mirror and leader, 82; sense of belonging and rights, 173; violence on, 69–70, 84n30
television commercials: apartheid-era commercials, 38–41
television commercials and branding South Africa, **35–57**; during 2010 World Cup tournament, 55–57, 62n83; branding as good for government and business, 5; Brand South Africa, 53–57; depicting South African collective effort, 1; idea of heritage in, 45–49; new national identity in, 41–45; political rhetoric in, 5, 35, 36–38; as public spaces, 4; racial reversals in, 49–52
Terre'Blanche, Eugène, 24, 158
text messaging, 7
third-world societies and texts, 9, 11
Thugwane, Josia, 55
Time magazine's "100 Most Influential People," 128
Toit, Natalie du, 54
Toto, "Africa," 43–44, 60n44
Toyota car commercial, 39
Die Transvaler, 92, 151
TRC. *See* Truth and Reconciliation Commission (TRC)
Treatment Action Campaign (TAC), **109–32**; about, 7–8; AIDS crisis and government actions, 110–14; battling pharmaceutical

Treatment Action Campaign (TAC) (*cont.*)
  industry, 116–17; demands and goals
  of, 109, 115, 117; launching of, 114–15;
  media production of, 118–19, 126–30, 131;
  networking with journalists, 117–18; online
  treatment literacy infrastructure, 120–23;
  use of media cult of personality, 125–30; use
  of media spectacle, 110, 123–25; website as
  organizing board, 119–20
Truth and Reconciliation Commission (TRC),
  3, 27–29; apartheid ministers and officials,
  144–45; mass media as actors in public
  hearings, 28; and new mediated politics, 5,
  15; report on violence during transition from
  apartheid, 173–74; white South Africans in
  transition, 143–44
Tshabalala-Msimang, Manto, 109, 111, 112, 116,
  124, 129
Tsha Tsha [Cha Cha] (SABC, 2003), 69
Tutu, Desmond: aftermath of Chris Hani's
  murder, 25; and new political consciousness,
  2; and "rainbow nation," 3, 42; "Today I woke
  up . . ." commercial, 54
Twitter coverage, 131–32, 175
Twitter users in Africa, 176

Ubuntu, 36
Unilever Institute of Strategic Marketing,
  40–41
Unite Behind, 110
United Democratic Front (UDF), 20, 117
University of Capetown, black student protest, 131
US television serials, 176

Van Blerk, Bok (née Louis Andreas Pepler),
  137–38, 153, 159
Verwoerd, Hendrik, 92
victimhood: Afrikaner, 147, 148, 149, 150;
  discourses of white victimhood, 152; media's
  role in identity, 8; minority rights, white
  genocide, and, 139–40; victims of crime, 160
video on demand service, 104n5
viewers: aspirational, 6; impact of American
  soap operas, 73; impact of television on
  national life, 15–16, 21–22, 26; and interactive
  technologies, 7; new kind of audience, 81;
  one-nation viewing, 6; and public reaction
  to socially conscious television, 69–70. See
  also *Generations*; *Isidingo* (SABC, 1998 to
  present); M-Net (cable TV); MultiChoice;
  soap operas on SABC; television
  commercials and branding South Africa
Viljoen, Constand, 145
Villagers, The (SABC, 1976–78), 71–72
violence: by Afrikaners, 143; xenophobic, 171–75
Virodene, 116
Vlaams Belang (Flemish Interest), 152
Voëlvry (outlaw) Afrikaans music movement,
  142, 158
Volkswagen Corporation advertising, 41
Vries, Fred de, 150–51
Vrye Afrikaan (Free Afrikaan), 141, 154–55,
  156–57
Vundla, Mfundi, 74, 75, 76

Waetjen, Thembisa, 140
Wainaina, Binyavanga, 9
Waluś, Janusz, 24
Wasserman, Herman, 132
Welz, Martin, 111
Western support of South Africa, 19
Westgate (SABC, 1981–85), 72
Westhuizen, Christi van der, 141
white privilege, 141, 143
Williams, Chester, 26
Wolpe, Harold, 167n69
World Conference Against Racism (Durban,
  2001), 153
World Cup (football), 2010, 55–56, 62n83
World Economic Forum, 93

xenophobic violence, 171–75

Yizo Yizo (This Is It) (SABC, 1998, 2001, and
  2004), 30n14, 69, 84n30
YouTube videos, 176

Zambia and reality television, 99, 107n65
Zola, "Today I woke up . . ." commercial, 54
Zulu, Lindiwe, 172
Zulu and "Africanization" of South Africa, 75
Zuma, Jacob, 42, 112, 130, 162, 174, 175, 176
Zwedala, Nontsikelelo, 122–23, 127
Zwelithini, Goodwill, 171, 172, 173, 174, 176

SEAN JACOBS

is Associate Professor of International
Affairs at The New School in New
York City. He is founder and editor
of the opinion and analysis site
Africa Is a Country.

www.ingramcontent.com/pod-product-compliance
Lightning Source LLC
Chambersburg PA
CBHW020737230426
43665CB00009B/469